Immigration, Diversity, and Broadcasting in the United States, 1990–2001

This series of publications on Africa, Latin America, Southeast Asia, and Global and Comparative Studies is designed to present significant research, translation, and opinion to area specialists and to a wide community of persons interested in world affairs. The editor seeks manuscripts of quality on any subject and can usually make a decision regarding publication within three months of receipt of the original work. Production methods generally permit a work to appear within one year of acceptance. The editor works closely with authors to produce a high-quality book. The series appears in a paperback format and is distributed worldwide. For more information, contact the executive editor at Ohio University Press, Scott Quadrangle, University Terrace, Athens, Ohio 45701.

Executive editor: Gillian Berchowitz
AREA CONSULTANTS
Africa: Diane M. Ciekawy
Latin America: Thomas Walker
Southeast Asia: William H. Frederick
Global and Comparative Studies: Ann R. Tickamyer

The Ohio University Research in International Studies series is published for the Center for International Studies by Ohio University Press. The views expressed in individual volumes are those of the authors and should not be considered to represent the policies or beliefs of the Center for International Studies, Ohio University Press, or Ohio University.

Immigration, Diversity, and Broadcasting in the United States, 1990–2001

VIBERT C. CAMBRIDGE

Ohio University Research in International Studies
Global and Comparative Studies Series No. 3

Ohio University Press
Athens

© 2005 by the
Center for International Studies
Ohio University
www.ohio.edu/oupress

12 11 10 09 08 07 06 05   5 4 3 2 1

The books in the Ohio University Research in International Studies Series
are printed on acid-free paper ⊚ ™

Library of Congress Cataloging-in-Publication Data

Cambridge, Vibert C.
 Immigration, diversity, and broadcasting in the United States, 1990–2001/ Vibert C.
Cambridge.
    p. cm.—(Research in international studies. Global and comparative studies se-
ries ; no. 3)   Includes bibliographical references and index.
  ISBN 0-89680-236-1 (pbk. : alk. paper)
 1. Ethnic broadcasting—United States. I. Title. II. Series.
 PN1990.9.E74C36 2005
 384.54'089'00973—dc22

                                                                            2004023114

To my mother, Lennie Cambridge

Contents

Tables

Acknowledgments

In the late 1960s I first encountered Edward Kamau Brathwaite's epic poem *Rights of Passage,* which told the tale of "Columbus's new world mariners"—the West Indian immigrant. I personally related to the cry of the exhausted immigrant—the "landless, harbourless spade"—seeking a place to call home. I, too, had come from many generations of New World immigrants that had crisscrossed and circulated through the Atlantic world. My maternal grandfather was born in Barbados, and my maternal grandmother was born in Dominica. My mother was born in Gold Coast. My paternal grandmother was born in Suriname and my father was born in British Guiana. Both branches of the family—the Simmons and the Cambridges—had been dispersed across the globe. Family memories speak of relatives in Antigua, Barbados, Canada, Cuba, Dominica, England, Ghana, Panama, Scotland, St. Vincent, Suriname, Trinidad and Tobago, Wales, and the United States.

Immigration has been a dominant narrative in the reality of my generation, and the United States has been the preferred destination. Prior to migrating to the United States in 1986 from Guyana, I had a career in broadcasting and was very conscious of its potency in that multiracial postcolonial society. When I was a doctoral student at the Ohio University School of Telecommunications during the late 1980s, questions about the state of international broadcasting and the role of broadcasting in America's multicultural society were salient. After graduating in 1989 and joining the faculty at Ohio University, I decided to explore the intersection of immigration, the discourse on diversity, and broadcasting in the United States. The origins of this book can be traced to the paper "Immigration, Race, and Ethnicity in

U.S. Broadcasting," presented at the International Conference on Immigration and Communication in Tallinn, Estonia, in August 1993.

I must extend thanks to following institutions and persons who helped me during my research for this book, among them the Ohio University Research Committee for a grant in 1992; the Museum of Television and Radio, New York, for providing research privileges; Dr. Hal Himmelstein, Brooklyn College; the Guyana Broadcasters in North America; Ms. Jackie Smart, for helping me to meet with immigrant broadcasters in New York during my field research in 2001; and Mr. Annan Boodram, for sharing his research and insights on immigrant radio broadcasting in New York. Special thanks are extended to my wife and trusted colleague, Dr. Patricia Cambridge, and to our children Nadine and Nigel.

I am truly grateful for all the support and assistance provided by so many persons—mentioned and unmentioned. I am responsible for any errors.

Abbreviations

AFRS	U.S. Armed Forces Radio Service
AFRTS	U.S. Armed Forces Radio and Television Service
ANA	Arab Network of America
ART	Arab Radio and Television Network
BCAT	Brooklyn Cable Access Television
BET	Black Entertainment Television
CANA	Caribbean News Agency
CATV	community antenna television
CBU	Caribbean Broadcasting Union
CCTV	China Central Television
CNN	Cable News Network
CSN	Caribbean Satellite Network
CPB	Corporation for Public Broadcasting
DBS	direct broadcast satellite
EEO	Equal Employment Opportunity
ETV	educational television
FCC	Federal Communications Commission
HBO	Home Box Office
ICN	International Channel Networks
ITVS	Independent Television Service
LPB	Latino Public Broadcasting
LPFM	low-power FM
MSO	multiple-system operator
NAACP	National Association for the Advancement of Colored People
NAB	National Association of Broadcasters
NAMIC	National Association of Minorities in Communication

NAPT	Native American Public Telecommunications
NATPE	National Association of Television Program Executives
NBPC	National Black Programming Consortium
NCTA	National Cable Television Association
NLCC	National Latino Communications Center
NPR	National Public Radio
NTIA	National Telecommunications and Information Authority
PATV	public access television
PBS	Public Broadcasting Service
PIC	Pacific Islanders in Communications
PRI	Public Radio International
RTNDA	Radio and Television News Directors Association

1

Seeking a Voice in the Melting Pot

SINCE THE INTRODUCTION of broadcasting in the United States in the early 1920s, immigrants and native-born minority groups have adopted radio and other electronic media for a number of functions not provided by mainstream broadcasters. Among those functions have been providing news and information from their home countries and about their present communities, transmitting their cultural heritage, orienting their audiences to the American way of life, encouraging participation in the political and economic life of their new communities, providing entertainment, and overcoming stereotypes. In some cases, the programs aired by these broadcasters have provided a service for the wider American society.

Such a program was the radio program *The Forward Hour,* aired weekly since 1932 by the Yiddish newspaper *The Forward* (itself established in New York City in the late nineteenth century). The program was still on the air in 2001 and still on WEVD,[1] New York, making it probably the longest-running ethnic radio program in the United States. Within the Jewish community in New York, *The Forward Hour* mobilized support for labor and socialist causes, helped orient new immigrants to life in the City, and served as a resource for resolving psychological problems and domestic crises.[2] It also contributed to the growth of American popular culture. The dramas presented by *The Forward Hour* provided training and career opportunities for a generation of influential American actors such as Lauren Bacall and Richard Widmark. Nobel laureate Isaac Bashevis Singer adapted his novel *The Slave* into a dramatic series for the program. *The Forward Hour* has demonstrated that minority broadcasting[3] in the United States serves as political channel, cultural animator, and community animator.

Immigrant and native-born minority communities in the United States now use communication technologies such as satellites and the Internet to extend their broadcasting capabilities. They can now broadcast to their parent countries and to members of their global diaspora. For example, in 2000, West Indian broadcasters, such as LINKUP Media in New York, were providing radio simulcasts that connected West Indians in New York and Miami with West Indians in London, Toronto, and Jamaica, as well as delivering these programs through the Internet to West Indians all over the world—thus helping construct a global West Indian identity. Similar global identities are being developed by other racial, ethnic, religious, gender, and lifestyle communities in the United States. These communities have become attractive audiences for the mainstream American broadcasting industry.

America's multicultural communities constitute a significant and attractive economic and cultural force. These communities also hold increasingly important political and economic significance. Immigration is continuing to expand this diversity and influence. President George W. Bush's Spanish-language radio address on May 5, 2001, is emblematic of the current importance of Hispanics in American politics.[4] No president of the United States had ever broadcast an entire radio address in Spanish before. The increasing economic significance of immigrants and people of color is also evident in American television advertising.

The presence of racial and ethnic minority groups in American broadcasts has increased dramatically, especially on television and in advertising, but also on the radio. These images of racial and ethnic diversity are not found exclusively in the nation's major metropolitan areas—the faces of racial and ethnic America are evident in every media market in the United States, even in rural areas. Video and audio diversity have converged in the webcasts available on the Internet. Commercial broadcasters constantly seek to maximize market share. This requires them to seek opportunities in America's diversity. And public service broadcasters in the United States are required by law to respond to the needs of new immigrants and other disadvantaged groups. Community broadcasting makes it possible for nonprofessional broadcasters to have access to their communities. Broadcasters from immigrant and native-born minority communities also enter into relationships with commercial, public service, and community broadcasters as they seek to provide those services not provided by commercial, public service, and community broadcasters. These relationships are present in radio, television, and online and are local, national, and global in scope. It was this web of broadcasting that the Ad Council used to deliver its "I am an American—E Pluribus Unum" campaign in the aftermath of September 11, 2001, when the United States mobilized for national unity, solidarity, and tolerance.[5]

But immigration not only replenishes racial and ethnic communities, it also exacerbates old tensions and creates new solidarities. These relationships affect all sectors of the American broadcasting industry—the commercial, the public service, and the community, or alternative, sectors. This book is a contribution to our understanding of this web of relationships that exists at the intersection of immigration, race, and broadcasting. Specifically, this book seeks answers to the following questions:

- How has broadcasting in the United States, especially in the last decade (1990–2001), responded to the changing racial and ethnic composition of our society? What patterns can be drawn from these responses? What functions have been and are being served? What stimulates the changing of the roles of broadcasting?
- Have these responses conformed to society's expectations of the performance of broadcasting in a democratic and multicultural society? Do these responses advance the nation's founding ambitions

of opportunity for all, responsibility for all, and community for all? How should the American broadcasting industry's responses to diversity be assessed in view of theory and historical context?

- Can these responses by the American broadcasting industry contribute to the improvement of race and ethnic relations in other multiracial societies around the world?

I have selected the last decade of the twentieth century because it marks the maturing of the new racial and ethnic communities in the United States and the emergence of diversity, or multiculturalism,[6] as dominant discourses in legal, educational, and cultural contexts.

I will also examine contemporary race and ethnic relations in the United States. The problem of race relations has attracted the attention of many influential American thinkers, including W. E. B. DuBois, Walter Lippmann, and Robert Park. In *The Souls of Black Folk* (1903) DuBois, an influential Harvard-educated African American scholar and Pan-African activist, introduced the concept of the color line to describe the bigotry that separated whites from persons of African descent in the United States at the beginning of the twentieth century. He described how access to the possibilities of America was denied to people of color, especially black people. This condition, he stressed, created a psychological tension he described as "double consciousness"—the struggle of blacks to construct identities and "the crucible in which their African and American identities could be merged into a unity of which they and the nation could be proud."[7] DuBois expressed despair that the possibility of building human brotherhood in America was being undermined by bigotry and inequality.[8] He was correct. Racism and bigotry continue to be international problems— nazism, Jim Crow, apartheid, ethnic cleansing in Rwanda and the Balkans. It is now recognized that race is a social construction and that the mass media play an important role in this process.

In the 1920s, political commentator Lippmann, an astute scholar of propaganda practices, coined the phrase "pictures in our heads" to describe the process through which the mass media created and influenced public opinion and relationships in American society. He contended that gatekeeping processes in the mass media determined what was selected from the "outside world." A report by the Kerner Commission—appointed by President Johnson to investigate the causes of the riots in urban America and to make recommendations to prevent their recurrence—concluded that in addition to white racism, the mass media, especially broadcasting, had failed to make the nation aware of the crises that affected the lives of black people in the United States. The report stated that pictures of African Americans the mass media created in the heads of white America were distorted and biased—African Americans were depicted the way whites saw them, not as African Americans saw themselves.[9]

This was not a new situation. There is a tradition in American mainstream mass media to treat immigrant and minority communities inadequately. One response among minority communities has been to create their own media outlets. In *The Immigrant Press and Its Control* (1922), University of Chicago sociologist Robert Park concluded that the foreign-language press played an important role in constructing identities and orienting new immigrants to life in the United States. Global migration from the southern regions of the world and the proliferation of broadcasting have now added new dimensions to the dynamics of race and ethnicity in major settler societies such as the United States. Simon Cottle uses the term "problematics of race" to refer to this expanded influence of broadcasting.[10] Race relations—the quest for continuous improvement in the relations between and among races and ethnic groups—is a major plank in maintaining the community harmony needed for progress in American society. Broadcasting plays a role in this process. Racialization and racism are ideologies that sort humanity into socially determined categories called race and use those categories to determine access to resources—education, health care, housing, nutrition, and finance. Broadcasting influences this process of resource allocation. For example, during the welfare reform debates of the 1990s, the term *welfare mother* was a code used to brand some sectors of society, particularly black women, as undeserving beneficiaries. Advances in transportation and the new communication technologies, including broadcasting, have now made it possible for people to develop identities that are transnational and solidarities that are global. These identities and solidarities are politically significant. The jihad called for by Osama bin Laden has assumed a global identity.

The United States has been described by Ben Wattenberg as the "first universal nation."[11] Because of its popularity as a settler site, the United States has become a hub for most of the world's diasporas. The diaspora is a social formation that will assume substantial significance in the twenty-first century. Examining broadcasting at the intersection of immigration and diversity in the United States permits observation of the nature and practices of diasporas and the role broadcasting is playing in the construction of transnational identities. For example, South Asian broadcasting in the United States reveals how that community is interfacing with American political institutions, how they are valorized in the consumer marketplace, how the broadcasters are serving their community, and how they are linked with their parent society and its diaspora. Similar insights can be gleaned from observing West Indian, Polish, Arab, or Jewish broadcasting in the United States.

The examination of the intersection of immigration, diversity, and broadcasting in the United States also encompasses an examination of the programming of mainstream broadcasters, whose programming is globally influential. American mainstream broadcasting products exert a "pull" influence on immigration to the United States; they articulate and support a lifestyle. It is not extreme to conclude that American media products, especially television programs, serve a pre-Americanization role for potential immigrants. Ultimately, this book is also a contribution to the evaluation of the performance of the American broadcasting industry. The answers to this book's core questions will provide insights on how the American broadcasting industry has responded to the following essential evaluative criteria— freedom, equality, diversity, information quality, social order and solidarity, and cultural order during the last decade.

This study required an examination of the history of immigration to the United States and a survey of the nature and scope of the American broadcasting industry. I have drawn upon a number of midrange social scientific, critical-cultural, and normative theories. The social scientific theories include media systems dependency theory and media dependency theory. The critical-cultural theories include theories associated with political economy, representation, and identity. The normative theories include formulations such as free-market media theory, social responsibility, and democratic-participant theories. (This theoretical framework is explicated in chapter 4.)

The evaluation of American broadcasting and its responses to the nation's changing racial and ethnic composition required triangulated research, which employs both quantitative and qualitative methods. For this study several research methods were used over an eleven-year period: surveys of ethnic organizations, in-depth interviews with broadcasting professionals (human resource professionals, producers, ethnic media owners and operators), and focus group and in-depth sessions conducted with audience members. Starting in 1991, I conducted in-depth interviews with minorities on their impressions of minority broadcasting. In the spring of 2001, I was able to conduct in-depth interviews in New York City with twenty-five participants from Barbados, China, Guyana (including African and Indian Guyanese), India, Iran, Ireland, Israel, Italy, South Korea, and Venezuela. The participants, either students at Brooklyn College or employed on Wall Street and mostly male, had been in the United States for an average of just over eleven years.[12] From these interviews it is possible to identify three types of programming at the intersection of immigration and diversity. In the commercial sector we find programming aimed at representing America's diversity. In the noncommercial (public and public access television) we find programming that is produced for America's diversity. We can also identify programming produced by America's minorities in all three sectors of the American broadcasting industry—the commercial, the public service, and the community sectors.

Corporate reports and official government documents, especially those from the National Telecommunications and Information Administration (NTIA), the Federal Communications Commission (FCC), and the Corporation for Public Broadcasting (CPB) were also examined. Extensive use was made of online resources, especially those of corporations, networks, and professional organizations. Of particular value was the collection of radio, television, and advertising materials available at the Museum of Television and Radio in New York.

2

Immigration to the United States

FOR OVER FOUR hundred years the United States has been one of the
most attractive settler sites in the human migration route. Between
1820—the first year the U.S. Congress required the systematic compi-
lation of immigration statistics—and 1997, nearly 64 million persons
settled in the United States legally.[1] Religious freedom, access to
land, employment, and the opportunity to enjoy life, liberty, and the
pursuit of happiness have all attracted people to settle here. Three
processes: "colonization, coercion and immigration" facilitated the
creation of the "first universal nation."[2] The English were the most
successful of the early European colonizers. During the seventeenth
and eighteenth centuries, they established communities in Virginia
and Massachusetts, established English as the language of the nation,
and laid the foundations for America's legal system and government.
Other early colonizers came from France, Spain, and the Netherlands.

The primary example of coercion in the peopling of the United
States is African slavery. In 1790, 19 percent of the population were
enslaved Africans. In the 2000 census, African Americans accounted
for 12.3 percent of the population. Other populations were forcibly

absorbed following war settlements, political deals, and land purchases. For example, when the Louisiana Purchase was concluded in 1803, all the French residents became Americans, as did Mexicans in California, New Mexico, and Texas at the end of the Mexican War in 1848 and Puerto Ricans after the Spanish American War.[3] But by far the most significant influx of population has come from successive waves of immigration.

The First Wave, 1607–1820

The term *immigrant*, first used in the United States in 1789, referred to people who came to the new nation voluntarily. The first wave of immigration consisted primarily of northern Europeans. Of these, the dominant group was the English. In 1790, they accounted for 60 percent of the population. Other immigrants in this wave included Scots, Scots-Irish, Germans, Dutch, French, and Spanish. The primary reasons for migration were to seek religious and political freedom and economic opportunity. The English settled in colonies on the East Coast and in the South. Print-based communication played an important role in attracting these early immigrants. During this period, the newspaper became important as a medium for spreading ideas and news. Benjamin Franklin, founder of one the first newspapers in the colonies, used that medium to comment on the apparent failure of German colonizers to conform to Anglo traditions, especially the use of English. He cited this failure to justify his support for restricting German immigration to the colonies.

But letters sent by immigrants back to their home countries were even more influential in stimulating further immigration. Letters in J. Hector St. John de Crevecoeur's *Letters from an American Farmer* (1782) make the point that the immigrant who was beaten down by poverty, war, and hunger in Europe found that in America "everything has tended to regenerate them; new laws, a new mode of living, a new social system; here they become [new] men."[4] These new men were Americans. America was the land of opportunity. This idea about America has remained constant across all major waves of immigration—from the earliest advertisement to the current multimedia environment.

The Second Wave, 1820–1860

The second wave also was dominated by immigrants from northern Europe, primarily from Ireland, England, and Germany. However, significant numbers were starting to come from eastern and southern Europe. From 1820 to 1840, over three-quarters of a million immigrants arrived in the United States. Forty percent came from Ireland, propelled mainly by poverty and famine. This wave of immigrants nourished the pioneering movement that opened the American West and established the communities that grew to become the states of the upper Midwest and the West. Print was the dominant medium. The foreign-language newspapers established during this period reflected the growing linguistic and ethnic diversity of the nation. These newspapers not only provided information and orientation, but in some cases, such as the Yiddish newspapers, helped rejuvenate languages that were dying in Europe.[5]

The Third Wave, 1860–1914

More than 20 million immigrants came to the United States during the third wave. Most came from eastern and southern Europe and were employed in the industrial sectors. They settled primarily in urban areas—especially New York, Chicago, and Detroit—creating ethnic enclaves. In addition, substantial numbers of Asian immigrants, especially Chinese and Japanese, settled primarily in the Western states to work in industrial occupations and to provide labor for the building of the transcontinental railway system.

The European migrants who dominated the third wave were fleeing violence, oppression, and suppression. The new immigrants from eastern Europe differed from earlier European immigrant groups. They were primarily Jewish and Slavic. The racial and ethnic differences of the new immigrant wave energized racist and nativist traditions in American society, resulting in the introduction of a number of immigration laws aimed at excluding certain racial and ethnic groups. Among the first such laws was the Chinese Exclusion Act of 1882. After extensions in 1892 and 1902, the act was extended indefinitely in 1904. Other people of Asian origin were subject to exclusion under the so-called Gentlemen's Agreement of 1907, signed with Japan.[6]

The Immigration Pause, 1915–1964

By the first decades of the twentieth century the exclusion of immigrants because of race and national origins had become a central feature of U.S. immigration law. Despite the presence of Africans virtually from the founding of the colonies, an attempt was made in 1915 to "exclude all members of the African or black race from admission to the United States." An act to this effect was introduced in the Senate and was approved. The act later was defeated in the House after actions by the NAACP. The codification of American immigration laws in 1917 maintained all the exclusions based on race and added illiterates to the list of persons excluded from immigration. The latter development was described as a "response to the influx of immigrants from southern and eastern Europe." The immigrants from southern and eastern European were characterized as "the dullest and dumbest people in Europe, as the dregs of the earth . . . who would erode, destroy and mongrelize American society." Rita Simon's analysis of a century of American newspaper coverage of immigration (1880–1980) revealed that the mainstream print media reflected these anti-immigrant and racist sentiments. This reality no doubt reinforced the necessity for developing the ethnic press and subsequently ethnic radio.[7]

World War I, restrictions to immigration, and pervasive anti-immigrant sentiments contributed to the decline of immigration to the United States during this period. In 1921 the national quota system was introduced, initially as a temporary act, to limit immigration from any country to 3 percent of the U.S. residents of that country already living here in 1910. Immigrants from the Western Hemisphere were exempted from the quota. Simon suggests that "the clear intent of the 1921 quota law was to confine immigration as much as possible to western and northern European stock" (41–42). The temporary quota became permanent under the 1924 National Origins Act, which limited the number of immigrants to one hundred fifty per year per country and introduced visa requirements. Again, potential immigrants from the Western Hemisphere were exempted. Clearly, the 1924 law was discriminatory (ibid.), a situation President Kennedy would seek to rectify in 1963.

There were periods when this exclusionary tendency was modified, especially during labor shortages, such as after the end of World War I and during the preparations for World War II. During these periods immigrants were welcomed to the United States—only to be expelled during economic downturns and as an appeasement to nativist, racist, and xenophobic tendencies. For example, "more than 1 million persons of Mexican descent were expelled from this country in 1954 at the height of Operation Wetback." The dislocations caused by World War II contributed to what has been termed the "erosion of certain discriminatory barriers." Among the outstanding developments was the repeal of the Chinese Exclusion Act in 1943. The War Brides Act of 1945 facilitated the "immigration of 118,000 spouses and children of military servicemen" (ibid.). In 1946, Congress permitted the naturalization of people from the Philippines and India, and under the 1948 Displaced Persons Act more than six hundred thousand refugees from Germany and Austria were admitted.

The McCarran-Walter Act of 1952 laid the foundation for contemporary immigration law but still contained race-based exclusion conditions. Not only was preference given to the European immigrant, the dominant ethos still sought to ensure that all immigrants met "Anglo conformity" (42). The civil rights movement of the 1960s demanded the end to discrimination in all aspects of American life. The changes to the immigration laws that took place in 1965 removed barriers based on race, color, and national origin.

Before that President Kennedy had sent to Congress legislation aimed at "revising and modernizing" U.S. immigration laws to ensure that "those with the greatest ability to add to the national welfare, no matter where they were born, [be] granted the highest priority."[8] The system he sought to modify had been in place since 1924 and was the result of many forces, among them fears that the nation's Anglo-Saxon traditions were being threatened by the huge influx of immigrants from eastern and southern Europe.

Kennedy pointed out that immigration policy had always been a prominent and controversial topic of discussion in America (69). On the one hand, there always had been a call for more liberal immigration policies—England's restriction of immigration to the colonies was one of the factors that led to the Declaration of Independence (69). This tendency to advocate more immigration has been referred to as "the admissionist tendency." The opposing call for limits to immigration is the "restrictionist tendency."[9]

Kennedy's recommendations for immigration reform were accepted in 1965, almost two years after his death. His assassination was symptomatic of the social turbulence that dominated American society in the sixties. The decade started with nonviolent protests against American apartheid, such as the sit-ins staged by students at whites-only lunch counters in Greensboro, North Carolina. By 1963, these actions had attracted a violent white backlash, including police brutality. The tide of violence escalated and brought in its wake the assassinations of Martin Luther King Jr. and Robert Kennedy and destructive riots across urban America during the mid-sixties. It was clear that resistance to three hundred years of legally sanctioned racial segregation was a major factor in the civil disorder.

The National Advisory Commission on Civil Disorder, also known as the Kerner Commission, was established by President Johnson to examine the causes of this disorder. The commission concluded that the mass media, especially broadcasting, played influential roles in supporting the conditions of discrimination and marginalization of African Americans and other minority communities in the United States. According to the commission, broadcasting in the United States was expected to reflect the nation's racial and ethnic diversity—in news rooms, in editing suites, as voices on radio, and as faces on television. In essence, the American broadcasting environment was to provide its audiences with programs that promoted solidarity and understanding and discouraged the divisiveness that emerges from the use of negative stereotypes and disengaged reporting. The modification in the immigration laws in 1965 would create conditions that would complicate the situation.

The Fourth Wave, 1965–Present

William Henry's term "the browning of America" describes one of the consequences of the fourth wave of immigration to the United States. In fact, the northward migration of peoples from the southern regions of the world has become commonplace. Henry concludes that by 2056, as a result of increased migration and birth rates, people of color—Asians, Arabs, Latinos, and peoples of the Caribbean—will be the majority population of the United States. The 2000 census confirms that trend. For example, the New York Times for Sunday, March 11, 2001, citing 2000 census numbers, reported that Latinos were about to replace African Americans as the nation's largest minority of color. And the Asian American community increased by nearly 50 percent between 1990 and 2000. Asian Americans now account for 3.6 percent of the population, up from 2.8 percent in 1990. The Asian Indian population grew by over 100 percent in the same period (table 2.1).[10]

Table 2.1. Growth of Select Asian American Populations, 1990–2000

Group	1990	2000	% Growth	% of U.S. Pop.
Asian Indian	815,447	1,678,785	105.9	0.6
Chinese	1,645,472	2,432,585	47.5	0.9
Filipino	1,406,770	1,850,314	31.5	0.7
Korean	798,849	1,076,872	34.8	0.4
Vietnamese	614,547	1,222,528	98.9	0.4
Other Asian (Pakistani, Bangladeshi, Sri Lankan)	779,992	1,285,234	64.8	0.5

Source: U.S. Census Bureau, cited in India Abroad Online Edition, May 18, 2001, available at http://www.indiaabroaddaily.com.

The black population also grew in the United States as a result of immigration from Africa, the Caribbean, and Latin America. The dominant immigrant groups from Africa were from Ethiopia, Ghana, Kenya, Nigeria, and Somalia. Ethiopians and Somalis came primarily as refugees. The immigrants from the Caribbean came primarily from Haiti, Jamaica, Trinidad and Tobago, and Guyana. The black Hispanic population grew to 1.3 million in 1992 (from 391,000 in 1980) as a result of immigration from the Dominican Republic.

Until the nineties the dominant Hispanic groups in the United States were Mexicans, Puerto Ricans, and Cubans. Since then Spanish-speaking immigrants from Central America, South America, and the Dominican Republic have become more numerous. Fourth-wave immigration to the United States is also contributing to increases in the Native American population. The 1990 census identified 148,000 Hispanic Indians.

Increasingly, fourth-wave immigrants to the United States manifest the characteristics of "transnational immigration": the operation of international networks of business organizations, new forms of transnational employment, the formation of transnational communities, and the formation of collective identities not confined by territory.[11] International networks of business organizations are usually accompanied by the proliferation of joint ventures between immigrants and American capital. These transactions are facilitated by the global communication infrastructure and encouraged by national governments and international organizations such as the World Bank and the United Nations Development Programme. One emerging area is that of transnational broadcasting enterprises like the previously mentioned LINKUP Media in New York and others that we will encounter later in this book. The new forms of transnational employment are evident among highly skilled workers in areas such as business, finance, science, and academia. The information-based sectors of the American economy, especially Silicon Valley, encouraged the migration of information technology professionals from India.

Mass communications has contributed directly to the last two characteristics of the transnational migration. The new communication technologies have made geography relatively insignificant in the distribution of information, knowledge, and entertainment. According to Oliver Schmidtke, "Global distribution of news, cultural productions, and goods has given birth to patterns of communication not defined by the nation" (6). This means that human beings can develop identities that are global, not purely local. Fourth-wave immigrants to the United States are therefore not under as much pressure as immigrants from previous waves to become Americanized. In Europe, another site of transnational immigration, immigrants no longer develop an identity with their new homes. The new nation-state they live in is "no longer the exclusive agent for creating the psychological bonds needed for community" (7). The new communication technologies and the global mass communication networks are facilitating the development of networks and interactions across borders, maintaining old cultural ties and developing new communal ties that do not follow the boundaries of the host nation-state (in this case the United States).

Each wave of immigrants to America has affected demographics, society, the economy, and public policy issues.[12] These effects frame media coverage and contribute to how native-born Americans picture immigrants. During the last decade of the twentieth century, the mainstream media's treatment of immigration reflected both admissionist and restrictionist tendencies. However, the dominant tendency was to be negatively biased and sometimes hysterical—focusing on undocumented aliens.

The Demographic Effects of Immigration

In the fourth wave of immigration to the United States, four issues have been salient: population size, age and sex composition, racial and ethnic composition, and settlement patterns. The fourth wave of immigration did not reach the levels of previous waves, and it has been different in several other ways. First, it is younger. In 1980, 41.3 percent of the U.S. population was between the ages of fifteen and thirty-nine, but more than 57 percent of the immigrants arriving that year were in that group. By 1994, more than 71 percent of undocumented aliens were between the ages of fifteen and thirty-nine. The 2000 census reaffirmed this youthfulness of immigrants to the United States. Second, more women are migrating to the United States, probably due to the uniting of families and the continuation of arranged marriages (particularly among Indians, Filipinos, and Koreans).[13]

Nearly three-quarters of new immigrants indicated that they intended to reside in California, Florida, Illinois, New Jersey, New York City, and Texas, conforming to a pattern established since the turn of the twentieth century and explaining the creation of ethnic enclaves. Immigrants from northern Europe tend to settle in all regions of the United States and are more inclined to "live in suburbs and metropolitan areas and rural areas than [are] other foreign-born groups." However, "[i]mmigrants from Asia are highly concentrated in the West region and in central cities of other regions. . . . Immigrants from . . . Eastern and Southern Europe are most inclined to live in the Northeast and North Central (Midwest) regions, in central cities, or in metropolitan rings. . . . Immigrants from Mexico and Latin America are inclined to concentrate in the South and West and in central cities of all regions."[14]

These demographic attributes—age, gender, and settlement patterns—exert significant influence on the American broadcasting industry. From a settlement point of view, immigrant communities coincide with major media markets and have influenced broadcasting, consumer marketing, and advertising. Other demographic features—residence in metropolitan areas, relative youth, and feminization—are sought-after mass consumer attributes and a significant determinant of commercial broadcasting performance in the United States.

The Social Effects of Immigration

Of the many issues associated with this category—language, education, residential segregation, social inequality, public health—the most relevant for our purposes are language and residential segregation. In the last quarter century Spanish has become a major language in Florida, Texas, and southern California, contributing to the dramatic growth of Spanish-language media. The advertising and marketing industries (key determinants of the health of commercial broadcasting in the United States) have also recognized the importance of foreign languages and accents in their market segmentation strategies. In Asian ethnic communities, the media and the mainstream economy are increasingly using Asian languages.

The settlement patterns of immigrants contribute to social segregation into ethnic enclaves. Indeed, some of the new immigrants have taken over enclaves developed by second- and third-wave groups. For example, Caribbean immigrants have replaced Jews in some parts of New York City. Ethnic enclaves have continued to serve a number of functions for immigrants in American society, the central function being the provision of social networks. Social networks are important organizing structures in the lives of America's diversity. They provide "material and physical assistance, making possible close social interaction, guiding individual activities, giving feedback and encouraging community participation. Likewise they operate as important channels of communication from individuals to communities and vice versa. In this sense they form mediating mechanisms between the individual and structural levels."[15]

There is also evidence to suggest that ethnic enclaves in the United States generate considerable employment for both native-born and immigrant workers. During the last quarter century, the ethnic sector of the economy has increased in importance and in attractiveness for the American broadcasting industry—both mainstream and minority. Further, transnational immigration has given these ethnic social networks a global scope. The scope of some of these networks, such as the Somali and Islamic money transferring system, was revealed in 2001 during the early days of the war against terrorism.

The economic activities in some ethnic enclaves have triggered significant tensions and racial conflicts between some fourth-wave immigrants and some native-born minorities, especially African Americans. The racial conflicts that exploded in New York and Los Angeles during the eighties and nineties are emblematic. At their core were the liquor stores and small businesses owned by Koreans that predominated in traditionally African American communities. Black community leaders argued that the Korean presence was due to racial discrimination—because practices like redlining and restrictive covenants made it difficult for African Americans to access the capital required for developing businesses in their communities. The tensions led to boycotts and were implicated in the racial violence in Los Angeles during 1992.

The Economic Effects of Immigration

The economic effects of the fourth wave of immigration to the United States appear to have generated the most biased media coverage, which in turn has encouraged powerful—and mostly inaccurate—perceptions about immigrants. Among the popular perceptions is that immigrants depress wages and, by extension, take jobs away from native workers. Another popular perception is that immigrants consume a disproportionate amount of the welfare pie and contribute little to the national tax pool. At the micro level, evidence suggests that immigrants are indeed creators of jobs, not only in their enclave communities but also in the wider economy. Despite some evidence that illegal immigrants may depress the wage market, this effect may well stimulate our economy by giving American industry a competitive edge in the global economy. There is even less evidence to support the perception that immigrants, both legal and illegal, are a drain on the welfare system and are noncontributors to the tax pool. Because of the fear of deportation, illegal immigrants have tended to be reluctant to apply for welfare benefits and services. Immigration scholars who have examined evidence from the U.S. Council of Economic Advisers and the Immigration and Naturalization Service during the early 1990s have concluded that "the overall contribution of immigrants is positive. Aliens may provide a net fiscal benefit to the nation, often paying more in taxes than they use in public services." Because of the youthfulness of fourth-wave immigrants, they have more to contribute to social funds such as Social Security.[16]

Nevertheless, the perceived economic effects of immigration are important news items in local and national media. In the last decade the more sensational aspects have been emphasized—such is the nature of the "tabloidization" of the news media. These negative images are held as truths and nourish the ebb and flow of admissionist and restrictionist positions on immigration. In the eighties, the immigration debate became even more contested as increasing numbers of refugees, asylum seekers, and undocumented aliens arrived in the United States. In response the Immigration Reform and Control Act of 1986 legalized 2.7 million unauthorized aliens and introduced penalties for businesses that hired illegal immigrants.[17] And the United States continued to modify its immigration laws. In 1996, Congress passed three major immigration-related laws—the Antiterrorism and Effective Death Penalty Act, the Personal Responsibility and Work Opportunity Reconciliation Act, and the Illegal Immigration Reform and Immigrant Responsibility Act—all motivated by three hot-button issues—responding to terrorism in America after the first bombing of the World Trade Center, the welfare reform movement, and efforts to curb illegal immigration.

The United States is in competition with other industrial nations for skilled workers in the information technology industries. To permit this, laws have been relaxed. The resulting relaxation in the immigration and naturalization laws indicates a new tendency in U.S. immigration policy, similar to models from Australia, Canada, and the European Union—one that tends to "favor young, skilled, educated and employable persons." Since 1990, the United States has introduced a diversity program—the Visa Lottery, which permits "up to 55,000 immigrants a year from countries that sent fewer than 50,000 immigrants in the past five years." Most of these visas go to European and African countries.[18]

Refugees and Asylum Seekers

The United States has prided itself in providing a safe haven for persons who are persecuted for their religious and political views. Under the Refugee Act of 1980, the United States accepted the United Nations definition of a refugee as the framework for the national refugee policy. According to this formulation, a refugee is a "person living outside his or her country of citizenship who was unwilling to return because of a well-founded fear of persecution because of race, religion, nationality, membership in a particular social group, or political opinion." American refugee policy includes the provision of cash, medical assistance, and job and language training for refugees.[19] Between 1961 and 1997, more than 2.5 million persons were admitted as refugees and asylees (see table 2.2). Some groups, such as the Cubans, have influenced the operations of the broadcasting industry. Like other immigrant groups, refugees and asylum seekers have also developed discrete residential patterns and have a number of linguistic, economic, and cultural challenges. Haitian refugees have tended to reside in Miami, New York, and Boston. Hmong refugees are located in Minneapolis, and Somalis in Columbus, Ohio.

Tourists and Other Sojourners

Tourists and sojourners—international students, academics, entertainers, and employees of international firms—also influence broad-

Table 2.2. Refugees and Asylees Admitted to the
United States, by Region, 1961–1997

Region	1961–1970	1971–1980	1981–1990	1991–1997
All countries	212,843	539,447	1,013,620	860,280
Europe	55,235	71,858	155,512	352,610
Asia	19,895	210,683	712,092	316,960
Africa	5,486	2,991	22,149	41,875
Oceania	21	37	22	245
North America (Cuba, El Salvador, Nicaragua)	132,068	252,633	121,840	144,642
South America (Chile, Colombia, Peru, Venezuela)	123	1,244	1,986	3,915

Source: Department of Justice, Immigration and Naturalization Service, *Statistical Yearbook of the Immigration and Naturalization Service* (Washington, D.C.: INS, 1997).

casting practices in the United States. All these categories of nonimmigrants have increased in size (see table 2.3).

Tourism is a major industry in the United States. In 1990, it amounted to $90 billion, up from $26 billion in 1986. In 1996, 46 million international visitors spent just under $21 billion in passenger fares to get here and then spent almost $70 billion on goods and services. Taken together, the tourist and sojourner presence in the United States is a significant economic and cultural reality. The importance of tourism for the American economy is attested by the downturn in the industry that resulted from the terrorist attacks of September 11, 2002. The U.S. Department of Commerce reported that tourism supported over a million jobs in 1996. Further, tourism provides an avenue for intercultural contact, makes demands on the domestic media environment, and encourages the creation of specialized broadcasting outlets.

Immigrants refresh and extend the racial and ethnic diversity of America. Immigrants and sojourners are sought after as audiences for the American broadcasting industry. Of special importance are their residential patterns (which usually coincide with the major media

Table 2.3. Nonimmigrant Visitors to the United States,
by Region, 1981–1996 (in thousands)

Region	1981	1985	1990	1995	1996
All countries	11,757	9,540	17,574	22,641	24,843
Europe	4,537	3,129	6,875	8,777	9, 387
Asia	2,290	2,627	4,937	7,000	6,913
Africa	225	177	186	228	258
Oceania	379	365	679	611	651
North America (Canada, Mexico)	2,817	2,189	3,245	3,091	3,187
Caribbean	614	774	1,231	1,088	1,154
Central America	300	316	449	536	531
South America	1,449	832	1,343	2,481	2,539

Source: Department of Justice, Immigration and Naturalization Service, *Statistical Yearbook of the Immigration and Naturalization Service* (Washington, D.C.: INS, 1997)

markets), their viewing habits, and their consumption patterns. Further, because of the emerging importance of transnational identities, immigrants in the United States are clearly important potential partners in global broadcasting ventures. Immigrants are not only important consumers but also producers of goods and services. They continue to leave indelible marks on American education, science, culture, and entertainment, including broadcasting. For example, David Sarnoff, the legendary head of NBC, was a Russian immigrant.

Rita Simon considers the millions of immigrants who have come to America to "be something of a miracle," considering that "at best [the country] was ambivalent toward them and at worst erected barriers to their entry."[20] The United States will continue to be an attractive settler site for the foreseeable future. The reunification of families will continue to be an ongoing factor in immigration to the United States. The trend of immigration of people of color to the United States will continue and there will be challenges associated with this development.

A significant challenge in the future will be the place of broadcasting in the formulation of an enlightened race relations regime, one that can respond effectively to the "problematics of race"—racism, racialization, and transnational identities. But these are complex, multidimensional problems. Old strategies, such as expanding the definition of whiteness and extending white privilege, would be unacceptable and dangerous. In our country's history there were times when the Irish, Italians, and Jews were not considered white. In the future, light-skinned Latinos and Asians will most likely be seen as white.[21] Accompanying whiteness, however, is the unfortunate tendency to devalorize African Americans, to reproduce practices that revile blackness and energize white supremacy. This hate takes on very virulent forms: "Since blackness is reviled in the United States, why would an immigrant, of whatever skin color, want to associate with those who are racially oppressed, particularly when the transit into the United States promises the dream of gold and glory? The immigrant seeks a form of vertical integration, to climb from the darkest echelon on the stepladder of tyranny into the bright whiteness. In U.S. history the Irish, Italians, Jews, and—in small steps with some hesitation on the part of white America—Asians and Latinos have all tried to barter their varied cultural worlds for the privileges of whiteness."[22]

The American broadcasting industry has responded in a number of ways to the changing racial and ethnic composition of the United States since the modification of the immigration and naturalization laws in 1965. Recent responses are in many ways mere extensions of practices adopted by American mass media in the late nineteenth and early twentieth centuries, to which we turn in chapter 3.

3

Immigration, Diversity, and the Media in the United States

The Immigrant Press

THE RECENT VARIED responses of the American broadcasting industry to America's diversity have been informed by the responses to diversity of the mass media in the late nineteenth and early twentieth centuries, especially the foreign-language press. Immigrants continued to develop newspapers during this phase. In addition to providing news from home countries, newspapers became important channels for advertising by "the priest, the doctor, and the lawyer." Immigrant newspapers carried advertisements for various professionals and for real estate, books, foods, occult services, matrimony, immigrant organizations, cultural events, and employment. The foreign-language press also connected the immigrant with the American economy and government. The ethnic press was also used by the United States to mobilize support for the American effort during World War I. By the start of the war, however, dependence on advertising also had made the ethnic press in the United States susceptible to foreign propaganda. By the end of the war, there was concern about the place of foreign-language newspapers in American society as there was clear evidence that Germany, the Soviet Union, and their allies had manipulated this press for their propaganda goals during the hostilities. Foreign-language newspapers that ran pro-German and pro-Soviet propaganda were rewarded by advertising supplied by Louis N. Hammerling and his agency, the American Association of Foreign Language Newspapers. The manipulation was so substantial that the immigrant press came under the scrutiny of several U.S. government agencies.[1]

THE IMMIGRANT PRESS IN THE 1920S

National security was only one manifestation of a wider concern about the immigrant presence in American society after World War I. Park's work was also motivated by national reaction to the dramatic shift that had taken place in the ethnic composition of the United States as a result of the Great Migration (mid-nineteenth to early twentieth centuries). These new immigrants, primarily from eastern and southern Europe and mostly unskilled, provided the manual labor required by the coal, railway, and steel industries that dominated the American economy. During the Great Migration, more than five million immigrants settled in what Park called "little language colonies" in urban areas (see tables 3.1 and 3.2).

Table 3.1 U.S. Immigration by Region of Last Residence, 1821–1930

Region of Last Residence	1821–1830	1841–1850	1861–1870	1881–1890	1901–1910	1921–1930
All countries	143,439	1,713,251	2,314,824	5,246,613	8,795,386	4,107,209
Europe	98,797	1,597,442	2,065,141	4,735,484	8,056,040	2,463,194
Asia	30	141	64,759	69,942	323,543	112,059
Caribbean	3,834	13,528	9,046	29,042	107,548	74,899
Latin America	13	3,947	1,492	2,708	25,472	57,984
Africa	1	55	312	857	7,368	6,286

Source: Compiled from tables 17, 18, and 19 in Department of Justice, Immigration and Naturalization Service, Statistical Yearbook of the Immigration and Naturalization Service (Washington, D.C.: INS, 1997), 58–66.

Table 3.2. Diversity of European Immigrants to the United States, 1821–1930

Region	1821–1830	1841–1850	1861–1870	1881–1890	1901–1910	1921–1930
All Europe	98,787	1,597,442	2,065,141	4,735,484	8,056,040	2,463,194
Northern and western Europe	85,102 (86%)	86,262 (54%)	2,046,566 (99%)	4,132,352 (87%)	4,055,301 (50%)	1,346,844 (55%
Southern and eastern Europe	13,695 (14%)	73,482 (46%)	18,575 (1%)	4,000,739 (13%)	4,000,739 (50%)	1,116,350 (45%)

Source: Compiled from tables 17, 18, 19 in Department of Justice, Immigration and Naturalization Service, *Statistical Yearbook of the Immigration and Naturalization Service* (Washington, D.C.: INS, 1997), 58–66.

When Park started his work, there were about "forty-three or forty-four languages and dialects spoken by immigrant peoples in the United States," and each language group created a cultural enclave and tended to support a press.[2] His study of more than one hundred foreign-language newspapers found that they served several specific functions for the immigrants. These functions included

reinforcing nationalism

preserving national languages and traditions

teaching English and improving literacy

stimulating intellectual growth

responding to the specific needs of immigrants living in rural and cosmopolitan communities by providing information on medical services, cultural performances, financial services, and other topics of interest

serving as a ventilator of frustrations and grievances

reflecting internal community tensions

providing visions of the future

articulating the host society's values and norms

commenting on American foreign and domestic policy

promoting naturalization and citizenship

offering reflections and comments on the state of race relations in the United States

Park used the terms *brake* and *accelerator* to summarize the functions of the foreign-language press in the United States. The brake helped immigrants maintain their language and other mores from their parent societies but retarded their entry into the American community, where, in the 1920s, Anglo-Saxon values took precedence. The accelerator facilitated the Americanization of immigrant communities through acculturation and assimilation. At that time the melting pot idea, with its basis in Anglo-Saxon conformity, dominated the national discourse on immigration and the expectations of immigrants when they arrived in American society. Generally, the idea was that all immigrants would enter the "bubbling cauldron" and emerge as new Americans. However, according to Park, "the proportions that go into the mix are not discussed. As the balance shifted and immigrants from Eastern and Southern Europe outnumbered those from Northern Europe, the pot seemed to cool. It appeared 'unable' to absorb such different elements as Italians, Russians, Slavs and Jews, for example. Orientals and blacks were rarely, if ever, associated with this concept" (3).

For Park, the task was not the eradication of the immigrant press but its incorporation into the wider communication environment, so that editors and readers would know that their publications were read outside their language groups and that their opinions were being noted. Park concluded that the immigrant press in the United States was a tool that allowed immigrants to negotiate their "double consciousness." He did not think the foreign-language press would disappear from American society.

THE IMMIGRANT PRESS SINCE ROBERT PARK

When Marion Marzolf revisited the ethnic press in the 1970s, almost fifty years after Park's work, she found an "enduring presence" of European ethnic media in the United States. The reasons she offered for this persistence were similar to those Park had suggested. They included

- a means for allowing non-English-speaking citizens to access "vital information"
- a means for strengthening community
- a means to "ease adjustment to the new life"
- a means of providing a sensitive mirror of the immigrants' views of the society
- a vehicle to maintain contact with the parent society
- a vehicle to promote economic development in the parent society.[3]

Early Ethnic Radio

Today the American mass media environment is more complex than it was in the twenties. Television and radio broadcasting have replaced the newspaper as the dominant mass media. This process started with the introduction of radio in the early twenties. Since its introduction, radio has responded in various ways to environmental factors such as race, ethnicity, demographics, the dynamics of the marketplace, and advances in communication technology. Radio broadcasting has been used by both immigrants and native-born minority communities for cultural transmission, maintenance of identity, orientation to a new community, support of economic enterprises in ethnic enclaves, mobilization, and, for immigrant groups, maintenance of a link with parent societies. For some émigré communities in the United States, such as Poles, radio has served as a vehicle to resist oppressive political conditions in the "old country."

It did not take long for radio station owners to recognize the commercial potential of ethnic and foreign-language communities. The dominant strategy of exploiting that potential was through brokerage, the renting of radio time by stations to independent producers (brokers) who produced programs and sold advertising to go with them. "[T]he only obligation of the broker toward the station was to pay a weekly fee for the rented block of time."[4] This model continues, and radio stations using this economic model are called time-brokered stations. African American, Polish, and Yiddish radio are among the earliest examples of the radio industry's response to diversity in America. Their practices and experiences, especially with brokerage, have influenced the broadcasting practices and patterns used by other immigrant communities.

AFRICAN AMERICAN RADIO

The development of African American radio in the United States is associated with the internal migration of African Americans from the South to the industrial cities of the Midwest and the Northeast. This internal migration started at the end of the Civil War and accelerated during the 1920s, '30s, and '40s. Radio became an important factor in the construction of the new black communities that were developing in the Midwest and the North. Janette Dates and William Barlow provide a framework for understanding the relationships between mainstream commercial broadcasters and minority-owned and operated radio. This framework is particularly useful in explaining the major investments that have been made in Spanish-language radio in recent decades.[5]

From its inception, African American radio has played three distinct roles: orientation to the new community, cultural transmission, and resistance to racism. The orientation role is exemplified by two shows created by Jack L. Cooper. In 1927, he started the first black news program in Chicago on radio station WGBC. He also developed the *Missing Persons Program*, which helped African American immigrants from the South reestablish contact with relatives and friends who had preceded them to Chicago (185). The primary vehicle for cultural maintenance and transmission in the early days of African American radio was the music program, facilitated by the segregation of the airwaves and the presence of an industry that produced what was euphemistically called race music. In the strictly segregated America of the twenties and thirties, commercial radio simply did not cater to African Americans. When music composed by African Americans was broadcast, it tended not to be performed by African Americans. When African Americans did start to produce their own programs on time-brokered stations, race music recordings were an accessible form of programming. This practice is an early example of the parsimony principle—the goal of minimizing the cost of program production and increasing the scope of profits—and an indicator of the linkage that exists between radio and the recorded music industry.

By the sixties, reflecting changes in American society, African American radio had become an important segment in mainstream radio broadcasting. Dates and Barlow identify four phases in this movement of African American radio from the Negro enclave to the mainstream: "blackface radio" (1920–39), "the middle passage" (1939–49), "black oriented radio" (1950–65), and "black controlled radio" (1965–present). Each phase provides a valuable lens to observe practices of racism—from the blatant to the subtle—in the American broadcasting industry and the concomitant strategies of resistance, incorporation, and appropriation.

When radio broadcasting began substantial shifts were occurring in America's social and cultural life. During the Roaring Twenties the country, especially the North, cast off its parochial Victorian shell and celebrated. America had emerged from World War I as one of the world's great powers and its richest nation. Radio delivered the era's soundtrack and played a major role in defining American race relations. Music and comedy programs were very popular on the emerging networks. Music composed or stylistically influenced by blacks had a substantial presence on the airwaves, even though black musicians were generally excluded from the airwaves.

The comedy programs prevalent in American radio in the twenties and the thirties have been described as minstrel radio. Radio appropriated the format of race-based comedy from the minstrel and vaudeville shows that had dominated American entertainment immediately before the advent of radio. In these shows, white characters in blackface caricatured African Americans. There were the docile Sambo and Mammy, the ungrateful and vicious Zip Coon, the overambitious mulatto—all with a proclivity for malapropisms. The exemplar of minstrel radio was *Amos 'n' Andy*, in which white actors portrayed African Americans. The show, which aired on the American Broadcasting Company's network, was extremely popular, regularly attracting up to 53 percent of the audience and stimulating the sale of radio sets. The formula was copied by other networks. CBS aired *Two Black Crows*, and NBC broadcast *Watermelon and Cantaloupe, Moonshine and Sawdust*, and *Molasses and January*. These shows presented African Americans as irresponsible, blundering fools. Through media reinforcement, these comedic representations have persisted along with other stereotypes of the African American. Racist representations on television have become much more subtle and may be considered to have been naturalized to the new medium. Such is the nature of "new racism" in the United States.[6]

The exclusion and stereotyping that dominated blackface radio triggered resistance by the African American community and a coalition of progressive forces in society as a whole. Leading the resistance were African American newspapers, civic organizations such as the NAACP, community leaders, and government agencies. The resistance took many forms, including the development of alternative radio programs and the development of African American–owned broadcasting companies.

Brokerage was the dominant practice in the development of early black radio in the United States. In 1927, two newspapers—the *Pittsburgh Courier* and the *Chicago Defender*—began to sponsor black-oriented programs on radio stations in their cities, both of which were important destinations for African Americans migrating from the South. In 1929, the Harlem Broadcasting Corporation was established to profile African American talent. The corporation used brokerage as its operating strategy. Its success with brokerage, and that of Jack L. Cooper, led to its adoption in Detroit, Chicago, Washington, D.C., and other cities with significant black populations. The NAACP adopted similar strategies and sponsored similar programs in 1931. World War II brought blackface radio to an end.[7]

Racial harmony in the United States, at least superficially, was a prerequisite for successful mobilization for World War II. Axis propaganda broadcast by shortwave to U.S. forces overseas and to Americans at home used American racism as a wedge.[8] Axis propaganda also targeted the German, Italian, and Japanese communities in the United States and aimed at enrolling their support in the war effort on the side of the Axis powers. Japanese propaganda broadcasts that targeted African Americans "often depicted the actual situation in the [United States]: lynching, discrimination against Blacks and other minorities, [and] Jim Crow laws." Japanese propaganda was effective in that it "threatened the United States Government with concrete evidence of its own hypocrisy [and] forced the American military to reevaluate its racial hierarchy if it wished to maintain domestic tranquility while pursuing total war."[9]

In response to these challenges to national security, mainstream American radio stations became more inclusive in their programming practices. Soap operas, one of the staples of radio programming at that time, became patriotic in tone and portrayed African Americans in a positive light. Governmental agencies such as the U.S. Office of Education and the Office of War Information produced programs aimed at integrating African Americans into the wider society. The

Armed Forces Radio Service not only aired programs to U.S. forces overseas to counter Axis propaganda but also broadcast black music performed by black musicians. Ethnic European radio programs were mobilized in the war effort as well. And although there was a return to segregationist practices after the war, the seeds of change had been sown.

The period right after World War II saw an acceleration in the growth of the American economy and increased efforts by manufacturers to stimulate consumption. These efforts were promoted by manufacturers of automobiles and domestic appliances and by providers of leisure goods and services. The African American—now no longer primarily an agricultural sharecropper but a wage earner in major metropolitan markets such as Detroit, Chicago, Philadelphia, New York, and Washington—became an increasingly important consumer and therefore a target for advertisers. This pattern has been repeated for other racial and ethnic communities—especially European ethnic groups and Spanish-language and Asian consumers.

By the early fifties, the radio market was depressed due to the arrival of television. However, the continued popularity of black music among another generation of white America and the demographics of African Americans led to the emergence of a new phase in radio broadcasting in the U.S.—black-oriented radio. William Barlow associates this reinvention of radio with developments at WDIA, a Memphis station established in 1947. The white owners of WDIA began to program black music as its format, emphasizing rhythm and blues and gospel (209–12). This programming shift attracted both black and white audiences and proved to be profitable. The format was quickly adopted in important national media markets.

By the mid-sixties, dramatic changes were afoot in all aspects of American society. The civil rights movement contributed to the legal dismantling of segregation and other race-based obstacles to black progress. Among the consequences of this dismantling was the emergence of black-owned radio stations—aided by the popularity of black music, the style of black disc jockeys (DJs), significant audiences in major media markets, and demonstrations of profitability by the black-oriented radio phenomenon, along with the amelioration of structural obstacles such as access to finance. Several genres are associated with the African American radio presence in the United States, including urban contemporary, jazz, blues, gospel, and hiphop. *Broadcasting and Cable Yearbook 2000* reports 140 radio stations with formats associated with African Americans (119 commercial and 21 noncommercial; 100 are AM). African American radio has been mainstreamed in the major radio markets in the United States. In many of these markets, African Americans are the majority of the audience. However, despite the importance of the radio market, the size of the audience, and the popularity of the formats, stations owned or formatted by African Americans generate only about three-quarters of the revenue "as similarly situated general market stations."[10]

In 1999, the FCC commissioned a study on discriminatory practices by the advertising industry vis-à-vis African American and other minority radio stations in markets where they held the top rankings. The report, *When Being Number One Is Not Enough,* concludes that the advertising industry had in place practices—"no urban dictates" and "minority discounts"—that were inhibiting the "ability of minority broadcasters to generate advertising revenues." "No urban dictates" refers to instructions by advertisers and advertising agencies to media buyers not to purchase advertisements on urban-formatted radio stations. (In the radio industry, *urban* refers to a music format targeting predominately black audiences.) "Minority discounts" refers to the practice of paying less money for commercial time on stations that target minority listeners. This practice, according to minority broadcasters, especially African American and Hispanic broadcasters, "accounts for a substantial loss of revenue from the sale of advertisements."[11]

The path taken by America's largest minority community in the field of radio broadcasting reflects that group's movement from the margins of the industry to the mainstream. In its growth, African American radio has served as a provider of community service, a provider of unserved cultural programming, and a creator of crossover audiences. African American radio in the United States has demonstrated social, cultural, and economic relevance. Some of the patterns in the African American experience are also evident in the experiences of other ethnic and racial communities in their relations with the radio industry in the United States.

Polish radio in the United States is a clear example of radio's role in the creation and maintenance of identity by a European ethnic community in the United States. The first Polish radio program in the United States was broadcast on station WJAY in Cleveland in 1926. Polish radio was still very much alive at the start of the twenty-first century. In 1999, four stations had a Polish format and almost 190 more offered more than 750 hours of Polish programming per week.[12] The first program was developed by a bilingual Pole, John M. Lewandowski, in response to a request from the management of WJAY. The program featured live performances of Polish songs sung by Paul Faut, a Pole who came to the United States in 1922 (119). Since then, Polish radio has grown from an occasional program to an established presence in American broadcasting. As with most ethnic broadcasting in the United States, records for the early years of Polish broadcasting are virtually nonexistent. In the 1980s, there were more than 260 stations in twenty-seven states broadcasting almost 700 hours of programs for Polish-speaking audiences located mostly in the Midwest and the Northeast.

Polish broadcasting has consolidated its position over the past two decades. Polish radio programming follows the Polish American population, which is fairly stable. In 1999, there were 188 stations in twenty-five states broadcasting more than 750 hours of programming for Polish audiences. Although there was a decline in the number of stations, there was an increase in the number of hours of programming. Most of the stations remained in the Midwest and the Northeast. The programming patterns support the conclusion that immigrants from eastern and southeastern Europe "are most inclined to live in the Northeast and North Central (Midwest) regions, in central cities, or in metropolitan rings." Polish radio in the United States has been central to the construction of Polonia—a cultural, political, and economic force representing peoples of Polish descent in the

United States. Indeed, Polonia is global, as it also refers to the Polish diaspora.[13]

Polish radio programming has also played an important role in the maintenance of the Polish language in America. George and Eugenia Stolarczyk, who began producing and airing radio programs in 1961, are credited as the first to broadcast Polish language lessons on the air.[14] Radio's role in promoting and sustaining culture Polish culture and popularizing polka music in the United States is also indisputable. Among the first to broadcast this musical genre were Chester J. Zablocki's *Chet's Polka Party* on WTOD in Toledo and Frank Swita's bilingual program *The International Polka Parade* on WXEN-FM in Cleveland. In the late seventies and early eighties, the dominant musical genre on Polish radio was polka music, an American phenomenon that has its roots in Czechoslovakian music of the 1800s. Its popularity is due in no small part to the fact that many producers of Polish radio shows were also leaders of orchestras. Walter Jagiello (Li'l Wally) started the first polka show in 1950 on WCRW in Chicago. The Polka King recorded several hits and toured the United States and Europe, and his program was so popular that stations with stronger signals competed for his program.

Much has happened since Li'l Wally started his show in 1950. There is now an International Polka Association, a Polka Hall of Fame, and January has been declared National Polka Month.[15] Polka music is among the top-selling genres of recorded music in America. The popularity of polka music illustrates three related concepts—cultural proximity, cultural similarity, and cultural shareability—among eastern Europeans in the United States. The ease of sharing could be a function of geographic proximity or religious similarity.

Polka music is another example of ethnic music having cross-over appeal—no doubt a function of radio programming and spillover audiences (audiences not intended by the programmers). In addition to music, Polish radio provided an avenue for Polish literature, drama, comedy, and religion and delivered news and information from Poland and the United States in the Polish language. Polish-language programs also served as an outreach vehicle for Polish educational and cultural groups. One such group, the Golden Age Committee in Chicago is credited with launching Polish-language radio in Chicago. And the Polish newspaper *Rekord codzienny* (Daily record) established Polish radio in Detroit in 1930 (177).

Polish radio also served as a valuable channel for promoting Polish businesses to Polish consumers. Some stores in Polish neighborhoods created their own radio programs, Chicago's New Grand Leader department store being the first to do so (126). Other programs, such as those aired by the Bruno Kujawski Piano Company and Star West Wash Laundry, mirrored commercial developments in mainstream radio at the time. For example, the term *soap opera* is a result of the fact that most serial drama on early America radio was produced by the soap and detergent companies, such as Ohio's Procter and Gamble.

Polish radio also provided a venue for political action. The Polish National Alliance (PNA), a "fraternal insurance benefit association," was associated with the formative years of Polish radio in the United States. The PNA was founded in 1880 in Philadelphia by Polish émigrés "to support the independence of their partitioned Polish homeland and to give humanitarian assistance to its people." Those ideas were not particularly new, but the PNA succeeded because of the phenomenal growth of Polish immigration to the United States (30,000 Poles in America in 1860; 2 million in 1900) and the commitment of its founders to "the betterment of the conditions of the immigrant population." PNA is the largest of all fraternals in the United States "formed on the basis of the nåtional origins of their members."[16] Membership is secured by the purchase of life insurance. In 1998, PNA had assets totaling $304 million and was providing insurance coverage in excess of $721 million.

On May 1, 1987, the Polish National Alliance started the operation of the radio station WPNA in Chicago. The station's signals are heard in Chicago and in the surrounding suburbs, "broadcasting the most Polish language and Polka (in English) broadcasts in the United States." The station provides twenty-four-hour Polish programming Monday through Friday. As a time-brokered station, it sells air time for other ethnic-language programs that are aired on the weekend. The station describes its weekend schedule as "balanced with Polish,

Irish, Ukrainian, Arabic, Blues, Gospel, Polka, and Public Affairs." Including its Internet presence, the station's Chicago listenership is estimated at 1 million.[17]

Polish radio in the United States has played an important role in mobilizing Polonian public opinion in the United States. It mobilized the Polish American community to support resistance against the domination of their homeland by fascists and communists. Polish radio also served a major role in orienting Polish Americans to American life and values. In its early days, many of these programs were of poor quality, examples of "cultural hideousness." As one early critic stated, "There are programs so absurd, so badly hosted, so idiotically planned, that they evoke only pity and a feeling of shame." But Polish radio survived. In the process, Polish broadcasters developed strategies to manage competition for limited advertising revenues. The earliest example of this form of collaboration was the Polish Radio Syndicate, established in Illinois in 1938. The Polish American Radio Network also broadcasts radio programs across the nation.[18]

Among the motivations for the founders of Polish radio was the need for a vehicle to deliver propaganda to support patriotic and nationalist goals such as Polish independence. In the process of utilizing radio for patriotic and nationalistic ends, John Lewandowski also refined the financial practices and ethics through which Polish radio programs operated. "Lewandowski ran those programs at his own cost. The programs neither belonged to a sponsoring firm nor to the broadcasting radio station as was customary at the time. In relation to the radio station, Lewandowski was an independent 'broker' who worked for himself. He paid the radio station a certain designated sum of money, found advertisers himself, paid the orchestra and any performing artists who appeared on his show and also paid for any recorded music during the programs" (207). Lewandowski's model has become the preferred model for independent ethnic broadcasters.

Another motivation for Polish broadcasters was to develop a vehicle to promote national culture and their own creativity and talent. Paul Faut, for example, became so successful as a Polish broadcaster and radio performer that he went on to establish radio programs for other European immigrant communities in the United States (among them Hungarian, Romanian, Italian, German, and Lithuanian). These programs, like the Polish ones he developed, served the function of cultural transmission: the popularization of a national culture and its music, traditions, and language (210). Other Polish broadcasters used their programs to orient Polish-speaking immigrants to American life and values.

Polish radio did not exist in isolation. It was part of the network of institutions that made up Polonia. It had links with the church and with labor. Bulletin boards in churches and union halls served as program guides. Polish radio permitted intergenerational dialogue between Polish immigrants and persons of Polish ancestry born in the United States. The shows also provided an outlet for talent and creativity and gave Polish Americans training opportunities. It is probable that Vincent Wasilewski, former president of the National Association of Broadcasters, and celebrated television writer Paddy Chayefsky entered broadcasting via Polish radio.

The arrival of the Internet, the World Wide Web, and digital technologies has added new capacity to the three sectors of the broadcasting environment in the United States. These new technologies provide citizens with more options for participation in broadcasting. This has contributed to the creation of a complex, multidimensional, public communication environment in which there are clear patterns of interaction between America's minority communities and the broadcasting industry. Immigrant and other minority communities continue to be important and attractive consumers in the American economy. More and more advertising is being delivered by mainstream commercial broadcasters to these communities. Commercial broadcasters have been developing niche channels and programming in response to the diversity present in American society. The faces of immigrants and America's native-born minorities are becoming more evident in the national broadcasting environment.

4

Broadcasting in the United States

THE UNITED STATES is a media-rich society. Ninety-nine percent of Americans had a radio set in 1999; the average household had at least five. Ninety-eight percent of all American households had television sets in 1999. In 78 percent of the households there was more than one set (the average is slightly more than two), and most sets were color. In that same period, approximately four out of five American households had at least one VCR. During this period the average American home watched television nearly seven and a half hours per day. African Americans viewed just over ten and a half hours, and Hispanics just over eight hours per day.[1]

The Economic Dimensions of Broadcasting in the United States

The broadcasting industry in the United States is complex. In addition to broadcasting outlets—radio and television stations, cable services, and their associated industries—the industry is closely allied with a number of other entities. These include producers and distributors of broadcasting equipment, producers and distributors of music and of radio and television programs, advertising and public relations agencies, and marketing enterprises. The broadcasting industry is one of the vibrant sectors of the U.S. economy. In 1998, expenditures on broadcasting totaled $290.7 billion, or 3.8 percent of the nation's gross domestic product. In 1996, the broadcasting industry generated over $25 billion in trade, up more than 200 percent from 1995. In 2000, there were over thirteen thousand radio stations and sixteen hundred television stations. Eighty-three percent of the radio stations were operated commercially. The remaining 17 percent were operated by the noncommercial public service sector. Of the 1,663 television stations in operation in 2000, 1,288 (77 percent) were commercial operations. Three hundred and seventy-five (375), or 22.5 percent, operated as noncommercial outlets. Sixty-four percent of the television stations—1,065—were affiliated with the major television networks. The remaining 598 (36 percent) operated as independent stations.[2]

Since the late fifties, television has become the dominant broadcasting medium in America in terms of advertising revenue, audience share, and actual influence. In 1990, commercial advertising revenues totaled $29.7 billion. Television attracted $21.3 billion, or 71.7 percent, of this total. Public broadcasting (both radio and television) generated $1.5 billion in income, of which 17 percent came from the federal government. In 2000, the commercial broadcasting sector had advertising revenues of $57.6 billion, and television still earned nearly 70 percent of the advertising pie. In 1999, public broadcasting income amounted to $2.1 billion, of which the federal government provided 14.6 percent. And in 2000, 11,800 cable systems were operating in the United States, a growth of 9 percent since 1990.[3] In 1999, over two-thirds of America's TV households were cable subscribers, generating approximately $42 billion in revenues. This is an attractive economic environment.

Over 98 percent of all American television households are capable of receiving cable television. Cable was originally developed for places that did not receive broadcast television or that had poor reception. Currently, 80 percent of cable subscribers have access to fifty or more channels. Although it is praised for increasing the range of programming options for American audiences, cable is also criticized for regurgitating old program materials, which have been shown to reanimate negative racial, ethic, and gender stereotypes. In 1988, the National Telecommunications and Information Authority (NTIA) predicted that cable would "expand beyond video programming to offer a variety of electronic interactive services, such as electronic shopping, electronic mail, videotext, and security alarm services. Thus, such services are currently being offered by newly constructed and newly upgraded cable systems." Those predictions have come true. Furthermore, cable television is an important site for multicultural broadcasting in the United States (see chapter 7).[4]

The removal of ownership restrictions under the 1996 Telecommunications Act and the attendant rash of megamergers have accelerated the concentration of ownership in the American broadcasting environment. In 1998, twelve companies—the "Mega-Media Twelve"— dominated the U.S. broadcasting and entertainment industries: Time Warner, Disney, NewsCorp, Viacom, Tele-Communications, Inc. (TCI), Sony, General Electric, Westinghouse, Gannett, General Motors, Comcast, and Seagram.[5] By 2001, with AT&T's acquisition of TCI, and the acquisition of Time Warner by America Online, AT&T and AOL had become members.

The Mega-Media Twelve exert a powerful influence on broadcasting in the United States. They own the majority of television stations in the top ten media markets and they own and operate more than six hundred radio stations. As a result, they wield "enormous influence over the nature and amount of news disseminated to the American people" (7–9). In addition, they control the major film studios and practically all the producers of network entertainment broadcasting. (For TCI spin-off Liberty Media's influence on cable networks that target America's minorities, see chapter 5).

Through this pattern of ownership, the Mega-Media Twelve control what is seen by more than half of all cable subscribers—over a million viewers each week (ibid.). Through their control of the major production facilities, the Mega-Media Twelve influence what is developed, what is sold, and what is purchased and how America's racial and ethnic diversity is presented. The Mega-Media Twelve are intimately engaged in the economic and cultural transactions that take place at the intersection of immigration, diversity, and broadcasting in the United States.

The power and influence of this group of companies is global: they have "significant interests in the Scandinavia Broadcasting System; in cable channels in Germany; children's programming in China, Nickelodeon UK; HBO Olé and El Canal in South America; NBC Super Channel in Europe; satellite channels in Europe, Asia, South America; and numerous other interests in many other countries. . . . [Rupert Murdoch's NewsCorp.] empire includes 123 daily newspapers around the world as well as [the Fox Network and] BSkyB, the direct broadcast satellite system in Northern Europe. He also has control of the largest potential television audience, the 1.6 billion persons in the footprint of STAR TV" (ibid.). This reality illustrates the infrastructure associated with the pre-Americanization process. Foreign policy scholars use the term *soft power* to describe the influence that American media products exert globally.[6]

The mergers and acquisitions that characterize contemporary broadcasting in the United States are primarily a function of two factors—ownership deregulation and developments in communication technology—developments that fostered the convergence of broadcasting companies, phone companies, and cable television services.[7] The economic power of American broadcasting and its national and global reach are consequences of the industry's rapid adoption of new communication technologies to enhance geographic reach, transmission quality, audiences, and profits. This capacity determines what we see and hear and controls what and who are represented and how. In this economic model, there are constant pressures to expand markets, reduce above- and below-the-line costs, and find new audiences.

Technology and Broadcasting in the United States

The United States has been among the world's leaders in the development and application of new communication technologies for broadcasting. This pattern began in the late nineteenth century, when the term *broadcasting* was coined by the United States Navy to describe their use of radiotelegraphy (wireless) for disseminating orders to the fleet.[8] By 1922, radiotelegraphy had migrated from purely military purposes and was emerging as experimental broadcast networks. Similar patterns are evident with the transistor, the satellite, and the Internet—each used first by the military.

The broadcasting industry's tradition of appropriating new communication technologies, which began with radio in the twenties, has accelerated since the mid-seventies. Some observers of U.S. technological developments have associated Home Box Office's use of INTELSAT 4 and Weststar satellites to distribute the Ali-Frazier heavyweight title fight on October 1, 1975, as launching the Information Age. Through these satellites, HBO was able to deliver the Thrilla in Manila from the Philippines to homes in the United States through pay-per-view cable services. (First-quarter earnings for pay-per-view television in 1999 were $207 million.)[9]

Since 1975, American broadcasters have sought to improve quality and extend reach by appropriating several other technological developments, including the VCR and the microchip.[10] The rapid diffusion of the VCR and improvements in its capability have triggered changes in television viewing patterns—"time shifting" and "take-out media"—and provided another revenue stream for the broadcasting industry. Immigrant communities also have appropriated the VCR. For example, in the late eighties and mid-nineties, the influential Indian newspaper *India Today* distributed *Newstrack*—a weekly videotape newsmagazine—to the Indian diaspora in the United States. Similarly, in the last decade or so, videotapes of popular Korean, Chinese, Pakistani, and Jamaican soap operas and situation comedies (mostly illegal copies) were available for rent from grocery stores that served those ethnic enclaves in the United States. This practice has been described as piracy in reverse, since the general tendency in video piracy has been the copying of programming from the United States and other developed regions of the north for use in the developing regions in the south. Native-born minorities, especially religious groups, have also appropriated the VCR because it permits the distribution of sermons and entire services to shut-ins and other group members unable to attend. Church-related videotapes have been important revenue streams for African American churches.

Likewise, the microchip, which enabled the development of the home computer, has had a profound impact on all aspects of the American broadcasting industry—management, production, and distribution. The digital, or information, age is the result of the microchip. As early as 1988, Wilbur Schramm noted six emerging trends: "(1) more information, increasing both knowledge potential and the chance of information overload; (2) faster arriving information requiring more efficient scanning, sorting, and processing mechanisms and institutions; (3) more long-distance communication, either mass or point-to-point, improving opportunities for intercultural relationships; (4) more point-to-point rather than point-to-mass communication, enabling cheaper, easier, tailored messages; (5) computers assuming tasks previously done by people; and (6) power increasingly accruing to people who gather, store, retrieve, and process information."[11]

These trends have given new power and scope to the American broadcasting industry as the utilization of computers, satellite distribution and receiving systems, integrated circuits, digital audio and video recording and transmission, and broadband distribution technologies in broadcasting have converged. In 1993, when *Electronic Media* reported Time Warner's plans for its national introduction of a digital computerized cable network that would deliver hundreds of channels of interactive entertainment, data, consumer and telephone services on viewer demand, there was general astonishment and some skepticism.[12] Those attributes since have become the standard expectation of cable broadcasting in the United States. Time Warner's digital cable service, with Road Runner broadband Internet, has been deployed in virtually all major U.S. media markets.

Technological convergence has rearranged the American information and communication environment. At the center of this development are inexpensive, fast, and powerful computers that are facilitating interactivity. The marketing and promotion industries already exploit interactivity as they refine their market segmentation techniques to target preferred audiences and potential consumers. Technological convergence, and changes in federal regulations have brought new players to broadcasting. The significant new players included the telephone companies (telcos) who already had the infrastructure that connected them to 99 percent of American households. Conversely, the cable companies, with "drop capacity" to almost 90 percent of American homes, have applied the same convergence to compete in the voice and data markets, once the exclusive domain of the telcos. America's minority communities also have been appropriating this capacity. As with previous leaps in the development of human communication, the consequences of technological convergence will have significant cultural and social implications for America and the world.[13]

Communication technologies have two tendencies—one empowers people, and the other leads to their domination. All societies, concerned about these possibilities, have articulated expectations on the roles of information and communication institutions because of the consequences of their performance. These concerns are amplified in multiracial and multiethnic societies such as the United States.

The Cultural Implications of American Broadcasting

Broadcasting has a significant place both in the lives of individuals and in society as a whole. Broadcasting performs an important socializing role, especially for children, adolescents, and, increasingly, for immigrants and other newcomers to American society. French philosopher Jacques Ellul has used the term "propaganda of integration" to describe the process whose aim is developing societal conformity: "Propaganda of integration . . . aims at making the individual participate in his society in every way. It is a long-term propaganda, a self-reproducing propaganda that seeks to obtain stable behavior, to adapt the individual to his everyday life, to reshape his thoughts and behavior in terms of the permanent social setting."[14]

Broadcasting helps Americans learn about the world and how to interact socially. Broadcasting also plays an important role in determining relationships among social, economic, and political institutions. Broadcasting is itself a central institution in contemporary American society. Other institutions—government, education, business, law—depend on broadcasting to provide access to the audiences and markets they need to achieve their missions. Broadcasters likewise depend on social, economic, and political institutions. Media systems dependency theory explains these reciprocal relationships and explains how media content can be influenced by their strength.[15]

The following list suggests several metaphors for the central position held by broadcasting in contemporary industrialized and post-industrial societies:

a *window* on events and experience, which extends our vision, enabling us to see for ourselves what is going on, without interference from others;

a *mirror* of events in society and the world, implying a faithful reflection (albeit with inversion and possible distortion of the image), although the angle and direction of the mirror are decided by others, and we are less free to see what we want;

a *filter* or *gatekeeper,* acting to select parts of experience for special attention and closing off other views and voices, whether deliberately or not;

a *signpost, guide,* or *interpreter,* pointing the way and making sense of what is otherwise puzzling or fragmentary;

a *screen* or *barrier,* indicating the possibility that the media might cut us off from reality, by providing a false view of the world, through either escapist fantasy or propaganda.[16]

Consider radio—an "old" technology that continues to hold an important place in American society. "Wake-up" and drive time radio are important elements in the daily life of most Americans. The continued proliferation of "walk-along" sets, such as Sony's Walkman, and special-format programming ensures that most Americans have daily contact with this medium. Satellite radio, cable radio, and Internet radio—all digital technologies—have given this medium new vitality. Minority communities in the United States also have appropriated these technologies. An example of this is Radio Demerara, a web radio station dedicated to Indo-Guyanese culture in the United States and around the world.

The place of television in American society is even more dramatic. In its 1988 review of commercial television in the United States, the NTIA concluded that "television, for good or ill, has helped to homogenize American society by providing a common cultural frame of reference for Americans of all regions, incomes, and backgrounds." Since 1959, Roper Starch Worldwide has been studying the role of television in the lives of the American public. Its 1997 report concluded that "television remains America's primary and most credible source of news and product information, as well as a source of information on important social issues." For 55 percent of the respondents, watching television together was the second most frequent activity done as a family.[17]

Network television appears to have the power to define what is "real" and "true" for substantial sectors of the population. According to the 1997 Roper Starch report, 53 percent of the respondents indicated that they would be "most inclined" to choose television over other media if they were to receive conflicting reports. Newspapers were favored by only 23 percent, and radio by 7 percent. Network television is an essential element of the American electronic media environment. According to George Gerbner, television has "reshaped the way our children are reared and socialized, the way we manage our lives, and the way we conduct our public affairs. A child is born into a home in which television is on an average of almost eight hours per day. For the first time in human history, most of the stories are told not by parents, schools, churches, or others in the community who have something to tell, but by a group of distant conglomerates that have something to sell."[18]

Television is undoubtedly a principal provider of entertainment for Americans. Gerbner's report on characters in prime-time and daytime entertainment American television from 1994 to 1997 concluded that the stories told on television misrepresent the racial, ethnic, or gender composition of the United States. For example, African American males (but not females) were overrepresented on American television. By 1997, their presence had increased to 171 percent of its real-life proportion. White males and females were also overrepresented. Asian or Pacific characters were less than one-half of their proportion of the U.S. population, and Latino characters, less than one-third. Mentally ill or "foreign" characters were likely the ones that had failed in life or were the most violent.[19]

The way television presents America's diversity in news, information, and entertainment programming has significant consequences, because it may be the only contact that some Americans have with this diversity. The cumulative effect of these representations can construct social perceptions of people of color and other minorities. A consistent criticism of American television is that it tends to exclude, trivialize, and marginalize people of color, women, and the old. The central mechanism in broadcasting is the story. In commercial television, the story is presented in various packages—program genres. The structure and content of these socializing stories appear to be constant. They are formulaic. We can anticipate the conclusions.[20] The cop will always get the bad guy. In old westerns, the guys who wore white hats always got the bad guys, who tended to wear black hats. These are the dominant structures of the contemporary story and they can influence the way we perceive reality.

The term *representation* is complex and central to the discussions in this book. Jeffrey Escoffier identifies two dimensions to the term that will be useful. Both senses are clearly examples of the act of communicating something about a particular group to the larger society. The first, political representation, refers to roles as delegate or spokesperson for a particular community. The second, cultural representation, is a particularly sensitive matter in this country and is more relevant here. Specifically, it is the "symbolic content of various cultural formats and the ways that particular social groups are portrayed in fiction, movies, or television."[21] For example, in 1999 the NAACP, the oldest civil rights organization in the United States, launched its Television and Film Diversity Initiative to address the lack of representation of African Americans and other people of color in prime-time television (see chapter 6).

Theorizing American Broadcasting

Most mass communication theories have been developed during the twentieth century and have cumulatively sought to describe and explain many aspects of the phenomenon—the process of exchanging information (including ideas, opinions, values, and entertainment) via a mass medium, the power of the media corporations, the effects of media products on individuals and society, the impact of the mass media on democratic institutions, their impact on morality and values, their role in race relations and representations of "the other," and their role in the construction of social reality.[22] Theories of mass communication also seek to predict outcomes that result from the process. Further, these theoretical formulations inform public policies aimed at directing and controlling the mass communication phenomenon.

Theories useful in discussions of the intersection of immigration, diversity, and broadcasting may be divided into four categories: social scientific theory, normative theory, working theory, and commonsense theory. The theories used so far in this chapter may be described as social scientific theories, that is, formulations that "permit [systematic] statements about the nature, workings, and effects of mass communication." Normative theories articulate a society's expectations of the role of the mass media in the promotion and maintenance of that society's social values. Working theories have been described as normative theories with a practical bent. They concern "not only how media should really operate, but how they can operate to meet specific ends."[23] Commonsense theories are those positions that individuals in a society hold about matters such as the quality of programming and are based on their individual experiences as consumers of the mass media.

Some theories of mass communication have focused on the individual, or micro, level and others on the societal, or macro, level. Still others have focused on the mid-range. These latter theories—developed by social scientists, social critics, politicians, and ordinary citizens—are guided by various "philosophies of science" (approaches to generating and sharing knowledge) and various "theories of society" (orientations to the nature of human society).[24] Mass communication scholars have to grapple with four categories of profound and interrelated questions as they articulate their philosophy of science: ontological questions, epistemological questions, questions about human nature, and questions of methodology. For the sake of explanation I will pose the polar opposite positions associated with these four questions.

Ontological questions are concerned with the nature of the mass communication phenomenon: Is it a reality that is external to the individual, and therefore objective? Or is it a product of the human mind, and therefore subjective? Epistemological questions ask how certain we are that the knowledge we have generated about the mass communication phenomenon is true or false. Is the knowledge based on objective patterns? Or is it subjective and based on personal and individual experience? Of equal importance are questions associated with human nature: Are human beings influenced and passively determined by their environment (determinism)? Or do human beings create and influence their environments—"the controller as opposed to the controlled, the master rather than the marionette" (2)? The latter position is referred to as voluntarism.

The ontological stance, the epistemological position, and perspectives on human nature inform methodological practices. At the heart of the methodology discourse are strategic questions and practices. At one extreme is the *nomothetic stance,* which "lays emphasis on the importance of basing research upon systematic protocol and technique. . . . It is preoccupied with the construction of scientific tests and the use of quantitative techniques for the analysis of data" (7). At the other extreme is the *ideographic stance,* which is "based on the view that one can only understand the social world by obtaining firsthand knowledge of the subject under examination." This orientation emphasizes "getting close to one's subject and exploring its detailed background and life history. The ideographic approach emphasizes the analysis of the subjective accounts which one generates by 'getting inside' situations and involving oneself in the everyday flow of life— the detailed analysis of the insights generated by such encounters with one's subject and the insights revealed in impressionistic accounts found in diaries, biographies and journalistic records" (7).

Theories of mass communication also consider the nature of society. Do societies strive to maintain stability? Or are they impelled by conflict? One model divides theories about society into two categories. Regulatory theories emphasize maintaining the status quo, social order, consensus, solidarity, social integration, and cohesion. Radical change theories examine the structural conflicts, modes of domination, and contradictions in society; they also seek to identify strategies for emancipation and the promotion of human potential.

The phenomena we are examining in this book require us to take an integrated approach to the questions of "philosophy of science" and the nature of society. Therefore, all four categories of theory (social scientific theory, normative theory, working theory, and commonsense theory) are relevant in a book such as this one. This inclusive approach to the construction of this theoretical framework is associated with the way in which mass communication theory has developed in the United States.

FOUR PHASES IN THE DEVELOPMENT OF MASS COMMUNICATION THEORY IN THE UNITED STATES

As it is possible to identify four categories of theories that are associated with the theorizing of mass communication, it is also possible to identify four phases or eras in the development of mass communication theory in the United States.[25] Each of these eras is associated with advances in research methods and more sophisticated interpretative options. These advances, in turn, have influenced the articulation of normative theory.

The first era has been described as the era of mass society and mass culture. The essential idea is that industrialization, urbanization, and other civilizational shifts have turned American society into a mass society. As a result, the average American has lost his social and cultural moorings and has become alienated. This condition has allowed the new mass media to have powerful and direct effects. Emblematic of the era are the Magic Bullet theory (which holds that the mass media have direct, immediate, powerful, and lasting effects) and the Payne Fund studies.

The first mass medium in the United States to come under systematic scrutiny for its influence was film. By the twenties, motion pictures had become a major part of American life. They were an inexpensive and popular form of family recreation. In 1922, over 40 million movie tickets were sold. By the end of the twenties, over 90 million tickets were sold annually, of which "an estimated 40 million were sold to minors, and among them were approximately 17 million children under the age of fourteen."[26] Film was catalyzing substantial shifts in American society. Specifically, it was feared that film was eroding the nation's Victorian moorings and that the new openness evident in the cinema would undermine "established moral standards."

More important was the application of early social science research methods to the study of the effects of film on American society. The vehicles for this research were the thirteen studies conducted between 1929 and 1933 that were initiated by the Motion Pictures Research Council, conducted by academicians, and funded by the Payne Fund, a philanthropic foundation. The Payne Fund Studies had two goals: to find out more about the content of films and the size and composition of their audiences and to "assess the effects on those audiences of their exposures to the themes and messages of motion pictures," especially the "acquisition of information, change in attitudes, stimulation of emotions, harm to health, erosion of moral standards, and influence on conduct" (35). Of particular relevance were the findings that exposure to movies had produced significant attitudinal changes in the area of race and ethnic relations. Children who were exposed to films that showed nonwhite characters in a positive light demonstrated positive attitudes toward those groups. Conversely, films that projected nonwhite characters in a negative light resulted in negative attitudes (40). These early studies, using the most sophisticated methods available at that time, indicated that film—a mass medium—had the power to influence the audience's beliefs, emotions, and behaviors, as well as relations between the races. Those findings resonated with the conclusions of Walter Lippmann, who earlier had concluded that the concentration of power in the hands of the owners of the mass media meant they could create the pictures of reality in the minds of Americans.

Social scientific theories of the late thirties, forties, and fifties, as well as emerging social theory, characterize the second era. These theories propose that the mass media has limited effects but serves important functional roles. In the forties, scholarly attention shifted to radio. The research methods available to mass communication researchers were more robust, which allowed researchers to explore more complex aspects of mass media's power and influence. Emblematic of the research at that time is the idea that audiences had developed a dependency on radio for information, entertainment, and education. That conclusion was incorporated into what became known as the Classical Four Functions of the Media, developed by Harold Lasswell and Charles Wright: surveillance of the environment—indicating what was going on, correlation of the parts of society in responding to the environment—how things fit together, transmission of the social heritage from one generation to the next, and entertainment.[27]

By the start of World War II, American mass media, and especially broadcasting, were predominantly commercial. Profit maximization and rapid returns on investment were among the core practices—working theory. These practices supported what Sydney Head has described as the parsimony principle—the production of programs for the lowest cost that would allow maximum profits—and led to the homogenization of content that has cultural consequences. This reality reenergized the criticisms articulated by Lippmann and others since the twenties. In addition to these practices, there were concerns about the concentration of ownership and political bias. These tendencies were considered to be detrimental to the wider society and led to establishment in 1942 of a private commission under Robert Hutchins, then chancellor of the University of Chicago. The commission's report would be one of the major articulations of normative media theory in the United States during the twentieth century.

The mission of the commission was "to examine areas of and circumstances under which the press of the United States is succeeding or failing; to discover where free expression is or is not limited, whether by government censorship pressure from readers or advertisers or the unwisdom of its proprietors or the timidity of the management."[28]

The commission's report in 1947 found that the press tended to privilege the voices of a small and powerful minority in American society. The voices of groups outside of that circle were muted if not silent. The commission used the term *social responsibility* to articulate the role mass media should strive to maintain in America. Specifically, the Hutchins Commission advocated the idea that the media environment in the United States should support diversity of views; should be objective, informative, and independent; and should avoid causing offense or encouraging crime, violence, or disorder. For the commission, social responsibility should not only allow freedom, it should actively promote freedom. The commission also expressed the position that media ownership should be considered a form of public trust and not be controlled exclusively by private interests.

In summary, social responsibility theory holds that "(a) the media have obligations to society and media ownership is a public trust; (b) news media should be truthful, accurate, fair, objective, and relevant; (c) the media should be free but self-regulated; (d) media should follow agreed codes of ethics and professional conduct; and (e) under some circumstances government may need to intervene to safeguard the public interest" (150). These views, although initially articulated for the press, have formed the underpinnings for what is expected from all mass media in the United States. It is evident that the Hutchins Report was guided by a theory of society—libertarianism. Libertarianism originates in the proposition that humans are capable of reasoned thought without relying on a monarch, priest, or anyone else who claims to have a special relationship with God.

By the fifties, the study of mass communication had become a major academic enterprise, attracting support from government and industry.[29] The dominant theorizing held that the mass media have only limited effects. Changes to American society in the sixties ushered in another phase in mass communication theorizing in the United States, "cultural criticism and the challenge to the limited effects paradigm."[30] During this era, theorizing dominated by positivism gave way to theorizing that focused on the concentration of ownership of mass media properties and the tendency to exclude minority groups from participation in the mass media, as well as on the role the mass media played in ensuring that the dominant elites maintained power and the consequences of that hegemony on culture, politics, and international relations. The combined weight of this scholarship reinvigorated the conclusion that the mass media in the United States had significant effects at individual and societal levels.

The social unrest of the sixties, especially the urban disturbances, led to the creation of the Kerner Commission (see chapter 1), which in 1968 called upon the mass media to live up to the expectations of libertarianism. Despite its many internal contradictions, such as facilitating the concentration of ownership, marginalizing voices, and encouraging formulaic programming, libertarianism is the essential core of American normative theory. Since then, successive administrations have introduced many policies and programs aimed at encouraging the participation of minority groups in the broadcasting industry, including setting aside spectrum space (frequencies for broadcasting) for educational programming, creating opportunities for ethnic minorities and women to acquire media properties, encouraging the production of programs by minority groups through special funding, and ensuring community access through the regulations that guide cable operations in municipalities. Further, it appears that these actions have been justified by the proposition that the construction of American community must allow for the expression of all its members. This is a right enshrined in the First Amendment of the Constitution. These policy interventions are dynamic translations of the nation's normative theories of the media and form part of the nation's expectations of media performance—their contributions to freedom, solidarity, equity, and social justice. Commitment to these values is expected to have a positive effect on race relations in the United States. We will return to these topics in subsequent chapters.

By the eighties, the fourth era had emerged, an era of moderate media effects. This development has been described as a function of "pressures from cultural studies and changes in the social research methods." Cultural studies brought to the fore the "active audience that uses media content to create meaningful experiences." Central to this theorizing is the notion that "important media effects can occur over longer periods of time as a direct consequence of viewer or reader intent."[31] The exploration of the effects of mass communication was not just limited to the individuals but was scaled up to include small groups, organizations, nations, and cultural communities, including diasporas. Moderate-effects theorizing reaffirmed the potency of the mass media in American society. The effectiveness of the mass media in promoting and supporting social change is evident in their central place in strategic communication practices—advertising, public relations, and public health communication. Mass communication researchers have recognized the multidimensional nature of broadcasting, its global scope, and the necessity of developing multiple theoretical frameworks to study it. These frameworks draw upon the functionalist and interpretive paradigms and utilize quantitative and qualitative methods.

LIBERTARIANISM AND AMERICAN BROADCASTING

Philosophically, all sectors of the American broadcasting industry—the commercial, the public service, and the community, or alternative—subscribe to libertarian ideals, which originate in the proposition that humans "come to know great truths through applying reason." In 1644, John Milton, an early pioneer of what has become known as libertarianism, argued in *Areopagitica* that all ideas should be freely shared in the "marketplace of ideas" as a prerequisite for allowing rational human beings an opportunity to find truth.[32]

The free sharing of ideas has been enshrined in the media practices of many societies that are culturally and historically connected to this concept. This European idea has flourished in the United States. The Constitution of the United States and its First Amendment, which caution against prior censorship, are guided by the principles of libertarianism. Under this system, broadcasting is controlled by the owners, who are expected to operate in the public interest in a free market of ideas. Associated with the public interest are freedom, diversity, social order, cultural order, and solidarity.

For example, the libertarian model seems to have encouraged the concentration of media ownership and increasing dependency on advertising and sponsorship revenues by broadcasting systems—

commercial and public service—in the United States. One result is the production of homogenized and formulaic programming, as when all the radio networks had programs that were copies of the *Amos 'n' Andy* show (see blackface radio, chapter 3). Such questionable programming practices have encouraged unidimensional and stereotypical representations of the racial and ethnic communities present in the United States.

The tendencies toward concentration of ownership and formulaic programming aimed at maximizing audience share have been evident from the genesis of broadcasting in the United States. These tendencies have been challenged by media scholars and critics, who expect broadcasting to play a more important role in nourishing the American democracy. These tendencies are seen as limiting diversity and thus muting public opinion. One outcome of this struggle between the philosophy of libertarianism and the practices of the marketplace has been the articulation of the social responsibility perspective. This perspective, whose origins were introduced above, informs all broadcasting in America. However, it finds its most consistent expression in public service broadcasting in the United States, as delivered through the Public Broadcasting Service (PBS) and supervised by the Corporation for Public Broadcasting (CPB).

The community broadcasting sector in the United States is guided by an offspring of libertarian philosophy—*democratic-participant media theory,* which emerged in the 1960s. This formulation, facilitated by declining costs and simplification in the operations of broadcasting technologies, emerged in Western Europe as a reaction to the domination of broadcasting by public and private monopolies and their failure to respond to local demands and expectations. According to European mass communication theorist Denis McQuail, democratic participant media theory "supports the right to relevant local information, the right to answer back and the right to use the new means of communication for interaction and social action in small-scale settings of community, interest group or subculture. Both theory and technology have challenged the necessity for and desirability of uniform, centralized, high cost, commercialized, professionalized or state-controlled media. In their place should be encouraged multiple, small-scale, local, non-institutional, committed media which link senders to receivers and also favour horizontal patterns of interaction."[33] Institutions such as community broadcasting, cable access, alternative broadcasting, microbroadcasting, and pirate radio typify this approach in the United States.

Libertarian ideals undergird the nation's normative theory of the media, our expectations about the interrelated issues of media ownership, media freedom, media equality, diversity in media content, information quality, and the role of the media in promoting social cohesion, solidarity, and harmony. These expectations not only guide the formulation of laws to regulate broadcast operations within the nation but also influence the formal and informal curriculum for educating and training media managers and other professionals. A society's normative media theory is an important indicator of its democratic life.

Given these origins, there is an expectation that broadcasters in the United States will facilitate the airing of a multiplicity of voices and ideas. Broadcasters are also expected to promote freedom, equality, and diversity, be mindful of the quality of information they disseminate, and be supportive of social order, solidarity, and cultural order. These commitments encourage fairness and social cohesion, nourish democracy, support emancipation, and promote human potential, attributes that have become essential criteria in evaluating the performance of broadcasting systems.

The intersection of immigration, diversity, and broadcasting in the United States is a complex and contested location that requires many theories to express. In this book, we draw upon such theories as media systems theory, media dependency theory, socialization theories (including theories of cultivation and representation), critical media theories (including Simon Cottle's formulation of the "problematics of race" and Roberta Astroff's "political economy of advertising"), and normative theories informed by libertarianism. The intersection of immigration, diversity, and broadcasting is also a location where human endeavors collide, interact, and re-create themselves. At the intersection we find the primal human response for survival and for improvements in the quality of life. It is a location that influences individual and social relations, individual and collective efficacy, and race relations. It is a location that produces cultural products that are powerful "soft" ammunition in international relations. Through its influence on consumption, it is a key player in the economy. It influences the allocation of power and plays an important role in the construction of a new America—polycultural America. The interactions at this intersection have consequences for all sectors of American life and for the world.

One of the universal attributes of broadcasting is its voraciousness—the insatiable demand for programs. In the United States, this insatiability has sustained the growth of program production and distribution enterprises. Their products are sold not only to broadcasters but directly to consumers. The 2000 Standard and Poor's Industrial Report estimated that American consumers would spend $82 billion for products such as TV programs, music videos, CDs, cassette tapes, and others, not including TV sets, recorders, and players. And in 1999 the United States exported $3.7 billion of television programming to Europe. We can conclude that the images provided by the various media products produced and distributed by the American broadcasting industry help define American life both at home and abroad. And the American identity and representation the industry helps shape are central to the understanding of race and ethnic relations. As a result of trends in international immigration, growth of minority populations, and increases in intermarriage, the issue of cultural identity will become more complex in the United States during the twenty-first century.[34]

Responses to Contradictions in the American Broadcasting Environment

Since 1965, several organizations and agencies in the United States have combated tendencies and practices—especially the negative portrayals of America's minority communities—in the broadcasting industry that undermine efforts to build a more inclusive America. Among them are federal and statutory organizations, academic and political institutions, industry-specific professional organizations, and organizations representing America's minority communities. The Kerner Commission's 1968 report on the organization and operation of mass media in the United States, for example, was emphatic when it concluded that "the news media have failed to analyze and report adequately on racial problems in the United States and, as a related matter, to meet the Negro's legitimate expectations in journalism. By and large, news organizations have failed to communicate to both black and white audiences a sense of the problems America faces and the sources of potential solutions. The media report and write from the standpoint of a white man's world. The ills of the ghetto, the difficulties of life there, the Negro's burning sense of grievance, are seldom conveyed. Slights and indignities are part of the Negro's daily life, and many of them come from what he now calls the 'white press'— a press that repeatedly, if unconsciously, reflects the biases, the paternalism, the indifference of white America. This may be understandable, but it is not excusable in an institution that has the mission to inform and educate the whole society." The report stated that the media "have not shown understanding or appreciation of—and thus have not communicated—a sense of Negro culture, thought, or history," and it directed attention to "the absence of Negro faces and activities from the media" and suggested that this affected white audiences also. "By failing to portray the Negro as a matter of routine and in the context of the total society, the news media have, we believe, contributed to the black-white schism in the country."[35]

Some have argued that American broadcasters, along with other institutions, have responded slowly to the commission's conclusions. However, Sharon Murphy, who has traced media practices after the Kerner Report, has identified some constructive responses on the national level that have helped shape current media practices. The FCC, for example, introduced "requirements for community ascertainment studies, to determine whether and how stations responded to the information needs and desires of their local audiences and for affirmative action in hiring staff." Other FCC initiatives included procedures to facilitate minority ownership of broadcast property.[36] Since 1965, industry associations such as the National Association of

Broadcasters, the Radio and Television and News Directors Association, and the Screen Writers Guild have all launched initiatives to improve the situation. Most were directed at hiring, on the assumption that hiring minorities will bring alternative perspectives to the decision-making and creative processes in American broadcasting. Another positive response was the passage of the Public Broadcasting Act in 1967, out of which came the establishment of statutory public broadcasting entities such as NPR, PBS, and the CPB, which are required by law to provide programming for America's diversity (see chapter 8). Since the Kerner Report, the Corporation for Public Broadcasting, along with the commercial networks and the cable broadcasting industry, has joined with professional organizations to recruit and retain minority talent.

Commercial radio broadcasters have likewise taken steps to increase the recruitment and participation of minority talent. These steps are the result of practices recommended by industry associations like the NAB, the RTNDA, and up to January 16, 2001, the Equal Employment Opportunities rules of the FCC. Organizations such as the National Association of Broadcasters and the Radio and Television News Directors Association have over the past three decades introduced a variety of initiatives aimed at improving the recruitment of minorities. Generally, the results have been spotty. It is now generally recognized that recruitment by itself is not sufficient to influence values and the programming output of mainstream media organizations. Training, corporate socializing, and career ambitions are factors that have influenced the performance of minority broadcasters. The variables orient them to the values of their organizations, and they appear to have more force than race, ethnicity, and gender.[37]

The community sector of the broadcasting industry also has responded to the changing racial and ethnic composition of American society. Minority broadcasters have individually, or in collaboration with commercial or public service broadcasters, crafted a fascinating broadcasting system in America.

5

Radio and America's Diversity

The Little Medium That Refuses to Be Squeezed Out

DESPITE THE POPULARITY of television and other means of mass communication, radio is still a significant medium in American society, partially because it has continued to reinvent itself. Immigrant and other minority audiences have played a role in this reinvention and reinvigoration. Radio is not as expensive as television and, unlike newspapers, it does not require literacy to be consumed. This makes it an attractive medium for new immigrants to the United States.

Radio—particularly commercial, public service, and community radio[1]—has responded strategically to diversity in the United States. In 2000, 9 percent of all American stations had formats that targeted specific racial and ethnic communities. (A format is defined as at least twenty hours per week of a given type of programming.[2] A radio station's format is its personality. For example, if a station airs more than twenty hours of polka programming, it is categorized as a polka station.) This was an increase of almost 2.6 percent since 1992.[3] In 2000, the radio industry had ninety-two radio programming formats. Of these, forty were clearly associated with racial and ethnic communities in the United States (an increase of 175 percent from 1990).[4] The ethnic formats included Albanian, Farsi, Finnish, German, Hindi, Jewish, Lithuanian, Scottish, Tejano, Ukrainian, and Vietnamese. Further, over twenty-two hundred stations (about one in six) indicated that they offered special programming (up to twenty hours per week) for distinct racial and ethnic groups—a total of more than eight thousand hours of programming per week. Radio stations catering to America's diversity can be found in every state and in U.S. territories, including Guam and the Virgin Islands, and they can be found on both AM and FM bands (although most are on the AM band—a legacy from the early days of radio, when AM was the dominant band). Such stations also have a presence on the Internet.

In 1965, U.S. radio stations offered special programming for African Americans, Spanish speakers, and Native Americans, as well as forty-four other distinct ethnic and foreign-language groups.[5] By 1975, there were fifty-nine such categories.[6] Although these formats were still predominantly European, there was more special programming for peoples from Asia and the Caribbean (Calypso, Haitian). Spanish-language special programming on the U.S. mainland had increased in 1975 to over two thousand hours per week (up from just over eight hundred in 1965).[7]

The amount of "special programming" targeted at ethnic and foreign language communities in the United States has been growing

Table 5.1. Ethnic and Foreign-Language Formats on U.S. Radio, 1965–2000

Year	No. of Stations
1965	170
1975	375
1985	428
1989	453
1995	602
1999	867
2000	877

Source: Broadcasting Publications, *Broadcasting Yearbook 1966, 1976, 1986, 1989* (Washington, D.C.: Broadcasting Publications, 1966, 1976, 1986, 1989); Bowker's Database Production Group, *Broadcasting and Cable Yearbook 1996, 2000, 2001* (Washington, D.C.: R. R. Bowker, 1996, 2000, 2001).

Table 5.2. Ethnic and Foreign-Language Special
Programming on U.S. Radio, 1965–2000

Year	Hours per Week
1965	4,384.25
1975	7,038.50
1999	8,387
2000	8,500

Source: Broadcasting Publications, *Broadcasting Yearbook 1966, 1976* (Washington, D.C.: Broadcasting Publications, 1966, 1976); Bowker's Database Production Group, *Broadcasting and Cable Yearbook 2000, 2001* (Washington, D.C.: R. R. Bowker, 2000, 2001).

consistently since 1965. It almost doubled after modifications to the United States immigration law in 1965 (see table 5.2). By 1999, special programming targeting African Americans exceeded twenty-two hundred hours per week, Spanish-language programming over fifteen hundred hours per week, and programming for Native Americans over five hundred hours. Thirty-four discrete ethnic and foreign-language communities were served. In all, 1,230 stations had formats that catered to America's diversity.[8] Since 1975, the number of stations that used the term "ethnic/foreign language" to describe their special programs increased over 160 percent (from 28 to 74). In addition, there were newcomers—reggae, Tejano, and Vietnamese—representing the new immigrants from the Caribbean, Latin America, and Asia. Similar developments also have occurred in American cable television programming since 1990.

Commercial Radio and Minority Communities

Immigrant and minority communities in the United States are internally diverse. For example, the Latino community is made up of many nationalities with Iberian ancestry, among them Cubans, Colombians, Nicaraguans, Dominicans, Mexicans, even Brazilians. Each group has particular residential patterns, musical tastes, religious practices—as do the Indians, Vietnamese, Thais, Filipinos, Cambodians, Japanese, Chinese, and others that make up the Asian immigrant community. African Americans (blacks born in the United States), continental Africans, and people of African ancestry from the Caribbean, Europe, and Latin America constitute black America. The differences of these groups in consumption practices, musical tastes, and residential patterns influence their relations with American broadcasters.

Despite the differences within ethnic and racial communities in the United States, there are very interesting patterns of solidarity. For example, although Indians, Pakistanis, Nepalese, Bangladeshis, and Sri Lankans have legacies of conflict with each other on the Indian subcontinent, they consume many of the same media products in the United States—a result of satellite broadcasting and a network of stores and shops—such as filmi music programs on radio, televised sports (especially cricket) and serials, film, music videos, and recorded music. These products are also being consumed by members of the Indian diaspora in the United States, especially those who have migrated from the Caribbean. The Indian diaspora, especially Indo-Caribbean peoples, are not passive consumers of media products from the Indian subcontinent; they are active participants, contributing materials that are in turn consumed by the global Indian community. This dynamic is evident in the Richmond Hill area in New York City. Here, chutney music—a fusion of Indo- and Afro-Caribbean musical traditions—is also circulated for consumption by global India (peoples from the subcontinent and its diaspora). This practice is a concrete example of what Cottle refers to as "new ethnicity"—one aspect of the three-dimensional problematic of race.

Consider the start-up of the Indo-Caribbean station WICR (89.3 FM) in New York City. Owned and operated by an Indo-Guyanese, its target audience was the city's rapidly growing community of Guyanese and Trinidadians of East Indian origin.[9] Its format was "largely music with a call-in talk show hosted by Dhanpaul Narine and Harry Bisson—*The Dan and Harry Show*—and a variety programme—the *RY Show*. Greetings and requests are encouraged, and news and weather updates are thrown in the mix. The music is predominantly Indian and Indo-Caribbean, with Caribbean music and English oldies added to the blend. The Friday and Saturday dance party mix is a delight with partygoers. The tenor of the radio station is, in principle, Indo-Caribbean."[10] This programming orientation also reflects developments in the political realm. For example, the Indo-Caribbean Federation, based in New York, is aimed at mobilizing the city's Indo-Caribbean political power.[11]

The commercial radio sector has responded cautiously to the changing ethnic composition in terms of investment. In the last two decades, although entrepreneurs appear to have invested in commercial radio properties that target racial and ethnic communities (particularly Asians, blacks, and Latinos), a 1997–98 survey of full-power minority-owned commercial radio and television stations in the United States found negligible increases in minority ownership. Hispanic-owned radio stations increased by nineteen during the period. Black ownership of FM stations increased by four, and Asian Americans acquired three AM stations. There was a decline in the ownership of radio stations by Native Americans.[12] High station prices and limited access to investment capital continued to restrict minority ownership. Further, minority ownership remained concentrated on the AM band and in small markets. In 2000, more than 65 percent of minority stations were AM operations.[13] (Only 44 percent of all U.S. stations were AM in 2000.) Another problem faced by minority-owned and minority-operated radio stations that attracted the attention of the FCC were "no buy" and "minority dictates and discount" advertising practices, that prevented minority-owned stations in urban markets from receiving market rates for the advertising they aired.

The key determinants for investing in commercial minority radio appear to be the size of the target population and their demographic and psychographic attributes—especially age, gender, and consumer behaviors. Remittances from some immigrant communities in the United States are not only important sources of foreign currency and an important plank in the economic life of their home countries, they also influence the nature of radio broadcasting in the United States. For example, Guyanese in the United States remitted almost $97 million to Guyana in 2000.[14]

Some immigrant communities provide significant financial contributions to election campaigns in the home countries. As a result, the radio programming produced for some of these communities, such as those produced by Indo-Guyanese, are supported by the governments and private media businesses from both the home country and the minority community in the United States.[15] Similar practices occur in Canada, the United Kingdom, and other European countries with significant immigrant communities.

Another programming practice that is evident at the intersection of immigration, diversity, and radio broadcasting in the United States is the parsimony principle (see chapter 3). As "race music" supported the introduction and establishment of African American radio in the 1920s, the availability of ethnic music nourishes immigrant and ethnic radio programming currently. Annan Boodram, a New York–based media critic, has concluded that the ethnic music industry is behind all immigrant radio programs in New York.[16] In 1990, no U.S. station had a reggae format. In 1999, five of the six reggae-formatted stations in the United States were commercial operations, and more than 140 stations were providing more than five hundred hours of reggae music per week. This is clearly a function of the reggae music industry. Filmi music—the music from Bollywood, India's film industry—is serving a similar role in South Indian and Indo-Caribbean Indian radio programming in the United States.

The Telecommunications Act of 1996 removed caps on the number of radio stations that could be owned by any single operator, nationally or locally. There are now concerns about the consequences of this act, especially for the concentration of ownership in the American radio industry. For example, in 2001, Clear Channel Communications owned and operated 1,170 commercial radio stations in the United States (10.6 percent of the total).[17] Fears have been expressed that should this concentration of ownership continue, programming for America's diversity would be seen as being of limited economic significance and thus dropped from the program schedule of many stations.

All the participants at the intersection of diversity and the commercial radio sector are using new communication technologies. Satellite-delivered syndicated programs are replacing locally produced programs; computerized systems are reducing station staff.

Substantial aspects of station operations—such as announcing, logging, and the playing of commercials—are now computerized. Further, the Internet is allowing commercial radio to extend its reach. Satellite delivery and the Internet has allowed radio to reinvent itself. American commercial radio products are also consumed overseas. Some products are syndicated to the new commercial stations that are emerging in the developing world and in the former Soviet Union. For example, in 2000, Clear Channel Communication owned and operated 240 radio stations overseas. The Armed Forces Radio and Television Service (AFRTS), the Voice of America, and American Christian radio, especially the evangelical sector, were also rebroadcasting commercial radio products on their global networks. Commercial broadcasters that served America's minority communities—such as New Jersey–based Internet station Radio Demerara and New York's LINKUP Radio—were also appropriating these technologies to reach audiences in the United States and in their home countries.

Public Service Radio and Minority Communities

The services provided under the Public Telecommunications Act of 1988 are the only radio services in the United States that are required by law to respond to the needs of immigrants and other minority groups. The act specifically requires the Corporation for Public Broadcasting (CPB) to respond to the needs of minority and diverse audiences (defined as "racial and ethnic minorities, including African Americans, Asian Americans, Hispanics, Native Americans and Pacific Islanders; recent immigrants; persons who do not speak English as their native language; and adults who lack basic reading skills").[18] The origins of public service or noncommercial radio in the United States can be traced back to 1917, "when 9XM sent out America's first 'educational' broadcast signal from the University of Wisconsin." By 1925, this trend had taken root and led to the creation of the Association of College and University Broadcasting Stations, which later became the National Association of Educational Broadcasters.[19]

The early history of public radio is a record of efforts to marshal the power of radio for positive social ends, as opposed to the perceived crassness of commercial radio. Robert W. McChesney provides illuminating insights into this early period and the tensions that existed between commercial and "educational" broadcasting interests for access to the spectrum. Tona Hangen tells a similar story about the competition between commercial interests and America's religious community for access to the airwaves in the twenties and thirties."[20]

Over the years since the University of Wisconsin's efforts, noncommercial radio has become a significant sector of the radio industry. But this growth has been fraught with problems of human resources, technology, and finance. The Public Broadcasting Act of 1967, which authorized the establishment of the Corporation for Public Broadcasting, has provided organizational stability, facilitated technological improvements (such as satellite-based interconnection, which has allowed for better program exchange), and ensured a degree of guaranteed financial support.

Before signing the Public Broadcasting Act into law, President Lyndon B. Johnson expressed the view that the Corporation for Public Broadcasting, with its radio and television services, would help to advance American democracy by contributing to the "enlightenment of all people" and play an important role in preparing American society for the twenty-first century.[21] The achievement of these goals and ambitions required close and sensitive relationships with local communities. Localism, as this relationship is called, is the hallmark of public radio in the United States. This orientation has permitted the presence of different languages and music on the airwaves. For example, more Hindi, German, reggae, and so-called world music is available on public radio than on commercial radio.

Public service radio continues to grow in popularity. From 1986 to 1999 the number of stations grew from 295 to 650.[22] Most stations are owned and operated by educational organizations, particularly universities. Public radio is the sector most responsive to the changing racial and ethnic composition of the American society. And in 2000, most people surveyed rated public radio a good value for their tax dollar (table 5.3).

Table 5.3. Satisfaction with Taxes Spent on Public Broadcasting, 2000

Population Group	% for Radio	% for TV
General population	58	60
Generation X (b. 1965–80)	62	54
Baby boomers (b. 1946–64)	57	64
Silent generation (b. 1930–45)	54	65
G.I. generation (b. pre-1930)	57	56

Source: Roper Starch Worldwide poll, March 2002, available at http://www.cpb.org/program/pr.php?pm.

Compared to commercial radio in the United States, public radio is more accessible to the communities each station serves. This access allows more community members an opportunity to "make" radio. Public radio also depends on communities for financial and other resources. In 2000, 2.2 million supporters contributed over $185 million, one-third of public radio's revenue. Public radio's popularity is also supported by the networking infrastructure afforded by National Public Radio (NPR). NPR continues to be responsible for "managing the public radio satellite system, producing and distributing programming on the satellite system, and providing its membership with 'representation and support services, such as program advertising, public information, promotion, and audience research' for 650 stations."[23]

In addition to the network infrastructure, National Public Radio—along with other programming services such as Latino USA, American Indian Radio on Satellite, Radio Bilingue, and Public Radio International—provide programming tailored for diverse audiences and tastes. In addition, since 1986, CPB's Radio Program Fund has funded programs aimed at increasing diversity on public radio. Independent producers who produce programs for minority communities have received about 75 percent of the radio production awards from the CPB radio fund. In 1999, there were ninety applications, altogether seeking more than $15 million. Twenty applicants were awarded a total of $4.5 million.[24]

During the last two decades, long-lived programs like *Afropop Worldwide, Crossroads,* and *Horizons* have reflected America's diversity. *Afropop Worldwide,* produced by World Music Productions of

Brooklyn, celebrates the many dimensions of global African popular music on more than two hundred public radio stations. One reviewer remembers hearing a rough cut of *Afropop* for the initial application for the program's funding: "This really was the sense of the power of radio. . . . [T]he producer was not only teaching us about music, but he was taking us to the site of the creation of the music, and he was walking us through these different towns and villages, and talking to the artists. . . . We were getting educated about music, understanding this whole new world out there. This was before the concept of world music had emerged."[25] *Afropop Worldwide,* aired in Africa, the Caribbean, Europe, and Latin America, not only connects Africans around the globe but gives listeners an appreciation of the "contribution of Afro-Atlantic civilizations to world culture."[26]

For over two decades, public radio has organized programs aimed at improving human resources, especially providing training for women and minorities and enabling them to take on higher levels of leadership within the sector. CPB's Minority Recruitment and Professional Development Initiatives have been in operation since the eighties. One example of this initiative is the master's degree in public telecommunications offered by Ohio University's School of Telecommunications for women and minorities under the CPB Fellows program, begun in 1988 and still in operation in 2001. A similar program in "news and public affairs" was offered at Ohio State University during the 1980s. In 1986, CPB introduced the Production Fellows Project, providing on-site production experiences for women, minorities, and the physically challenged.

The public radio sector has continued to collaborate with external agencies to develop training opportunities for members of racial and ethnic communities. In 2000, NPR and the W. K. Kellogg Foundation, along with the Native American Journalists Association, the National Association of Black Journalists, the National Association of Hispanic Journalists, the Asian American Journalists Association, and the National Lesbian and Gay Journalists Association cosponsored training programs for young people interested in careers as radio journalists.[27] This program was in addition to NPR's ongoing internship program. These efforts are considered necessary as it was clear that public radio, especially urban public radio, was not as inclusive as expected. In 2002, Fairness and Accuracy in Reporting (FAIR) found that "the dominant voices on the leading public radio stations in seven U.S. urban markets are overwhelmingly white and predominantly male."[28]

The Corporation for Public Broadcasting has also given individual stations money to acquire technologies for reaching minority and ethnic audiences through projects like the 1990 Public Radio Expansion project, established through the Multicultural Programming Fund. The Rural and Minority Initiative, begun in 1991, sought to "help rural and minority audience stations extend the reach of their signal and expand service to new audiences, collect audience data, and develop training programs."[29]

Like commercial radio, American public radio has global connections. More than 140 hours per week of National Public Radio programs are distributed to radio stations in fifty countries worldwide.[30] Also like commercial radio, NPR programs are rebroadcast by the AFRTS and the Voice of America. In addition, the Internet and webcasting have made American public radio increasingly accessible around the globe.

Community Radio and Minority Communities

Community radio is probably the purest expression of the libertarian philosophy in radio broadcasting in the United States. Specifically, it is a manifestation of democratic-participant broadcasting ideals (see chapter 4). The Pacifica system, which was started in 1949 with station KPFA in Berkeley, California, is recognized as the genesis of community radio in the United States. The system was founded by nonsectarian pacifist Lewis Hill, who believed that "democracy requires a wide diversity of ideas." KPFA was expected to be the national model for "listener-supported, community-based radio." For five decades, the Pacifica system held to this model and grew to become a national network, with stations in California, New York, and Washington, D.C. The system provided access to minority broadcasters and independent producers. For more than fifteen years, Trinidadian-born Von Martin has been producing and presenting a weekly program of news, interviews, and music for the West Indian community in Washington, D.C. His program became so influential that West Indian governments sought access to his program to communicate with their nationals in the area. Martin was a regular guest of the government of Guyana in the eighties, and a guest of other West Indian governments in the nineties. In addition, he operates a private news agency that supplies materials to mainstream media outlets. According to Von Martin, these services are only used when there is a crisis in the region.[31]

By the late 1990s, the Pacifica system was in crisis as the national board attempted to curb what jazz critic Nat Hentoff described as Pacifica's "wild-eyed zealotry" and to replace it with a more commercial orientation.[32] The "treasonable" move by the national board was seen as an attempt to limit the diversity of ideas and as pandering to commercial interests, and the shift led to physical clashes at several stations in the Pacifica system. So Pacifica's dependency on foundation and philanthropic dollars has changed its operational style.

A more radical element in the community broadcasting family is "pirate" radio, sometimes referred to as microradio. One example of this tradition is San Francisco's Liberation Radio (93.7 FM) which serves the western San Francisco community. The station's mission statement indicated that the station was committed to freedom and social justice and "to giving our audience a politically progressive point of view, with a special emphasis on topics of local concern. As a non-commercial radio station, we will concentrate on airing voices and viewpoints that are now totally excluded from the airwaves. These include local citizens and citizen groups opposed to domination and control of our city by national and multi-national corporations. We will also broadcast independent music, call-in talk shows, uncensored news and children's programming. The vast majority of shows will be produced locally by our staff."[33]

Pirate radio has been part of the American broadcasting scene since the inception of radio, and there appears to have been a proliferation of these services over the past decade. According to the FCC, between 1996 and 1998, two hundred pirate stations were shut down.[34] Community activists see pirate radio as an antidote to the mergers that are dominating the American radio environment. Recently there have been concerns that all noncommercial radio—including state-supported public service radio, the Pacifica system, and other "alternative" radio operators—has lost its community moorings because it has increasingly depended on private-sector, governmental, and foundation resources. The pirate radio community was responding to a real problem.

Microradio advocates argue that there is "a need for neighborhood-scale information—ranging from the live broadcast of a school board meeting to ethnic folk music—that is harder and harder to come by as the radio industry is controlled by fewer and larger owners." One legal quest was for low-power FM stations. For Ralph Nader: "Low-power FM offers the opportunity to offset commercial radio's inadequacies, decentralize broadcasting and empower neighborhoods and communities. Labor union locals will be able to broadcast to their members; communities will have a radio forum to debate and discuss local issues; ethnic groups will be able to air programming to meet their particular needs, including non-English broadcasting; senior citizens centers will be able to reach seniors who cannot make it to the centers' physical facilities; local government meetings can be broadcast to the community."[35]

The community radio/microradio community is represented by the National Federation of Community Broadcasters (NFCB). This organization, established in 1975, came out of the National Alternative Radio Konvention, whose twenty-five participants have been described as "visionaries and counterculture types." The main goal of the federation in the late seventies was to support training through the development of manuals. There are close parallels between the activists in both community radio and community television. In 1982, the NFCB held the "first-ever Minority Producers Conference," which was "instrumental in bringing people of color into public [and community] radio."[36] By 2000, the federation's goals had expanded to include program exchanges and lobbying, in addition to the production of training manuals. Like commercial and public service radio, community radio has an Internet presence.

Responses to the Environment

The FCC's review of the radio industry in 2000 concluded that, since the passage of the 1996 Telecommunications Act, the number of commercial radio stations had increased by 5 percent and that the number of radio owners had declined by 22 percent. In 1996, the two largest owners of radio stations had fewer than 65 stations each. In early 2000, the two largest owners held more than 440 stations each. At the end of 2000, they merged: as a result, Clear Channel owned more than 1,000 stations. One outcome of the merger frenzy in the radio industry was a decline in the ownership of commercial radio by minority groups. For example, in 1996–97, African American–owned FM stations declined by 26 percent, and Hispanic-owned stations declined by 9 percent.[37]

In an effort to curb concentration of ownership and ensure the diversity of voices on the airwaves, the FCC proposed on January 28, 2000, rules for licensing approximately one thousand low-power FM (LPFM) stations that would transmit at less than a hundred watts and serve areas with a three-and-a-half-mile radius. In addition, the FCC also proposed licensing additional ten-watt stations serving a one-to-two-mile radius. This decision reversed a ban that the FCC had introduced about twenty years ago. The rules became effective on April 17, 2000. The philosophy behind the LPFM stations appeared to be in harmony with the wishes of the advocates for microradio. The decision was not received favorably by commercial broadcasters, however, and there is great fear that the National Association of Broadcasters (NAB) will use its lobbying muscle to thwart the plan in Congress. Resistance to LPFM, or legal microradio, is based on the notion that they will interfere with more powerful stations—both commercial and public. National Public Radio also joined the resistance against LPFM. FCC chairman William E. Kennard called NPR's resistance the "unkindest cut of all. . . . [A]lthough NPR has offered excellent quality public programming over the years, it must realize that 'All Things Considered' is not all things to all people."[38]

All sectors of the radio industry have responded to the changing racial and ethnic composition of the United States since 1980. Most immigrant and other minority groups have a radio presence in the United States. Some are established and others are transient. Most groups are served by the commercial sector through brokerage practices and are found on the AM dial. Some are present on public radio, particularly on college-operated stations, and some are present on community radio. Contemporary programs serve the same range of functions for America's diverse communities that the older ethnic radio programs did.

In the following case studies, note how these communities are utilizing new communication technologies, especially the Internet, to reach their members. Note also the relationships that exist between advertisers and broadcasters that target America's minorities and how radio broadcasting is influencing the problematics of race in the United States. The final goal is to contribute to the overall assessment of the performance of the American broadcasting system, especially in the crucial areas of access, equity, and solidarity. This assessment will include audience reactions to radio programming aimed at America's minority communities. As in television, three categories of programming are aimed at America's diversity. In the commercial sector we find programs aimed at *representing* America's diversity; in the public sector we find programming *produced for* America's diversity; and in all sectors of broadcasting we find programs *produced by* America's minorities.

Asian Radio in the United States

According to the 1990 census, the Asian community was the fastest-growing segment of the U.S. population (20 percent per year). In 2000, there were 10.5 million Asians in America; by 2050, Asian Americans are expected account for 10 percent of the population. Asian Americans are relatively young and are the country's most affluent ethnic group. In 2001, their spending power was estimated at $101 billion per year. This demographic and economic profile has made the Asian population very attractive to advertisers, as is evident from the trade literature. Financial services, producers of high-end consumer goods, telecommunications, and new technology firms have special interest in this sector. For example, South Asians are the primary ethnic focus for MetLife. In addition to being attractive to mainstream advertisers, the Asian community in the United States is also essential for Asian businesses here and in their countries of origin.[39]

The Asian population in the United States is diverse, and that diversity is important in several contexts. The advertising agency Admerasia identifies Vietnamese, Filipinos, South Asians, Chinese, Japanese, and Koreans as the dominant ethnic groups within the Asian community in the United States.[40] There are numerous subethnicities within these groups, each with its own linguistic and cultural particularities. Within the Vietnamese community are the Hmong. Among South Asians are speakers of Hindi, Urdu, Gujarati, and Punjabi, as well as followers of Hinduism, Islam, and Christianity. Cambodians, Laotians, and Vietnamese in the United States may have common religious practices and share cultural values because of the geographic proximity of their countries of origin. In addition, they share common histories, especially the history of the Vietnam War, which resulted in their migrations to the United States since the 1970s. Political conflicts, especially those informed by border conflicts and ethnic separatism, characterize relationships among the nation-states of South Asia—India, Pakistan, and Bangladesh. Some of these tensions are reproduced among the South Asian communities in the United States. However, there is evidence of cultural solidarity, especially in the consumption of media products.

The Asian population in the United States tends to congregate on the West Coast and in the Midwest. In addition to differences in country of origin, ethnicity, religion, and class, the Asian population in the United States can be distinguished by its "institutional completeness."[41] In other words, the strength and durability of the community's social network, including its ability to influence activities in the wider social, cultural, economic, and political spheres. The Jewish community in the United States also has a high degree of institutional completeness. Institutional completeness encourages collective efficacy—a community's belief that it can overcome any obstacle.

Asian American radio practice has a wide spectrum of practices, from "vanity productions" to the programming produced by federal, state, local, or volunteer agencies aimed at providing special groups, especially refugees, with essential information, to brokered programs, to the outright ownership of radio stations. Vanity productions are motivated by personal ambition and tend to profile a particular individual or group. In 2000, twelve stations, primarily AM stations, had formats that targeted the Asian community, and eighty-one stations provided 254 hours of special programming for Asian-language groups in the United States (see table 5.4).

In the early 1990s, the major program genre was the music program,[42] and the dominant advertisers and sponsors tended to be small businesses in Asian enclaves and mainstream entities that specialized in services needed by the community, such as telephone service. A decade later the music program was still dominant but more mainstream enterprises—financial services, food, communication companies, and manufacturers of automobiles and other big-ticket items were competing for this audience.

ASIAN INDIAN RADIO

Almost one million Indians live in the United States. Like most immigrants, Asian Indians maintain ties with their home country, and

Table 5.4. Asian-Language Special Programming
on U.S. Radio, 1990–2000

Language	Number of Stations		Hours per Week	
	1990	2000	1990	2000
Chinese	7	18	19	91
Farsi	1	2	1	6
Filipino	12	19	82	65
Hindi	13	13	25	34
Japanese	13	15	39	38
Korean	6	7	21	38
Vietnamese	6	7	7	20
Total	58	81	194	254

Source: Bowker's Database Production Group, *Broadcast and Cable Yearbook 1991, 2001* (Washington, D.C.: R. R. Bowker, 1991, 2001).

most want to return after retirement.[43] Indians, the wealthiest Asian group in America, are served by a complex media environment that includes newspapers, television networks, the Internet, and radio. Since 1990, Indian radio has been offering diverse programming tailored to the diverse needs of its audiences. The program guides in *India Abroad* for August through October 1990 reveal a total of forty-five regular radio programs. Some, like *Gateway to India, Jhankar, Sounds of India, Geet Gujarati,* and *Punjabi geet sangeet,* were distributed nationally. Most consisted primarily of music that reflects the ethnic diversity of the Indian community. Hindi music, especially filmi, dominated. Classic forms, such as the religious *bhajans,* were also common. Other genres of music, reflecting Indian ethnic diversity, were also evident. There were programs that profiled North and South Indian music (*Jhankar* and *Madhura Bharati*), Punjabi (*Punjabi geet sangeet*), and Gujarati (*Geet Gujarati*).

In the early 1990s, other Indian genres included dramas, community talk shows, and news and information programs. For example, Mel Ramswany produced the four-minute minidrama series *Pell-Mell. Swaranjali* was as an Indian community forum program, and *Punjabi Community Hour, Waves of Change,* and *The People's Voice* broadcast news and information. Most programs were broadcast on Saturday and Sunday (mostly Sunday) on college-operated public stations. The commercial radio stations that broadcast Asian Indian programs tended to be stations that described their formats as multiethnic. Most of the programs profiled in the program guides of *India Abroad* originated in the Midwest and the East Coast. Brokerage was clearly the dominant business model, and the primary advertisers were small Asian Indian businesses and providers of professional services.

The fact that both radio and television programs are promoted in the program guides of *India Abroad* suggested a high level of coordination in the Asian Indian media environment in the United States in the early nineties. That most programs were aired on weekends, especially on Sunday, also indicated that the programming responded to Indian listening habits and targeted the Indian family. The range of programs suggested that the programs served the classical roles of information, correlation, and orientation, but their emphasis was clearly cultural transmission.

A decade later, Indian radio in the United States was much more diversified. Radio programming was distributed through a variety of channels—shortwave, AM, FM, satellite, and the Internet. In the shortwave arena, Indians in the United States could choose from programs offered by All India Radio (the service operated by the government of India), several language services of the BBC World Service, the Voice of America, and Deutsche Welle. In 2000, Indians had access to 121 stations whose formats were described as ethnic or foreign/ethnic. Almost half were AM stations.[44] Also, according to the *Broadcasting and Cable Yearbook 2001,* Indian programming was part of the over 750 hours of special programming broadcasting per week on American radio stations during 2000.

A typical show was *Vividh Bharti Radio,* broadcast on WDCT (AM 1310), Fairfax, Virginia/Washington, D.C.[45] Indian radio now has an active presence on the FM dial with programs like *Sounds of the Subcontinent,* a call-in show on WCBN-FM (88.3), Ann Arbor, the radio station of the University of Michigan.

Also on FM is EBC Radio, a service offered by the Eastern Broadcasting Corporation on WCNJ-FM in Hazlet, New Jersey. Introduced in February 1999, this twenty-four-hour service claims to reach nearly four-fifths of the more than three hundred thousand Indians, Pakistanis, and Bangladeshis in the New Jersey and Metro New York City region. The system tells advertisers it can provide access to a growing community that is "highly educated and affluent, with a high savings rate and extremely high purchasing power." EBC Radio is owned and operated by Indian Americans. The EBC program schedule for July 2001 suggested diversity of genre, but most programs were music based. For example, *Bollywood Quiz Time* focused on the younger generation and emphasized entertainment. As Admerasia points out, "Asian Indians love entertainment. The Indian film industry, Bollywood, is the second largest in the world after Hollywood. Movies, film scores, videos, CDs and mega star shows from India are all the rage among Asian Indians."[46]

The Korean American community is emblematic of the new wave of immigrants from Asia.[47] The entrepreneurial activities of the Korean enclaves in Southern California and in other urban areas have attracted much attention, both positive and negative. Koreans are described as model immigrants, but their community also is seen as insular and culturally insensitive to blacks and Hispanics. The latter perception clearly added to the tension in urban America between blacks and Koreans that culminated in the Los Angeles riots of 1992.

An outstanding example of Korean American radio is Radio Korea in Los Angeles, a twenty-four-hour service launched in 1989 as a brokered service on KBLA-FM, then owned by Ron Thompson. Radio Korea is now owned by Korean Americans. The target audience in the early 1990s was first-generation Koreans, and all programming was in Korean. The programming of Radio Korea in the early 1990s was dominated by music programs that offered Korean opera, contemporary Korean pop, and golden oldies of American pop. The popularity of American oldies among Korean immigrants is associated with spillover from the music programs aired by AFRTS in South Korea. The many information and talk shows included *Learning English*, a ten-minute program broadcast twice a day to help new Korean immigrants develop their English. Other special programs included the daily (Monday–Friday) *Real Estate Information, Economic News*, and *Health Information*. Among the programs that targeted women was the one-hour Sunday show *Infant Rearing*. On Saturday and Sunday there were programs for English-speaking Koreans. Duncan Suh, a reporter with Radio Korea in the nineties, saw that programming strategy as a tactic to connect with those second-generation Koreans who used mainstream media extensively.

Over two hours of news were broadcast daily. The key to the popularity of these programs was up-to-date news from Korea, gleaned from wire services. The Korean national newspaper, *ChoSun*, had a reciprocal news-sharing relationship with Radio Korea. Stories on Radio Korea also were compiled by their reporters in Korean communities in Los Angeles. Articles were translated from America's prestige newspapers, such as the *Los Angeles Times*, the *New York Times*, and the *Washington Post*. The major advertisers on Radio Korea in the early 1990s were small businesses—restaurants, banks, and car dealerships.

In the early nineties, approximately 70 percent of the first-generation Koreans in Los Angeles listened to Radio Korea. Those numbers could not have been corroborated then because the standard rating services did not provide ratings on Korean audiences, but now the rating companies that measure the Korean audiences confirm Radio Korea's popularity. Suh offers two reasons for its early popularity: it was the only Korean-language service in the community, and its newscasts presented items translated from America's prestige newspapers.

In the early nineties, Radio Korea launched a number of community outreach initiatives aimed at harmonizing relationships among Koreans, blacks, and Hispanics. To increase contact among those groups, it sponsored sports events, food banks, and other activities aimed at undermining the negative stereotypes associated with being black and Hispanic in the United States. The outreach approach was obviously a better strategy because blacks and Hispanics do not listen to Korean-language radio. By 1996, the station had added call-in shows with black guests as a means of furthering dialogue.[48]

Radio Korea developed a network of stations across the United States and distributed its programming by satellite; it also broadcast globally via its Internet service. But Radio Korea is only one example of Korean radio in the United States. According to *Broadcasting and Cable 2000*, there were seven radio stations with Korean formats—five on the AM band—and all were commercial operations. Six other stations aired thirty-one hours of special programming a week. WONX-AM in Evanston, Illinois, was responsible for twenty hours a week.

Over a ten-year period, Radio Korea has demonstrated solid growth and development. The future of Radio Korea and other Korean radio in the United States is intertwined with the dynamic of the national economy and the acculturation and assimilation of the Korean American population. If current trends continue, there will be a need for Korean-language programming for some time. However, second-generation Koreans, who speak English, are more affluent than their parents. In the early nineties, Suh predicted that this audience eventually would push Radio Korea into full-time programming in English, but that has not yet happened.

The history of Radio Korea illustrates the working of an influential economic model in minority radio broadcasting in the United States. Ron Thompson's decision to lease KBLA to a Korean American in 1989 was based on economic sense. That decision had its roots in the brokerage tradition that has been evident in minority broadcasting since the early years of the medium. Radio Korea not only plays an important role in the acculturation of Korean immigrants in Los Angeles but achieves cultural transmission through its music programming and facilitates correlation by translating major stories from elite newspapers. The relationships between *ChoSun* and Radio Korea do not involve a mere exchange of news; they indicate the importance Korean immigrants in the United States place on maintaining linkages with Korea and the importance of Korea's diaspora to the Republic of Korea.

West Indian Radio in New York

From 1960 to 1997, almost three million Caribbean people migrated to the United States. West Indians—English-speaking immigrants from the Caribbean—were among the largest groups of immigrants settling in New York City during that period. Most came from Jamaica, but many were from Guyana and Trinidad and Tobago. West Indian radio in New York has both innovative and reactionary tendencies, but there are positive potentials even in the reactionary tendencies.[49]

In 1992, when asked to give their impressions of West Indian radio in New York, most interviewees responded that it was Jamaican.[50] After all, the dominant genre in West Indian programming was music, and the dominant musical genre was reggae and its dance hall/hip-hop derivatives. Reggae was so popular that it had migrated even to the playlists of urban pop, jazz, and other formats. In the same year, members of the West Indian community in New York who had embraced federation and the construction of the Caribbean community before immigrating expressed concern about the paucity of Pan-Caribbean news and information programming on West Indian radio. They felt that the news programs tended to be parochial and that it was only the sensational issues from other Caribbean nations that attracted attention.

Brokerage was the major strategy behind West Indian radio in New York, and that practice may explain the apparent Jamaicanness of West Indian radio in New York. Jamaicans have tended to be the most entrepreneurial of the West Indian immigrants and have an influential diaspora. Jamaican entrepreneurs operated stores that sold merchandise like West Indian foods and hair care products, offered basic services like barbershops and hairdressing salons, and promoted cultural events that featured popular Jamaican talent. In the final analysis, the other English-speaking audiences were frosting on the cake!

In the nineties, most West Indian radio was found in the commercial sector. There was also a weekend presence on public radio, especially those stations operated by universities and colleges with West Indian students. The Pacifica service in New York featured programs for English-speaking Caribbean audiences. The commercial radio service that emphasized West Indian radio in the early nineties was clearly WLIB-AM, the flagship of Percy Sutton's Inner City Broadcasting Corporation. Among the earliest of the black-owned radio services in the United States, WLIB provided a home for West Indian DJs, like Guyanese Claude Taitt.

Claude Taitt joined WLIB as a sports reporter in 1976 and is associated with bringing West Indian cricket reports to New York. Over the sixteen years he spent with the station he helped expand its Pan-Caribbean offerings. He went beyond cricket to become one of the first Caribbean broadcasters in the United States to incorporate materials from the Barbados-based Caribbean News Agency and the Caribbean Broadcasting Union. Taitt went on to become a major commentator on Caribbean politics and culture. His remote broadcasts from the Caribbean helped West Indian immigrants maintain linkages with their "old countries." Claude Taitt's work at WLIB[51] helped shift perceptions about West Indians in New York—there was more to the "coconut heads" than sun, sand, and surf!

Much has changed in West Indian radio in New York.[52] The vibrant Indo-Caribbean voice is present in all its diversity on West Indian radio in New York—through institutions like the Indo-Caribbean Federation, Indo-Caribbean radio is basically Pan-Caribbean, incorporating Guyanese, Trinidadian, and Surinamese culture. Indo-Caribbean radio is becoming global as it links its programming, especially music, with the global Indian community through the Internet.

Ishri Singh, one of the pioneers of Indo-Caribbean radio programming in New York, developed his broadcasting and marketing competencies in Guyana. Although broadcasting there was dominated by African Guyanese politics, a space was always open for Indian Guyanese on the Guyanese airwaves. Interestingly, this space was accessed through brokerage practices. So, in addition to having access to free space, Indian Guyanese were able to buy radio time to promote religious and cultural themes. They also depended on Indo-Guyanese religious institutions and businesses buying advertising. In Guyana, Ishri Singh was extremely influential; he was a popular voice on the air and a popular promoter.

Ishri Singh, Balwant Singh, and Robert Mohammed were among many the Indo-Guyanese who migrated to the United States and Canada between 1970 and 1990, fleeing political domination in Guyana. Many of them settled in New York and Toronto,[53] and Richmond Hill, New York, has an influential Indo-Guyanese community of professionals, businesses (food stores, jewelry shops, music and video stores, bakeries, restaurants, night clubs, and travel agencies), religious organizations (Hindu temples, mosques), and branches of Indo-Guyanese political parties. The community has the resources to support independent radio producers. Other influential Indo-Caribbean broadcasters there are Skamila Karim, Haji Zakir, Lake Persaud, Roshan, DJ Freddie, and Herman Singh. Their programs, especially those produced by Anil Parsnauth and aired by WLIB on Sunday mornings, are also popular among African Guyanese audiences in New York. This inclusive programming offers an alternative to the racial tensions between Indian and African Guyanese since their initial encounter in British Guiana in 1838, four months before the emancipation of enslaved Africans.[54] Indo-Caribbeans have also ventured into the ownership of radio properties. Mohammed and Balwant Singh have established radio services over the air and on the Internet. Mohammed's WICR and the station Balwant Singh operates on the Internet, Radio Demerara.

LINKUP RADIO

The distinctive Caribbean radio presence in New York and other sites of the Caribbean diaspora in North America is a function of the proliferation of independent radio program producers and the willingness of station owners to "offer" time to these producers. Caribbean radio is also appropriating the capabilities of new communication technologies, especially satellites, to create and deliver programs that serve a transnational audience. David Annakie, "DJ Squeeze," presents the extremely popular *LINKUP Show* on LINKUP Radio, WRTN-FM 93.5, broadcast simultaneously in New York, London, Toronto, and on Hot 102 FM in Jamaica. The format is so popular that other radio stations in the Jamaican diaspora—like Irie Jam FM in New York and FAME FM in Jamaica linkup—have similar arrangements. And WWRL 1600 AM in New York has linked up with Choice FM in London to deliver the *Saturday Afternoon Express,* a reggae program that features the Jamaican DJs Daddy Ernie and Phillip Smart.

OTHER CARIBBEAN RADIO

Across the United States many other Caribbean radio programs thrive. Haitian radio, for instance, is growing in Florida. The first Haitian station there, WRBF-120 AM, was launched in January 2001. Like Radio Korea, the station is a leased service. The operators of WRBF indicated at its launch that they anticipated expanding into Orlando, Boston, and New York, places where there are concentrations of Haitian immigrants. Boodram and Persaud indicate that there are many Haitian stations, most of them illegal. In Washington, D.C., Howard

Radio and America's Diversity | 89

University's WHUR-96.3 FM has been home to Barbadian American John Blake's *Caribbean Express* for more than two decades. Caribbean independent radio producers and brokers have to pay six to eight hundred dollars per hour for access to the radio waves. As Boodram and Persaud have reported, Caribbean brokers are a valuable revenue source for owners of radio properties in New York; they have rescued some companies from bankruptcy. Like the early Polish broadcasters, Caribbean broadcasters were also associated with other media-based activities such as, parties, boat rides, fashion shows, and cultural events.

Spanish-Language Radio

Spanish language radio, especially music programming, is very important to Hispanics in the United States. And although Hispanics may migrate from Spanish-language television to English-language television when they become comfortable with English, they do not abandon Spanish-language radio.[55] The Hispanic community is expected to become the largest minority in the United States by 2005, and, for that and several other reasons, it is very attractive to investors. Unlike other minority media, Spanish-language media properties tend to be owned by non-Hispanics. This tendency in ownership has some impact on programming.

The dominant genre in Spanish-speaking radio is the music program. More than 80 percent of all programs on Spanish-language radio in the United States are music—compared to less than 5 percent for news, 3 percent for talk, and 2 percent for drama. This fact is associated with many complex and controversial issues: production costs, relationships with the recording industry, ethnicity, and politics. The parsimony principle is very evident here: music programs are inexpensive to produce.[56] Another explanation is found in the internal diversity of the Hispanic community in the United States. The music programs on Spanish-language radio are important indicators of Hispanic ethnicity. Consider the following observation by Peter Manuel on the early nineties:

Working-class Puerto Ricans, Cubans, and Dominicans, concentrated in the northeastern United States and especially New York, prefer "tropical music"—*salsa* and *meringue*. Miami based Cuban Americans, while enjoying salsa, favor American salsa-pop fusions. People of Mexican and Chicano [*sic*] descent, comprising some two-thirds of Hispanics in the United States, prefer Tex-Mex *rancheras* or *musica norteña*. The growing numbers of Colombians and Central American immigrants, while not averse to these musics, retain a special fondness for Colombian *cumbia* and *vallenato* music. Finally, newer genres—particularly Latin jazz and Latin hip hop—have substantial followings in New York and elsewhere.[57]

These musical preferences influence programming practice. However, it is not as simple as that. Spanish-language music programming can become a site for conflict with major record producers and programmers. These conflicts invariably influence the music programming of those commercial stations that do not operate according to the brokerage system. Manuel provides an example of this conflict in his examination of the music policies of four Spanish-language stations in New York—WKDM, WJIT, WKAQ, and WADO:

> New York's four Spanish-language radio stations (all owned by Anglo corporations) were thus faced with the diverse musical tastes of an increasingly mixed listening public. One strategy would have been to divide their programming and audiences along ethnic musical lines, with one or two salsa stations, a Chicano-oriented station, a Dominican station, and so on. Instead, however, each station chose to follow the monopoly capitalism model by seeking the largest possible audience—and by extension, the greatest advertising revenue—rather than targeting a particular ethnic audience. In effect, each station decided to devote over half of its music programming to the common denominator music styles that are enjoyed by *some* members of *all* the Hispanic groups—in particular, the sentimental pop ballad (*balada romántica* or *canción romántica*) as sung by Julio Iglesias, Jose Jose, Emanuel, and other practitioners of this thoroughly international genre. (110; emphasis in original)

Manuel concludes that record companies controlled by conglomerates like Coca-Cola pressured the stations to change the musical content of their programs. This, he says, resulted in the creation of a "mass, homogenized audience" that was easy to exploit. The practice carried with it limited playlists, thus further marginalizing popular music, the music of the grass roots and the night clubs. Further, the manufactured popularity was re-exported to the parent culture of the immigrants and thus set in place the spread of this homogenization, exploitation, and domination.

When Manuel observed the Latin music scene in the early 1990s, musicians who had resisted the power of the corporations and appeared not to subscribe to the anti-Castro orthodoxies had to pay the price through the power and influence of right-wing Cubans in Spanish-language radio at that time: "Right-wing Cuban exiles, several of whom are powerful figures in radio broadcasting, have effectively banned the music of Oscar de Leon, Andy Montanez, Ruben Blades, and Willie Colón from the airwaves in Miami and elsewhere (de Leon and Montanez for visiting Cuba, and Blades and Colón for the anti-imperialist message of some of their songs). Other stations shun the music of singers like Blades because it is too 'controversial' in its attempts to address social reality" (112).

Because of increased competition for Spanish-speaking audiences in the United States, the number of Spanish-language stations has continued to increase. For example, there were 67 stations with a Spanish-language format in the United States in 1975, 261 in 1990, and 528 in 1999, of which over 90 percent were commercial operations. By the mid-nineties, other nationalities, such as the Colombians, had started to rival the Cubans for influence in the radio market.

CARACOL RADIO, MIAMI

Caracol Radio is an affiliate of the Colombia-based transnational conglomerate CARACOL, operated by Julio Mario Santodomingo.[58] Its origins in Miami are associated with the efforts of Colombian immigrants to break the Cuban domination of Spanish-language radio in Miami. Since 1965, Miami has become a preferred settlement site for many Latin Americans, especially those from Colombia, Nicaragua, Argentina, the Dominican Republic, Venezuela, and Puerto Rico.

These immigrants joined Cubans refugees and immigrants who settled there after the Cuban revolution, making the Miami region one of the most internally diverse Spanish-speaking regions in the United States.

By 1980, Hispanics represented more than 60 percent of Miami's population. However, political, economic, and cultural life—including the radio waves—was dominated by the Cubans. This meant that the media agenda was driven by Cuban realities, especially its anti-Castro discourse. Matters pertaining to other Spanish-speaking ethnic groups tended to be marginal. One group that decided to respond to this was the Colombians, who by 1990 made up nearly 6 percent of the foreign-born population in Miami. By the 1980s, Miami had become an important site for Colombian businessmen, politicians, and diplomats. This situation demanded a Colombian radio presence in Miami.

The first radio program dedicated to Colombians in Miami is associated with the work of Eucario Bermudez, who had been a broadcaster in Colombia before immigrating to the United States. His hour-long talk show, *Tierra colombiana*, was developed in collaboration with a Miami-based Colombian newspaper, *Acontecer colombiana*, and included news, music, and legal counseling. The show attracted an audience on the strength of the host's name recognition, although it was not an advertising success. Bermudez's work attracted much attention, and in 1989 he presented *Voz de Colombia*, a three-hour program on WVCG-1080 AM. One section, "Update Hour," was presented by Jaime Flórez, a correspondent for RCN, one of Colombia's influential radio networks and Caracol's main competitor.

Bermudez's work attracted competition. In 1989, two former Colombian broadcasters, Rudy García and Alberto Jiménez, launched seven hours of daily programming on station WAKT. Their programming provided the same elements—news, music, talk, and community counseling. One consequence of this competition was declining revenues and the failure of either service to make a profit. Advertisers bought time on these brokered shows based on prior friendships as opposed to a strategic position. But amazingly, the competitors decided to unite and the result was Radio Kalidad.

Radio Kalidad was operated by Rudy Garcia for two years at station WSUA-1260 AM. In 1993, Radio Kalidad was purchased by a Miami-based Colombian businessman, Herman Díaz, who renamed the service Radio Klaridad. The naming of radio services is a Colombian tradition, a branding strategy, and a prerequisite for brand loyalty. Very early in the operations of Radio Klaridad, Díaz began to develop relations with Caracol, the dominant radio service in Colombia. In addition, Radio Klaridad opened up 20 percent of its programming schedule to other Spanish-speaking groups, especially Cubans and Nicaraguans. By 1992, Radio Klaridad's programming schedule was similar to the design that guided Caracol Radio in Colombia.

In January 1993, Caracol Radio began to program Radio Klaridad completely. By November, Caracol Radio entered into a twenty-four-hour brokerage deal similar to the one that established Radio Korea in Los Angeles, and launched Radio Caracol. Radio Caracol continues to be a presence in the United States, drawing upon the resources of its parent, Caracol Radio in Colombia. Radio Caracol has access to satellite distribution technologies that allow it to be plugged into the Colombia diaspora. Since its establishment, Radio Caracol has been able to attract mainstream advertisers like AT&T, McDonald's, Coca-Cola, and Nike. It has also won and controlled the Spanish-language broadcasting rights for important world events like soccer's World Cup. The Radio Caracol experience, like that of Radio Korea, has demonstrated a flexibility in American broadcasting laws. In the United States noncitizens cannot own broadcast properties, but there appear to be no regulations limiting the amount of time foreign nationals can broker!

Other Ethnic Radio Services in the United States

So far, I have deliberately focused on the radio practices of the groups that have dominated immigration to the United States since 1965. This should not suggest that minority radio is dominated by these communities. *Broadcasting Yearbook 2000* identified 138 stations with formats for European ethnic communities (see table 5.5). In addition,

Table 5.5. Partial List of U.S. Radio Stations with European Ethnic Formats, 1999

Format	Total Stations	AM	FM	Commercial	Non-commercial
Foreign-language	88	38	50	78	10
French	4	3	1	4	0
Greek	4	4	0	4	0
Italian	4	2	2	2	2
Polish	4	3	1	4	0
Polka	8	4	4	7	1
Portuguese	5	4	1	4	1
Russian	1	1	0	1	0

Source: Compiled from Bowker's Database Production Group, *Broadcasting and Cable Yearbook 2000* (Washington, D.C.: R. R. Bowker, 2000).

more than two thousand hours of special programming per week are aired (table 5.6).

European ethnicity is alive and well in the United States. Most ethnic European radio programs are produced by independent producers using brokerage. As with other minorities, the dominant program genre tends to be music, but news and information and cultural performances are also aired. Advertising is mostly for small businesses and those goods and services not provided adequately by the mainstream economy. Ethnic European radio continues to serve several functions—orientation of new immigrants to the community, provision of ethnic entertainment, a source for learning English, contact with the home culture through news and information programs, a site of resistance and protest against political domination in the home culture, a vehicle for the transmission of cultural values to the younger members of the ethnic community, and, more recently, as a vehicle to promote economic relations with the parent culture. Presenters and producers of ethnic European radio programs have identified a variety of reasons for their activities, including the imperatives of community leadership, community need, and vanity. Similar motivations were found among independent producers in Asian, Caribbean, and Spanish-language radio.

Table 5.6. Partial List of U.S. Radio Stations with European Special Programming, 1999

Ethnicity	Number of Stations	Hours per Week (approx)
Albanian	1	1
Croatian	9	4
Czech	15	39
French	57	150
German	75	200
Greek	32	60
Hungarian	10	19
Irish	65	150
Italian	76	200
Lithuanian	10	15
Polish	188	750
Portuguese	23	60
Russian	19	49
Scottish	2	7
Serbian	7	9
Slovak	8	11
Slovenian	7	25
Ukrainian	11	20

Source: Compiled from Bowker's Database Production Group, *Broadcasting and Cable Yearbook 2000* (Washington, D.C.: R. R. Bowker, 2000).

Italian radio in the United States reveals another tendency in ethnic radio in the United States—the involvement of state-operated broadcast institutions from the old country. (Compare the involvement of the Colombian private sector in Colombian radio in Miami or of regional institutions in West Indian broadcasting.) In the Italian case, RAI—Radiotelevisione Italiana, the official broadcasting agency of the Italian government—plays a significant role in the media practices of the Italian radio community in the United States.

Italian radio has had a long presence in the United States. Italian radio soap operas broadcast in New York in the late thirties and early forties spread propaganda for Italy's fascist government.[59] *Broadcasting and Cable Yearbook 2001* identified two stations with Italian format, both on the AM dial. However, seventy-seven stations concentrated on the East Coast and in the Midwest were broadcasting more than two hundred hours of special programming per week. A key program in Italian radio in the United States is news from and about the old country, and RAI is actively involved in this service. One explanation for this popularity is "Italian neo-ethnicity," a renewed "search for self-identity."[60] Through satellite feeds, Italian Americans are able to receive daily newscasts from Italy and are presented with a range of positive Italian images, including the Italian renaissance man and the *contadino* (peasant). RAI's role in Italian American radio is not only related to an old tradition but is a recognition of the importance of the Italian American to the political and economic life of Italy.

The involvement of external agencies in the programming of minority broadcasting in the United States (as with Italian, Korean, and Colombian radio) is partially driven by commercial motives. But much of it, in both radio and television, is driven by the recognition that some minority groups, even second and third generations, in the United States have substantial influence on their parent society's politics, economy, and culture.

Responses to Radio Programs at the Intersection of Immigration and Diversity

In my in-depth interviews with minorities (see chapter 1), most had a favorite mainstream commercial radio station and a favorite radio personality. Furthermore, most of their listening to mainstream commercial radio took place during morning drive time. One respondent indicated that commercial drive time radio provided them with materials to use in conversations with native-born American colleagues. However, when asked to identify what channels they listened to when they wanted news, information, and entertainment from their home countries, the majority identified programming produced by independent producers on stations that catered to America's minorities.

My interviewees' major motivations for seeking news, information, and entertainment from their countries of origin were to "find out what is going on back home," "to stay in touch," and "to find cultural solace." An Indian male reported that he listened because "I love the songs and because I want to be in touch with what is going on back home."[61] When asked to identify their satisfaction with the news and information programs provided by independent producers, 60 percent described them as "acceptable," and 40 percent indicated that they were either "dissatisfied" or "very dissatisfied"; none chose "satisfied" or "very satisfied." The Venezuelan participant, who had been living in New York for more than ten years, expressed concern for the apparent loss of musical variety on Spanish-language radio in New York. She said that most of the music now tended to be Mexican in flavor and was an indication that Mexicans had replaced Puerto Ricans and Dominicans as the major Spanish-speaking groups in New York.

Forty-four percent of the interviewees indicated they were "satisfied" with the entertainment programs produced by the independent producers, 22 percent chose "acceptable," and the remaining 34 percent described themselves as either "dissatisfied" or "very dissatisfied." Caribbean respondents had higher levels of dissatisfaction than the other respondents.

I also asked interviewees the following questions:

> What impressions do you think Americans get about your country of origin and its culture from mainstream American radio programs?

> What impressions do you think Americans get about your country of origin and its culture from radio programs produced and presented by people from your home country or the region of the world you are from?

> What impressions do you think Americans get about your local community in the United States from radio programs produced and presented by people from your home country or the region of the world you are from?

The interviewees felt that mainstream radio tended to provide unidimensional and stereotypical treatments of non-American subjects and locales. Several of the interviewees felt that when their home countries were discussed, the treatment tended to be sensational and the focus was on elite members of their societies. That position was tempered, however, by the standing their home country enjoyed in the United States. For example, the Italian interviewee felt mainstream radio in New York presented Italy in a manner that was "generally, very positive."

Irish, Asian Indian, and East Indian Guyanese respondents were very satisfied with the programming of minority producers, as those programs gave American listeners a better understanding of their home countries. The Asian Indian interviewee indicated that Americans would appreciate India's rich cultural diversity from listening to the programs produced by Asian Indian radio producers. But the Afro-Caribbean interviewees were dissatisfied with the programming produced by Caribbean radio producers. One, a Barbadian American, felt that the emphasis on music reinforced the impression that Anglophone Caribbean people were just "party animals."

Likewise, in the perceptions of impressions about local community from minority-produced programs, there were two tendencies. The interviewees indicated that if American audiences paid attention to the commercials associated with minority-produced programs they would get the impression that minorities were hard working, religious, and proud of their cultural heritage. However, the interviewees, especially those from China and the Caribbean, also felt that with sensationalism becoming part of minority news broadcasting, Americans might think that their communities were dangerous.

Through our exploration of minority radio in the United States, some tentative conclusions can be drawn about the consequences of the interactions between immigration and broadcasting in the United States since 1965:

- The assertiveness of minority organizations and the minority community, especially their concerns about representation, will determine the degree of radio activity.
- The perceived economic power of the minority community will

determine the degree to which mainstream/commercial radio and the related "associated enterprises" will include it in their business.

- The closer the minority community is to the mainstream (structural and behavioral assimilation/acculturation) the more it will attract mainstream advertisers.

- The first level of response by the mainstream broadcast industry to diversity is through hiring. The assumption is that this will represent access by the community and provide a different point of view.

- Minority broadcasters, especially independent program producers, tend to copy mainstream programming formats. Further, there is also the tendency to appropriate the attitudes to professionalism and in turn restrict access by the less influential segments of the minority community. This phenomenon was demonstrated by Cuban broadcasters in Miami.

- Brokered programming tends to be done by those members of the ethnic community who are seen as community leaders, those of higher social standing who think that this is a duty, or those who were (or wanted to be) popular radio personalities in their parent societies.

- The functions of minority radio changes with time; from orientation to guidance (e.g., the Missing Person Program in Chicago during the black migration to the North) to promotion or active propaganda against home regimes in the case of refugees or other political exiles and immigrants.

- Ethnic programs are subject to influence by mainstream audiences. This means that mainstream audiences do listen to ethnic radio, and if the content of a show seems to be anti-mainstream, the mainstream audience can get it off the air.

- Minority programs are indicators of the internal diversity of the minority community.

- Some ethnic stations broadcast in their native languages, others in English. This is probably a function of how long the ethnic community has been in the United States and the degree of acculturation, assimilation, age, gender, and region of residence.

- The more "institutionally complete" an ethnic community is, the less will be dependency on the media, and the media will serve different functions.

- Associated enterprises, such as news agencies created by minority communities, tend to be used by the mainstream media only in times of crisis (e.g., the experiences of Von Martin).

- Old-country political, economic, and broadcasting institutions utilize ethnic media outlets and resources in the United States as vehicles for propaganda or to maintain contact with their nationals. This is important given the significance of remittances and forms of technology transfers. It can therefore be hypothesized that the more significant the ethnic community is to the economic, political, and technological development of their parent society, the more advanced will be the forms of media contacts between the parent society and its migrant groups.

- Ethnic programs subscribe to the parsimony principle.

- The new distribution technologies, especially satellites and the Internet, provide opportunities for increased broadcast contact between minority communities in the United States, their parent societies, and other parts of their diaspora, thus creating transnational identities and lessening acculturation pressures.

6

Commercial Television and America's Diversity

AS IN COMMERCIAL radio, there are several players in the commercial television industry in the United States, including independent program producers, federal and state regulators, transnational corporations, special interest groups, community activists, and foreign broadcasters. The interactions of these players have great significance for the intersection of immigration, diversity, and commercial television. Commercial television in the United States is dominated by two large sectors—network, or over-the-air, television and cable television—and the roots of the former extend back to well before the end of the twentieth century.

The Beginnings of Network Television

From its introduction in 1931, television has steadily established itself as the dominant medium in the United States in terms of reach and influence. In the forties, three million television sets were sold in the United States; in the fifties, more than five million. By 1956, over 70 percent of American households had television. Now 99.9 percent of

America's more than ninety million households have on average two color sets. In that journey, American commercial television has reluctantly provided a space for the nation's minorities, though mostly they were there to provide humor and encourage consumption.[1] Commercial network television has been criticized for its negative representation of minorities and has thus become a pivotal point in the dynamics of race and ethnic relations in the United States.

Three of the four major national television networks in the United States (ABC, CBS, NBC) "emerged from radio networks owned by their parent companies." Commercial television has thus followed many formulae used by radio. It embraced the practice of networking because networking ensured guaranteed income for affiliates. The contemporary commercial television network is "basically a programming service," whose success "depends on its ability to present programming which attracts large numbers of viewers who will be exposed to the advertising accompanying the programming."[2]

In his 1991 study of the "life cycles" of the mass media in the United States, Donald Shaw concludes that network television is in decline. He argues that the rapid growth of cable television, the energizing of public television, and the emergence of other media had reduced the network's prime-time audience share from 90 percent in 1980 to about 55 percent in 1991. At the turn of the century, the network's share had eroded to less than 50 percent.[3]

Declining audience share, however, does not necessarily imply a decline in influence. A 1997 Roper Starch study concluded that network "television remain[s] American's primary and most credible source of news and product information, as well as a source of information on important social issues." In addition, the report found that:

> Overwhelmingly, more Americans watch a network TV program than engage in a variety of "new media" activities, such as playing video games or going on-line.

> About two out of three Americans who make a special effort to watch certain TV shows do their "appointment viewing" on a major TV network.

Americans increasingly believe that viewers themselves rather than government or special interest groups should decide what they see on television.[4]

American Television Programming and America's Minorities

In *The Complete Directory of Prime Time Network TV Shows*, Tim Brooks and Earle Marsh identify seventy-eight entertainment genres.[5] Among the dominant genres are soap operas, game shows, situation comedies, and crime dramas, which, despite structural differences, convey similar themes. Brooks and Marsh identify seven eras in American television programming.

THE VAUDEO ERA, 1948–1957

During the vaudeo era, the stars of vaudeville came to television from radio, where they had been lured during the thirties—the so-called golden age of radio, when radio refined a range of program genres, among them "soap operas, comedies, dramas, quiz shows, and variety hours" (x–xx). These programs were developed for the mass market, primarily the working class, and were easily transferred to television. These radio genres also extended the popularity of the vaudeville stars.

Some outstanding artistes of this era had immigrant backgrounds: Milton Berle, Jack Benny, Sid Caesar, Eddie Cantor, Jimmy Durante, Jackie Gleason, Rosemary Rice, Ed Sullivan, Abbott and Costello, George Burns, and Gracie Allen. Brooks and Marsh consider Milton Berle's *Texaco Star Theater* an exemplar of the vaudeo era in commercial network television: "frantic, corny, but always highly visual. If ordinary people were going to spend $400 for a small-screen 'radio with pictures,' they wanted to see movement and action, and lots of it. Berle gave them fall-down slapstick with crazy costumes and sight gags galore." Ed Sullivan provided "a three-ring circus of comedians, acrobats, opera singers, scenes from plays, and dancing bears" (xiv). The visual and production style of most of the shows in this era resembled the old vaudeville, thus the term *vaudeo*.

Stage vaudeville has been recognized as one of the pivotal sites in the development of American popular culture. It is the origin of Jim Crow, Mammy, Sambo, and other negative black stereotypes. It was in vaudeville that the crystallization of a distinctly American humor and dance began. The heavy use of sight gags and slapstick, which transcended language, was probably a response to the multilingual working-class urban communities that arose in the United States as a result of immigration in the early decades of the twentieth century.

Another device expanded during the vaudeo era that has been transmitted to the other programming eras was the use of a speaker of broken English or one with a thick foreign accent in situation comedies. The exemplar was Ricky Ricardo on *I Love Lucy.* Lucy did crazy things, but equally funny was her manic Cuban husband who spoke with the funny accent. The fracturing of standard English was the core device in *Amos 'n' Andy,* as it was in the representation of European ethnic groups. In 1961, just after the vaudeo era, CBS aired *Angel,* whose star was a "petite French girl who had just moved to America and become the bride of a young architect, John Smith. Her efforts to adjust to the American way of life provided humor in the series. Her problems with English, misunderstanding of situations, and attempts to be a responsible housewife contributed to the amusement of her husband and their next door neighbors, Susie and George, who were also their closest friends" (45). And immigrants with difficulties in English are still a major comedic device in network entertainment television.

The all-knowing father show (of which *Father Knows Best* is a prime example) had its beginnings in the vaudeo era. *Make Room for Daddy* (*The Danny Thomas Show*) is seminal. The importance of this show does not reside in its endorsement of patriarchy, but in the fact that Danny Thomas was a Lebanese immigrant. This show reflected a completely assimilated immigrant. Indirectly, the show also reflected the porous nature of the boundary of what is defined as white in American society. Danny's assimilation and acculturation was so complete that he reflected mainstream values.

Ethnic soap operas and situation comedies dominated the vaudeo era. Each Friday night between 1949 and 1956 "millions of Americans" kept a date with Marta Hansen, the matriarch of CBS's *I Remember Mama*—a family comedy about a Norwegian immigrant working-class family. Other ethnic sitcoms included "*The Goldbergs*, depicting the experiences of Jews in the Bronx; *Amos 'n' Andy*, blacks in Harlem; *The Honeymooners* and *Hey, Jeannie*, Irish working-class families in Brooklyn; *Life with Luigi*, Italian immigrants in Chicago; and *The Life of Riley*, working-class migrants to Los Angeles during and after World War II."[6]

Lipsitz argues that these shows were not based on some idea of improving the representation of diversity in the United States but were the product of a deliberate partnership between the government and the manufacturing industries to increase consumer consumption immediately after World War II:

> [T]elevision's most important economic function came from its role as an instrument of legitimation for transformations in values initiated by the new economic imperatives of postwar America. For Americans to accept the new world of 1950s' consumerism, they had to make a break with the past. The depression years had helped generate fears about installment buying and excessive materialism, while the New Deal and wartime mobilization had provoked suspicions about individual acquisitiveness and upward mobility. Depression era and wartime scarcities of consumer goods had led workers to internalize discipline and frugality while nurturing networks of mutual support through family, ethnic, and class associations. Government policies after the war encouraged an atomized acquisitive consumerism at odds with lessons of the past. At the same time, federal home loan policies stimulated migrations to the suburbs from traditional, urban, ethnic working-class neighborhoods. The entry of television into the American home disrupted previous patterns of family life and encouraged fragmentation of the family into separate segments of the consumer market. The priority of consumerism in the economy at large and on television may have seemed organic and unplanned, but conscious policy decisions by officials from both private and public sectors shaped the contours of the consumer economy and television's role within it. (75)

The ethnic family sitcoms and soap operas appeared to have been among the primary vehicles. In them advertisers would directly or indirectly weave their messages: "tensions developed in the programs that found indirect resolutions in commercials . . . the content of the shows themselves offered even more emphasis on consumer spending" (78). In promoting consumerism, these programs portrayed the old ethnic extended families as out of step with the requirements of the new society. Fathers who could not provide the new gadgets for their families were portrayed as failures. They resolved those problems by entering into credit arrangements. The resolution to the tedium of mothers' lives was offered through the adoption of the new gadgets and consumerism.

It has also been suggested that these ethnic situation comedies also undermined working-class solidarity. "Blue-collar labor often appears as a stigma—a condition that retards the acquisition of desired goods" (88). This practice distorted the historical experience of working-class ethnic families in the United States: "Stripped of essential elements of ethnic and class identity, interpreted through perspectives most relevant to a consumer middle class, and pictured in isolation from the social connections that gave purpose and meaning to working-class lives, the televised working-class family summoned up only the vaguest contours of its historical counterpart. Even in comparison to depictions of class in other forms of communication, like folklore, theater, music, literature, or radio, television presented a desiccated version of working-class life" (92–93). Despite the disappearance of the ethnic family sitcoms in 1958, the subgenre reappeared in other programming eras, especially during the seventies with shows like *All in the Family, Chico and the Man,* and *Sanford and Son,* which followed the formula developed in the fifties (103).

An examination of the vaudeo era would be incomplete without reference to the marginalization and trivialization of Asians, African Americans, and Latinos. There was the Chinese cook or laundryman; unidimensional blacks like Amos and Andy, and Beulah; and the subservient sidekick, such as Tonto and El Toro, the Native American and Mexican companions of the Lone Ranger and Kit Carson. These characters reinforced the construction and promotion of negative stereotypes and unidimensional characters of color. The appropriation of the vaudeville by early commercial television reproduced the invisibility and stereotypes of people of color that were developed in stage vaudeville.[7]

Many shows popular during the vaudeo era enjoyed a resurgence on the cable television aftermarket and through home video, thus contributing to the reinvigoration of negative stereotypes.[8] These syndicated programs were also being consumed globally and contributed to the pre-Americanization of immigrants to the United States.

The second era of American prime-time television was relatively short, but the programs from that era can still be seen on cable television. Some of the outstanding programs of that era were *Big Valley, Rawhide,* and *Have Gun, Will Travel.* But the era's start was marked by the appearance of *Gunsmoke,* introduced on Saturday, September 10, 1955, by John Wayne, an enduring symbol of American machismo. The series remained on network television for twenty years.[9] The growth of this genre was phenomenal. In the 1955–56 season, there were nine westerns, and by 1959–60 there were thirty, but by 1964–65 there were only seven.

The adult western era continued the exclusion and marginalization of minorities, using negative racial and ethnic stereotypes, and the creation of unidimensional racial and ethnic characters. Another deficiency of the era was its blatant overrepresentation of white Americans in stories about the West. There was the occasional Chinese cook, such as Hop Sing in *Bonanza.* Blacks were virtually invisible, and Hispanics were projected as indolent and threatening. This blatant distortion led to the development and reinforcement of negative stereotypes. The opening up of the West was a multiracial reality: American Indians, enslaved Africans, African American buffalo soldiers, Arabs, and Chinese were all participants.[10]

But there is more to television criticism than the mere counting of characters. Television narratives carry ideological messages. The adult western was an effective metaphor for the Cold War. The image of the strong, just, white cowboy, the rugged individual who meted out swift justice, was consumed hungrily in the United States and abroad. The strong cowboy was associated with the United States of America— bright and young—saving the world from the "Red" Indian—communism. The adult western also reinforced ideological stances. It helped to color perceptions. The adult western on TV had its big-screen counterpart in *Shane* and *The Magnificent Seven*. For many a potential immigrant to the United States after World War II, the western film was the introduction to American values.

Another popular program genre during this period featured swinging detectives, who were "sexy, as fast with a wisecrack as with a gun, and usually operated in an exotic locale."[11] Generally, however, in shows like *Seventy-Seven Sunset Strip* and *Hawaiian Eye,* it was the urban context and urban violence that provided the backdrop. Like the adult western, this subgenre celebrated the victory of good over evil. In this formula the deracinated/nonethnic European American good guy, usually with a sidekick (invariably a loyal person of color), always won. The bad guys tended to be characters with less valorized ethnic origins, especially Italians, blacks, Latinos, and other people of color. The hero-sidekick formula has an enduring presence in American popular culture and articulates status and position in America's social hierarchy. The adult western era consolidated practices of exclusion and marginalization and justified the use of violence for dealing with the "other."

THE IDIOT SITCOM, MID- TO LATE SIXTIES

During the sitcom era, the range of genres on prime-time commercial network television was extended. The domination by westerns ended, and television entertainment began to reflect a wider spectrum of white American society. Taking center stage were *Gomer Pyle, USMC* and other "hayseed comedies" featuring an assortment of unsophisticated rural innocents. At the heart of these programs was one of the core aspirations of American society—the idea that with a little bit of luck, like discovering oil on your property, you could be propelled into a life of luxury, like the Clampetts in *The Beverly Hillbillies.*

Brooks and Marsh suggest that a key determinant of this shift in programming was the mood of the target audience. During this period, the baby boomers had become advertisers' preferred audience. They had gone to college, were building homes, were parenting, and had more disposable income. The preferred audience had grown up with television. It was a principal factor in their lives. It provided relaxation and escape.

Despite changed locales, the prime-time shows of this era continued the tradition of excluding, marginalizing, and trivializing the nation's multiracial and multiethnic reality. One implication from Brooks and Marsh's comments is that the audiences did not want to be disturbed with images of reality. The preferred fare was the Clampetts, Gomer Pyle, and other lovable misfits—socially or linguistically. Eva Gabor's role in *Green Acres* embodied both ideas; the social and the language misfit. Gabor played ditzy Hungarian socialite Lisa Douglas, reluctantly trying to navigate the idyllic American heartland with poor English language skills and "highbrow European social graces." Implied here was derision based on national origin. Lisa Douglas had some connection with reality. Starting during World War II and accelerating during the Cold War, large numbers of Hungarian and Eastern European elites came to the United States fleeing fascism and, later, Soviet communism. Another example of derision based on national origin was *Hogan's Heroes,* set in a German prisoner of war camp during World War II. Both German central characters, the haughty Colonel Klink and the bumbling Sergeant Schultz, were ridiculed.

Domestic detectives were joined by international Cold Warriors during this era of television programming. Outstanding examples of this genre included *The Man from U.N.C.L.E.* and *I Spy.* Both shows carried with them the kernel of ethnic inclusion, and *I Spy,* with Bill Cosby as agent Alexander Scott, signaled the beginning of a new era in the representation of blacks in American television.

In *The Man from U.N.C.L.E.* superagents Illya Kuryakin and Napoleon Solo, a Russian and an American, joined forces against the international criminal organization THRUSH. Although it was a spoof of the popular James Bond film series, the show reflected a tiredness with the Cold War tensions; its two superpower agents worked together to solve more global problems. The bad guys in the series tended to have Asiatic appearances. So the stereotyping continued. With the lenses of hindsight, the men from U.N.C.L.E. seem to be prescient—anticipating al-Qa'ida. Despite its pejorative description, the "idiot sitcom" era presaged a more inclusive era in U.S. television programming.

THE RELEVANCE ERA, LATE SIXTIES–1975

The relevance period encompasses the maturing of the civil rights movement and the beginning of the "politics of inclusion" in the United States. During this period, all major societal institutions—the government, judicial system, education, religion, economy, and immigration—were closely scrutinized with the intention of isolating and eradicating race-based practices that had hitherto characterized American society.

The scrutiny took many forms—violent and nonviolent. Because of the racial disorders in American cities in the summer of 1967, President Johnson established the Kerner Commission (see chapter 4). The commission "was directed to answer three basic questions: What happened? Why did it happen? and What could be done to prevent it from happening again?"[12] Among the causes of urban disorders the commission identified "white racism," "racial ghettos," "unemployment," unequal treatment of people of color (compared to European immigrants), and the media. The report emphasized that "white racism is essentially responsible for the explosive mixture that has been accumulating in our cities since the end of World War II" (5). Among their recommendations was a series of media development tasks, including the recruitment of blacks by the media and improvements in the representation of blacks in media products (10).

From a programming point of view, one response was the "anti-bigot" show, of which one outstanding example was Norman Lear's *All in the Family*, introduced in 1971 (and based on the BBC series *Till Death Us Do Part*):

> *All in the Family* changed the course of television comedy. It brought a sense of harsh reality to a TV world which previously had been

populated by homogenized, inoffensive characters and stories that seemed to have been laundered before they got on the air. Its chief character, Archie Bunker, was anything but bland. A typical working-class Joe, he was uneducated, prejudiced, and blatantly outspoken. He was constantly lambasting virtually every minority group in existence. His views on blacks [or, as he often called them, "jungle bunnies" or "spades"], Puerto Ricans ["spics"], Chinese ["chinks"], and any other racial or religious group not his own, were clear and consistent. Archie believed in every negative racial and ethnic stereotype he had ever heard. (29)

He was also unapologetically homophobic and a classic male chauvinist pig. There is evidence to suggest that, in addition to revealing the stupidity of bigotry, the show served to reinforce bigotry in some sectors of the society.[13]

Spinoffs from *All in the Family* included *Maude* (the liberated woman) and *The Jeffersons* (upwardly mobile African Americans). Other ethnic comedies of this era included *Sanford and Son* and *Bridget Loves Bernie*. *Sanford and Son,* a takeoff of the British show *Steptoe and Son,* was set in multicultural Los Angeles. On occasion, Fred Sanford's junk yard welcomed Latino visitors.

In *Bridget Loves Bernie,* "Bernie was Jewish, a struggling young writer who supplemented his income by driving a cab. Bridget, his young bride, was an elementary school teacher whose parents were wealthy Irish Catholics. The couple shared a small apartment above a New York City delicatessen owned by Bernie's parents. The widely divergent ethnic, cultural, and social backgrounds of the Steinberg and Fitzgerald families, and their attempts to reconcile for the sake of the young couple, provided most of the plot situations." *Bridget Loves Bernie* lasted for one season—September 1972 to September 1973. Brooks and Marsh suggest that "one contributing factor may have been the furor created by the unhappiness of religious groups, primarily Jewish, over the show's condoning and publicizing mixed marriages."[14]

Black ghetto life was the subject of *Good Times.* Possibilities of upward mobility for blacks were exhibited in *The Jeffersons* who had "moved on up" to Manhattan. White mainstream culture met Hispanic in *Chico and the Man*. The Polish American community applauded *Banacek*. The hero, a "cool, smooth [and] shrewd" Polish American freelance insurance investigator whose "Polish proverbs were liberally sprinkled throughout the series, and the positive image of its hero made the show very popular with such groups as the Polish American Congress."[15]

The relevance era of programming was, no doubt, a response to the tensions of the times. Despite obvious attempts at inclusion, the nature of the ethnic characters in prime-time entertainment television remained essentially the same. Black characters followed the old traditions—they were safe, either "bucks, mammies, or coons"[16]—a pattern still evident today.

THE ABC FANTASY ERA, 1975–1980

The fantasy era provided respite from the harsh realities and tensions of the relevance era through a basic pattern of U.S. television programming—escapism. The "thoroughly escapist . . . or sexually titillating"[17] shows that dominated this era included *The Love Boat, Fantasy Island,* and *Mork and Mindy.* But despite the prevalence of this genre, profound programming innovations took place in American television. One such innovation was the miniseries. The outstanding example, the spectacularly successful *Roots,* made substantial contributions to African American self-identity and helped stimulate major interest in genealogy and a resurgence in neoethnicity among European ethnic communities.[18]

THE ERA OF SOAP OPERAS AND REAL PEOPLE, EIGHTIES

There are two types of soap operas on American television—daytime and prime-time. In the eighties, the prime-time soap opera, whose origins can be traced to the golden age of radio, consolidated its popularity both nationally and internationally. Television and the VCR had diffused globally, and the prime-time American soap operas, along with other American television programs, had become regular viewing fare for many of the world's television audience. For many viewers, the glamour associated with *Dallas* and *Dynasty* was synonymous with life in America. Such was the nature of American soft power!

American soap operas, both daytime and prime-time, were critiqued for being exclusive. By the end of the eighties, the genre appeared to have become more inclusive, featuring more characters of color. There were attempts at developing network soap operas that put blacks at the center of the story, and it has been suggested that these moves toward inclusion and the creation of black soap operas were due in part to the recognition that blacks make up a substantial sector of the soap opera audience, especially the daytime soaps.

There were also two strands of "real people" television. Shows such as *Hill Street Blues, St. Elsewhere,* and *The Cosby Show,* though fictional, tended to be more reflective of social reality. Shows like *Emergency 911, Real People,* and *Cops,* on the other hand, have been described as video vigilante shows because they emphasized violent crime, creating an image of dangerous blacks and validating the use of force as the solution to urban problems.

One outstanding development of commercial network programming in the latter eighties was the significant prime-time exposure of people of color, especially African Americans.[19] Black shows had story lines that obviously related to the black experience, were set in a locale or context that was primarily black, or featured black characters whose role was central to the dynamics of the show. After holding steady with around two top-rated shows per season throughout the seventies, six black shows had top ratings during the 1989–90 season.

That development attracted both positive and negative evaluations. In essence, the positive perspective argued that the increased presence of African Americans on network television was having a positive influence on society. That presence was "light years removed from 1956, when Nat Cole became the first major black entertainer to host a network variety series—for 15 minutes a week, without a sponsor." Instrumental in the increased presence of blacks on commercial television was an African American market that had become "increasingly upscale, diverse, proud of its ethnic identity and loaded with disposable income." Furthermore, black households were larger than nonblack households, had a larger concentration of adults, and watched half again as much television.[20]

Television in this era—especially with shows like *The Cosby Show, A Different World,* and *In Living Color*—had "become more attuned to creating new, realistic perceptions of blacks, a direct result of placing more African Americans behind the camera as well as in front of them."[21] Furthermore, shows like *The Cosby Show, A Different World,* and *Roc* could be singled for their contribution to the field of edutainment (education-entertainment), the practice of embedding in entertainment programming educational and other informational resources aimed at promoting positive social change.[22]

The social issues addressed by African American television shows in the late eighties and early nineties included the role of women in society, the crisis of the young African American male, family planning, AIDS, and participation in the political process. African American leadership figures like Jesse Jackson served as role models, appearing in cameo roles. South Africans, Afro-Caribbeans, Afro-Brazilians, and other global Africans were presented to the mainstream audience in nonstereotypical roles, displaying the diversity of global Africa in the United States. Those representations may have also contributed to the expanding perceptions of what African Americans and other blacks are and can be—more than just entertainers and athletes. An African American professional has defined this orientation as *value-added entertainment*—"entertainment based programming that has a value and provides an opportunity to put across some values other than dancing or music."[23] During this period, African American women achieved significant successes in front of the camera, behind the camera, and in decision-making positions. Debbie Allen's work with *A Different World* was lauded by the industry.

The popular African American programs not only brought the rich diversity of the black experience into mainstream homes, they profiled other forms of black art. The set of the internationally popular *Cosby Show* always featured the works of artists like Varnette Honeywood, Jacob Lawrence, Charles White, or Romare Bearden. Such shows also demonstrated the continuing ability of African American themes to develop loyal audiences in the domestic and international marketplace. The Hispanic and Asian presence in front of and behind the camera also increased in the last quarter century, although not as substantially as the black presence. Despite these quantitative and qualitative improvements, many critics still contend that the more things change the more they remain the same. Thomas Tyrer argued that although blatant negative ethnic stereotypes were "fading from the small screen" during this era, they were being replaced by "more subtle stereotypes." Jesse Jackson suggested that "five [new] deadly stereotypes" had been introduced in the case of African Americans: "[W]e are projected as less intelligent than we are, less hardworking than we work [sic], less universal than we are, less patriotic than we are, and more violent than we are." Sut Jhally and Justin Lewis coined the term "enlightened racism" to describe the new phenomenon. Enlightened racism is one of the central elements of the problematics of race in the United States at the start of the twenty-first century.[24]

Richard G. Carter and Henry Louis Gates Jr. do not feel that the presence of blacks on American commercial network television improved in the eighties. In 1988, Carter concluded that "there has never been a hit 'black' series that wasn't a comedy, or more comedy than drama." He used the term "white comfort zone" to explain "the safe feeling [whites] experience when they watch [black comedy]." Because of the power and influence of the white audience and white advertisers, networks and program producers tend to produce shows that are safe (comedic) and nonthreatening (not dealing with serious issues). Carter also posits that a show like *The Cosby Show* "never discusses issues of real importance to real blacks. Like housing, job discrimination, unemployment, poverty, or the devastation the drug epidemic has heaped on many black communities." He argues that by operating according to the white comfort zone, black shows "help camouflage the hopelessness felt by millions of blacks . . . even those who are said to have 'made it.'"[25]

In 1989, Harvard's Gates took up the same issue:

Even black Americans sometimes need to be reminded about the deceptiveness of television. Blacks retain their fascination with black characters on TV. Many of us buy *Jet* magazine primarily to read its weekly television feature, which lists every black character (major or minor) to be seen on the screen that week. Yet our fixation with the *presence* of black characters on TV has blinded us to an important fact that "Cosby," which began in 1984, and its offshoots over the years demonstrate convincingly: There is very little connection between the social status of black Americans and the fabricated images of black people that Americans consume each day. Moreover, the representations of blacks on TV is a very poor index to our social advancement or political progress.

Gates also draws upon Sterling Brown's 1933 categorization of black characters in American popular culture to construct a genealogy of the black characters in situation comedies:

[I]n the history of black images on television, character types have distinct pasts, as is also the case with shows, series seem both to lead to other series and to spring from metaphorical ancestors.

Let's track the evolution of the "Cosby" type on television. While social engineering is easier on the little screen than in the big city, Sterling Brown's list of black stereotypes in American literature proves quite serviceable as a guide to the images TV has purveyed for the last two decades. Were we writing a new sitcom using these character types, our cast might look like this—contented slave: Andy (*Amos 'n' Andy*), Fred Sanford (*Sanford and Son*), J. J. (*Good Times*); wretched freeman: George Jefferson (*The Jeffersons*); comic Negro: Flip Wilson (*The Flip Wilson Show*); brute Negro: Mr. T (*The A Team*), Hawk (*Spencer for Hire*); tragic mulatto: *Julia*, Elvin (*Cosby*), Whitley (*A Different World*); local color Negro: Meschach Taylor (*Designing Women*); exotic primitive Link (*Mod Squad,* 1968–73), most black characters on MTV. If we add the category Noble Negro (Cliff Huxtable, Benson), our list might be complete.

I think of the evolution of the Huxtable character in this way: imagine if George Jefferson owned the tenement building in which Florida and her family from *Good Times* lived. After John Amos dies, Jefferson evicts them for nonpayment of rent. Florida, destitute and distraught, tries to kill George. The state puts her children up for adoption. They are adopted by Mr. Drummond (*Different Strokes*) and graduate from Dalton, Exeter and Howard. Gary Coleman's grandson becomes an obstetrician, marries a lovely lawyer named Clare, and they move to Brooklyn Heights. And there you have it: the transformation of the character type of the black male on television.[26]

Everyone agrees that black representation on TV regressed in the early nineties. Joshua Hammer points out that the 1992–93 season was "dominated by black characters." However, some of those shows, especially *Out All Night, Hangin' with Mr. Cooper, Martin,* and *Rhythm and Blues* have been "condemned . . . for having a simplistic, unreal view of black life." Hammer mentions a speech by Bill Cosby during his induction to the Academy of Television Arts and Sciences Hall of Fame. Cosby, he reports, "excoriated the networks for spewing out 'drive-by images' that . . . reinforce shallow stereotypes. TV blacks 'think funny about theft.'" Hammer suggests that "African-American buffoons" were undermining the "individualized, attractive black characters [that] pop up in dramas like NBC's *Law and Order,* and *I'll Fly Away* and comedies like NBC's socially conscious *A Different World* and Fox's *Roc.*"[27]

This apparent return to facileness was also evident in the representation of other ethnic groups on commercial network television programming in the nineties. Jewish situation comedies promoted the stereotype of the "nebbish Jew"[28] in the early nineties, when the dominant trend was the decentering of commercial network television and the rise of the cable channels (see chapter 7). As in the eighties, the visibility of Native Americans, Latinos, and Asians did not increase as rapidly as that of blacks, although some shows, such as *L.A. Law* and *Northern Exposure,* did portray Latinos and Native Americans in a more responsible manner.

Newer immigrants to the United States were not very visible on commercial television. When they were, they followed the current stereotypes—including that of the Asian brainiac. Asian Indian student Jawaharlal Choudhury was quite comfortable as an academic overachiever in ABC's *Head of the Class.* In the hierarchy among Asians, people from Korea, Taiwan, Vietnam, Hong Kong, and the

People's Republic of China were depicted as model immigrants, while images of lower-status Asian immigrants, such as Cambodians and Laotians, suggested the return of the triads and black hand gangs.

Jack G. Shaheen addresses the concerns of Arab Americans and their recent representation on commercial television:

> Turn to any channel, to any show from *Benson* to *Hart to Hart,* television is full of Arab baddies—billionaires, bombers and belly dancers. They are virtually the only TV images of Arabs viewers see. An episode of a popular entertainment program may be seen by 50 million people the first time it is telecast. With reruns, the program may attract a total of 150 million viewers.
>
> Television tends to perpetuate four basic myths about Arabs: they are all fabulously wealthy; they are barbaric and uncultured; they are sex maniacs with a penchant for white slavery; and they revel in acts of terrorism. Yet, just a little surface probing reveals that these notions are as false as the assertions that Blacks are lazy, Hispanics are dirty, Jews are greedy and Italians are criminals.[29]

The events of September 11, 2001, unfortunately have reinforced those perceptions of Arabs.

The growing importance of ethnic communities to advertisers and the refinement in the practices of audience segmentation led to the establishment of special services in the advertising industry. The Bravo Group is the Hispanic markets division of Young and Rubicam, Inc., one of the world's largest advertising agencies. Bravo's president described the unit, established in the early seventies, as a response to the developing multicultural and Hispanic market and said that its aim was "to be able not only to understand and respond to the specific communication needs of the different cultures, but to do this in a manner that is relevant and sensitive."[30]

Many organizations have attempted to address representation and other matters associated with diversity and the programming of commercial network television. Among them have been organizations representing America's racial and ethnic communities, such as the National Association for the Advancement of Colored People (NAACP); agencies of the federal government, such as the Federal

Communications Commission (FCC), and the National Telecommunications and Information Administration of the Department of Commerce (NTIA); and industry-based volunteer organizations, such as the National Association of Broadcasters (NAB), the Radio and Television News Directors Association (RTNDA), and the National Association of Television Program Executives (NATPE).

Responses to Commercial Network Programming in the United States

ORGANIZATIONS REPRESENTING AMERICA'S RACIAL AND ETHNIC COMMUNITIES

Several organizations representing minorities in the United States have challenged what they consider to be negative and trivial representations of their communities. In a survey of fifty U.S. ethnic organizations I conducted in 1992, only northern European groups expressed satisfaction with their representation on commercial television. Among the most vociferous critics were groups representing Arabs, Asians, blacks, Hispanics, and some European minorities, particularly Germans, Irish, and Italians.[31]

Groups adopted a range of interventions to deal with negative representations on network television. Besides traditional protest strategies, such as letter-writing campaigns and boycotts, some ethnic and minority groups (e.g., B'nai B'rith, the Arab Anti-Defamation League, and the NAACP) developed educational and legal interventions. Other strategies have included support for the production of programming or establishing alternative television channels (see chapters 7 and 8). By the turn of the century, concerns about the representation of America's diversity had become rather shrill. For example, at the annual convention of the NAACP in 1999, its president, Kweisi Mfume, announced the establishment of an industry watchdog—the Television and Film Diversity Initiative—to monitor how well the entertainment industry was reflecting America's multicultural base and to initiate litigation and civil action where necessary. Mfume called the present state of affairs a "virtual whitewash" and stated that "there is practically no representation of people of color in the top echelon of production, which is the nucleus of the industry. Whether the paucity of minority executives at the networks, studios, or other entities is because of nepotism or cronyism, or racial discrimination, the results are the same."[32]

The reaction by the NAACP was part of a tradition. In 1915, only six years after its founding, the NAACP protested against the racism in D. W. Griffith's motion picture *Birth of a Nation*. Since then, the NAACP has fought to end stereotypes in the mass media that create misunderstanding and prejudice. From the perspective of the NAACP, the absence of minorities in the fall 1999 prime-time television lineup was an extreme permutation of prejudice, given the centrality of broadcasting in American life. Since the NAACP was established, the racial and ethnic composition of the United States has changed. Asians and Latinos have joined African Americans as substantial minorities of color. For the NAACP, failure to address the problem of prejudice in broadcasting further undermined the possibility of achieving "the ideal of human brotherhood in America," a goal of one of its founders, W. E. B. DuBois.[33]

Legal remedies and civil action, including boycotts of advertisers for the 1999 fall shows, were among the strategies suggested by the NAACP. The reaction from the entertainment industry was immediate. The four major national television networks (ABC, CBS, NBC, and Fox) all acknowledged the importance of diversity and sought dialog. The remarks of the NAACP's president had attracted the media's attention. Prejudice in broadcasting was discussed on important national talk shows for over a week after the convention. Major national newspapers also carried reports. *USA Today*'s Robert Blanco headlined his August 6, 1999, article "The World According to TV: Everybody Is White, Sex-Crazed, Beautiful, and Young—Just Like Reality, Right?"

The NAACP focused the nation's attention on two of the themes associated with prejudice in American broadcasting: its cyclical nature and its responsiveness to the ascendancy of conservative forces in society. The American broadcasting system, especially the commercial television networks, has a fundamental influence on the economic, political, and cultural life of society and on the pillars of society—education, law, the family. Citizens develop dependencies on broadcasting for information, education, and entertainment. These dependencies, especially in times of tension and ambiguity, can exert significant influence on the way a society feels, thinks, and acts.[34] Broadcasting's central role in society has made it a central site for the demonstration of political power. The control of broadcasting, including the articulation of expectations, has been a central feature in American governance since the introduction of radio in the early decades of the twentieth century.

Michael R. Winston traces the marginalization of people of color in the media to "America's double consciousness . . . about the race problem." He also invokes the inherent qualities of television to explain

> why television has, on the whole, not only failed more than the print media to reflect social reality as far as race is concerned, but has helped also to perpetuate false or stereotypical images of blacks and some other minorities. In part, this is inherent. Television's basic communication technique—the transmission of information by a rapid succession of coded images—is neither discursive nor reflective. Although television can, of course, project ideas, it may be incapable of matching the capacity of print to develop complex ideas and arguments. Free of the restraints of syntax and linear discussion, television conveys a "sense of authenticity" through the intrinsic superiority of the visual image, giving the viewer the impression that he or she has grasped a matter intellectually, when in fact only the absorption of visual images that *suggest* ideas and conclusions has occurred. It is simply easier for television to give the viewer the feeling that the images are accurately reflective of a complex reality than it is to achieve the same effect of print.

Among the key techniques associated with these qualities of television is the use of code words. Since the 1960s, "inner city" has been used as a code to refer to areas that have been abandoned to black habitation. The term "blacks and other minorities" is used to describe populations in cities where these groups actually comprise a majority. Winston emphasizes, "These codes have often been studied simply as 'stereotyping devices,' with great emphasis laid on the more superficial aspects of particular images. But something of greater significance lies behind the specifically demeaning characteristics of stereotypical black images in American popular culture. These 'images' were not conceived as representations of reality, nor understood to be 'real' by audiences, but were ways of coding and rationalizing interracial behavior."[35]

So, television images and representation are more than shorthand devices. They are tools of valorization. They articulate race relations. They racialize—that is, they construct race and justify strategies for allocating resources based on race. Television images and representation are important variables in the problematics of race in the United States. Just over two decades ago, George Comstock commented on the impact of television on American institutions and identified six areas of significant influence: "family life and the socialization of children," "church and religion," "enforcement of laws and norms," "leisure," "public security," and "politics and public affairs." The degree of influence varies according to the level of media consumption, as well as racial, ethnic, and socioeconomic status. Comstock maintained that "[b]lack youths are much more likely to report that they obtain ideas for dating from television than are whites. Blacks and children from families of lower socioeconomic status more frequently report that they use television as a source for learning."[36] The Adbuyer Initiative Media report on American television viewing habits confirmed these differentials (table 6.1).

In addition to differences in the amount of television viewed by minority groups in the United States, there are differences in taste—in

Table 6.1. Television Viewing Habits of Blacks,
Hispanics, and Nonblacks, 2001

Group	Avg. Hours per Week	Avg. Overnight Hours
Blacks	73.6	10.3
Hispanics	56.9	3.7
Nonblacks	51.2	4.1

Source: Hispanic, November 2001, 16.

what is watched. There are also differences in programming preferences among different television audiences. For example, Nielsen Media Research reported that the ten highest-rated programs in all U.S. homes from September 1999 to May 2000 included *Who Wants to Be a Millionaire? E.R., Friends, Frasier, Sixty Minutes,* and *The Practice.* However, the highest-rated programs in African American households included *The Parkers, Malcolm and Eddie, City of Angels, The Steve Harvey Show, Moesha,* and *Grown Ups.* The only program that was popular across both groups was *NFL Monday Night Football* (third among African Americans and sixth among the overall audience). This difference in audience preferences is of substantial importance in understanding the intersection of diversity and broadcasting in America.

Network television plays an important role in defining preferred values and norms for American society. During the last decade, for example, network television appears to have preferred a particular family formation—the two-parent nuclear family. But that privileging failed to represent the structure of the families of different ethnic groups in the United States. For some ethnic groups the extended family is the preferred structure. The immigration literature comments on the "chain-link" phenomenon—the tendency for middle-class, high-skilled immigrants to sponsor the immigration of their parents and lower-skilled relatives. It is not uncommon for such families to share a common household. On the other hand, some ethnic groups, such as who came here as refugees or from the Caribbean, have a high number of single-parent households. This type of family diversity is not always evident on American television, especially in the programming offered by the influential commercial networks.

It has become popular during the last decade to say that the prime function of commercial television is to deliver its audiences to advertisers. Through advertising on commercial television, the audience is exposed to goods and services produced for mass consumption. In 1985, network advertising revenues amounted to $8.3 billion; in 2000, $40 billion.[37] Consistently, the dominant advertisers on commercial network television are the automobile industry, the food industry (especially the restaurant and drive-in sector), food stores and supermarkets, toiletries, and confectionery, snacks, and soft drinks.

Roberta Astroff has demonstrated that commercial television, in its quest to develop minority audiences as consumers, has the power to valorize or devalorize racial and ethnic communities in the United States. Her examination of practices during the last few decades in the development of the Latino market revealed the valorizing of attributes that were formerly perceived as negative. For example, large Latino families were no longer offered as indicators of parental irresponsibility but as valuable attributes of a "high consumer."[38]

Commercial network television, with its extensive national reach, has a large role in the web of dependency relationships that exist in American society. Central to this web of dependency is a competition among key societal institutions (including commerce, industry, government, and special interest groups) for scarce resources, especially access to the American audience as consumer or voter.[39] Commerce, industry, government, and religious institutions depend on the mass media, especially commercial network television, to access the marketplace. Commercial network television depends on advertising, and it requires a supportive regulatory environment to achieve its goals of profit maximization. The mass media, especially commercial network television, are therefore susceptible to the influence of both the public and private sectors. They also have been susceptible to the influence of special interest groups such as the NAACP and groups that represent Jews, Arabs, women, and the old—particularly if those groups threaten to organize boycotts. Because of these dependency relations, commercial television in the United States has been considered conservative in terms of ideology and programming practice. It tends not to rock the boat. In addition, entertainment programming on network television tends to privilege and reproduce the value systems of the capitalist class and other powerful interest groups in our society.

The mass media, especially broadcasting, have substantial power and influence in American society and have demonstrated their central role in the formulation and construction of American culture and civilization. Politicians and media professionals—such as advertising managers, program producers, and political consultants—operate from the position that the media, especially broadcasting, directly affect American society, particularly for the achievement of their goals of increased sales, sustained consumption, and the election of their candidates. After September 11, 2001, confidence in this power was demonstrated when the media were used to mobilize the nation in the war against terrorism, especially in the task of maintaining national solidarity, maintaining the alliance against terrorism, and winning the hearts and minds of Muslims across the world.[40]

Over the past three decades the FCC and other federal agencies have promulgated regulations that have influenced the structure and output of commercial network television in the United States. These regulations, reflecting the ideological orientation of American society, have targeted areas such as "management and ownership and programming and advertising."[41] The First Amendment of the Constitution prohibits federal agencies from directly influencing the content of commercial network television. However, some regulations and programs administered by the FCC, the NTIA, and the Equal Employment Opportunity Commission—especially those oriented to minority employment, ownership, and advertising—have indirect influence.

The origins of many of these regulations and programs can be traced back to the report of the Kerner Commission in 1968 and to the ideological spirit of those times. Since the Kerner Commission report, the dominant approach has been informed by the assumption that increased engagement of minorities in the broadcasting industry would bring the perspectives and sensitivities necessary for more responsible programming. The dominant strategies to achieve that goal were recruitment and increased opportunities to own and operate broadcasting outlets.

Evidence from the National Association of Broadcasting has suggested that the recruitment strategy has not been as effective as was hoped, due to glass ceilings and other environmental tensions. The 1990 report from the NAB showed that, since 1988, there had been a decline in the number of black males in the industry. Despite these failings, the industry continues to use recruitment as the primary vehicle to ensure diversity in commercial network television. One report indicates that the American mass communication sector would be unable to meet its goal of recruiting minorities in numbers proportionate to their population size.[42]

The FCC is the principal federal agency involved in the regulation of broadcasting in the United States. Although it is constrained by the First Amendment from interfering with program content, it can influence the general operating environment and can thus affect the organization and output of commercial television in America. Two clusters of regulatory issues have direct bearing on race and ethnicity in commercial network television: management and ownership issues and programming and advertising issues. In 1991, the chief of the Policy and Rules Division of the Mass Media Bureau summarized the situation:

> The Commission does, however, have a commitment to minority participation in employment within the industry. The Commission has rules that require that equal opportunity shall be afforded by licensees to all qualified persons and that no person shall be discriminated against in employment because of race, color, religion, national origin or sex. Broadcast licensees are required to file annual employment reports with the FCC, and licensees who have more than five or more full-time employees provide data on staff composition by job categories and by gender, race or national origin. In addition, each license renewal applicant and new application for a broadcast license who has or will have five or more employees must submit to the Commission an EEO [Equal Employment Opportunity] program designed to ensure equal employment opportunity for women and minorities. Copies of the annual employment report and EEO program filed with the Commission must be available in a station's local public file.[43]

Failure to follow the EEO regulations and employment practices attracted sanctions that included "the imposition [of] reporting requirements on the station, forfeitures, shorter renewals and the designation of an EEO issue for evidentiary hearing which could lead to a denial of renewal." In further support of the recruitment paradigm, the FCC in 2000 had articulated a body of rules referred to as the

Equal Employment Opportunity rules. These rules, especially the requirements for making vacancies known to wide communities, were declared unconstitutional by the District of Columbia Circuit Court of Appeals in 2001. On December 13, 2001, the FCC announced that it was in the process of articulating a new set of rules to ensure adherence to its "long-standing anti-discrimination rule." The commission also announced that it was in the process of developing rules that would "require broad outreach to all qualified job candidates for positions at radio, television, and cable companies."[44]

In addition to the EEO regulations the FCC also instituted regulations that aimed at encouraging minority ownership of commercial television property. This goal was embodied in the "distress sale" policy, which was "designed to promote minority ownership by making it possible for a minority to buy a station that would otherwise be priced out of reach, by creating an opportunity for ownership that would not otherwise exist and by creating additional incentive for a licensee to sell to a minority." This policy and the attendant regulations were challenged in the courts and in March 1989 were found to be unconstitutional. Nevertheless, support for this strategy continues. This court decision and the rollback of the EEO rules in 2001 are indicative of the impact of ideology on the broadcasting environment. Since 1980, the United States has entered a conservative phase of governance that appears to be rolling back decisions associated with constructing a more inclusive society. Despite these reversals, the NAB supports minority employment at all levels of the industry and remains "concerned about the under-representation of minorities in telecommunications and therefore favor[s] initiatives designed to promote minority ownership."[45]

The Minority Telecommunications Development Program, established in 1978 and administered by the NTIA, was also oriented toward helping minority ownership. Specifically, the program was introduced to

> increase minority participation in all phases of telecommunications. Through this program, minority business persons, educational institutions, and organizations are helped in the creation and expansion of telecommunications businesses.

The MTDP helps minority entrepreneurs and noncommercial entities through a variety of incentives: (1) providing, through its broadcast technical services project, initial engineering assistance in starting a broadcast facility; (2) analyzing and participating in industry developments, legislative and regulatory policymaking, and FCC proceedings to ensure that policies will adequately consider minority interests; (3) holding seminars and briefings for minority entrepreneurs and other organizations interested in business, manufacturing, and ownership opportunities available in telecommunications.

In 1992, the program had been extended to include a training program for minority owners and there were plans afoot to launch an access to capital program. Today the MTDP is still in place and continues to "develop programs and policies that increase minority ownership of broadcast and telecommunications businesses." The MTDP also aims to support businesses owned by women.[46]

The NTIA's 1998 report on the state of minority ownership of full-powered television stations was not inspiring. Altogether, minorities owned thirty-two commercial stations and two networks in 1997. This represented 2.7 percent of all commercial television stations in the United States. Blacks owned twenty-six stations (2.2 percent) and Hispanics owned six (0.5 percent). Asian Americans and Native Americans owned no commercial stations.[47] Besides the demands from minority organizations and programs by the federal government, commercial television in the United States responds to internal factors in its response to diversity. Commercial network television appears to have adopted a range of internal practices, both formal and informal, in response to the many issues at the intersection of diversity and commercial network television.

Industry Responses

STANDARDS AND PRACTICES UNITS

Their titles may vary, but in each of the commercial television networks in the United States there is a unit that ensures that common standards of decency and good taste are followed. At the American

Broadcasting Corporation (ABC), the Standards and Practices Unit was established in 1942 and "is independent of any other department in the company." ABC's *Broadcast Standards and Practices* provides insights on that company's responses to the increasing multicultural composition of the United States. The unit has expertise across a range of fields—"law, teaching, English, social sciences, communication, psychology, journalism, and early childhood education"—and must "see that all . . . entertainment programming and commercials meet standards of good taste and community acceptability." This requires the prescreening of all programs, advertisements, and public service announcements to ensure that they satisfy ABC's own policies and the rules of the FCC.[48]

The policy document also states that ABC recognizes television's "extraordinary impact and power" and is therefore "sensitive to [its] obligation to present a wide range of programming that meets the needs of all viewers." In isolating factors that determine "the needs of all viewers," ABC identifies "age, education, interests, tastes, [race, and ethnicity]." The document explicitly states, "we also strive to avoid the ethnic stereotyping of individuals by subjecting all shows to the rigorous scrutiny required by our basic guidelines. Our objective is to encourage fair ethnic representation. If we don't have sufficient expertise within our staff to deal with a particular ethnic group, we seek advice from those who are knowledgeable" (7).

In 1991, Albert R. Kroeger, director of Editorial Service, corporate communication for NBC, reported that NBC had "no explicit rules or polices on programming for . . . society's new entrants." He, did say, however, that

[i]ndividual TV stations, whether the NBC owned and managed stations or the independently-owned NBC affiliated stations, have a specific community service obligation, and it obviously depends on the ethnic/cultural mix in the market being served whether it would be meaningful to purchase or develop programs targeted to a specific population sector. In New York, Los Angeles and Miami, areas with major Hispanic concentration, NBC stations do, very deliberately, carry some Hispanic-oriented programs. . . . Part of the local public

service messages broadcast in some markets may also have a specific ethnic/cultural orientation.

On the national network level, a different situation applies, since the mission here is to serve a mass, very homogenized audience. TV entertainment programs on the commercial networks are not produced or selected to accomplish a particular societal objective, nor is the programming approach educational or instructional in nature, as it might be with specialized local stations or with public broadcasting outlets.

Kroeger recognized that "mass appeal, mainstream programming without a doubt does offer a viewer unfamiliar with American lifestyles and customs the opportunity to watch what is portrayed, and to gain insights and information on life in the U.S. Conversely, mainstream audiences do get to see a certain amount of programming dealing with the ethnic and racial minorities." Finally, he suggested that "entertainment programs on NBC for upwards of two decades— from Chico and the Man up through Miami Vice, L.A. Law, and episodes of various dramatic shows—have introduced Hispanic themes and characters." He added that this practice "is almost common today as the ongoing presentation of blacks and black cultural themes." He stated that "Asian immigration has certainly increased, but this group today still only comprises 3% of the total population. As writers and producers learn more about Asians in American society, we have no doubt that Asian-American themes will become more common." He pointed out that the practices he had mentioned earlier were not formalized but added, "it is the nature of TV storytelling to look for new and novel themes out of the total society, and NBC certainly welcomes themes that are and will be derived from the more varied cultural makeup of this country." Kroeger's predictions were correct: by 2000, NBC programs had started to present Asian Americans responsibly.[49]

Another example of the response by commercial network television to diversity has been diversity in the economic relations the sector has with external suppliers (see esp. chapter 7). Despite individual efforts by the commercial television networks, there are some issues such as recruitment and retention and programming that require an industry-wide response. The principal mechanisms involved in the development of these responses include the pan-industry institutions such as the NAB, the RTNDA, the National Association of Television Program Executives (NATPE), and the Screen Actors Guild (SAG).

In 1991, I asked Dwight M. Ellis, the NAB's vice president of human resources, what significant challenges faced his organization because of the multicultural makeup of the media environment. His response is provided in its entirety:

1) Assisting the NAB membership in maintaining a balanced workplace as to gender, race and culture during periods of economic hardships brought on by increased marketplace competition and a rapidly changing media environment.

2) Maintaining climates of encouragement and opportunity for attracting and retaining quality minority and women employees to careers in broadcasting.

3) Protecting and enhancing the image of broadcast entities in volatile economic times where staff downsizing has become more prevalent than ever before.

4) Providing realistic broadcasting career guidance to colleges and universities involved in teaching and training prospective broadcast employees.

When asked how he and his organization had responded or planned to respond to the changing multicultural makeup of the United States, Ellis replied,

1) Creation of useful materials designed to assist broadcasters in attracting, hiring and promoting minorities and women to productive careers in broadcasting (e.g., *Diversity in Broadcasting: Actions Toward Better Business* brochure).

2) Maintaining initiatives for bringing broadcasters and prospective workers together for career and business opportunities (e.g., Em-

ployment Clearinghouse of the Department of Human Resource Development; conducting free broadcast job seminars; and developing liaisons with minority and women's communication professional organizations; publication of a booklet explaining procedures for purchasing broadcast stations).

3) Providing EEO guidance and materials to broadcasters to help ensure awareness and proper implementation of fair employment practice and polices in the broadcast workplace (e.g., publication of a broadcast EEO manual; conducting EEO-related presentations before [state broadcast] associations).

4) Sustaining a positive presence with media professional and community organizations, and other vital groups having interest in broadcast matters (e.g., participation on committees and ad hoc initiatives charged with improving diversity in broadcasting and allied media; serving as a resource to governmental bodies, such as the Telecommunications forum of the Congressional Black Caucus, to assist in presenting productive strategies for career development).

5) Serving on advisory boards, and accepting speaking assignments . . . at colleges and universities with communications and journalism divisions.

The NAB continues to adopt and support policies and programs aimed at ensuring that America's diversity is evident in the broadcasting industry. Particular emphasis is placed on internship and other human resource development strategies.[50]

THE RADIO AND TELEVISION NEWS DIRECTORS ASSOCIATION AND THE NATIONAL ASSOCIATION OF TELEVISION PROGRAMMING EXECUTIVES

The RTNDA and the NATPE have also emphasized human resource development. They provide seminars, have established job banks, and coordinate internship programs. However, despite these efforts in the area of recruitment, which were supposed to influence news and entertainment production, there are problems associated with recruitment, retention, and promotion. As mentioned earlier, the National

Association of Television Programming Executives is also involved with the issues of ethnicity and race in the industry. The three key main goals of the NATPE are: "(1)To promote the professionalism of television program executives; (2) to enhance the industry's image; and (3) to ensure the current and future viability of television."[51] All three of those goals are influenced by the industry's responses to the changing composition of American society.

THE SCREEN ACTORS GUILD

Another industry-related organization whose work has influenced commercial television's engagement with America's diversity is the Screen Actors Guild (SAG), which "represents 81,000 professional performers working in theatrical and television films, commercials and industrial/educational films." This organization has responded to the changing ethnic composition of American society in a variety of ways, as indicated by the following excerpts from SAG policy documents:

> For more than a decade now, SAG has recognized that the American scene is increasingly multicultural and multiracial. Moreover, performers of color comprise about 15 percent of the SAG membership and deserve nothing less than fair and equal employment opportunity. In response to this reality SAG has developed and negotiated contract language with producers and advertising agencies which urges them to increase employment opportunities and eliminate negative stereotyping of African-Americans, Asian/Pacific, Latino/Hispanic and American Indian performers in films and commercials. In this regard, the Guild's challenge is to ensure producer and ad agency compliance with SAG's Policy of Non-Discrimination and Affirmative Action. In short our primary objective is to ensure that the American scene, with its ever growing cultural and racial diversity, be portrayed realistically in films and commercials.

SAG has developed a variety of initiatives to achieve these goals. For example, in the early nineties it

> adopted a multi-faceted approach aimed at improved casting opportunities and character portrayals. In Hollywood, where the bulk of television and feature motion pictures are produced, Rodney Mitchell,

executive administrator of Affirmative Action, routinely initiates meetings with studio, producer and casting representatives to discuss and ensure compliance with SAG's Policy on Non-Discrimination and Affirmative Action. As a result, modest gains in the employment of performers of color in film and television projects have been observed. Yet much remains to be done before we can report that reasonable and satisfactory progress in minority hiring has been achieved. . . .

In New York, Elaine Brodey, administrator of Affirmative Action, has developed a comprehensive educational seminar program focusing on non-traditional casting and balanced imagery and directed toward all advertising agency personnel involved in the creation and production of television commercials. Seminars have been conducted at the major agencies in New York, Chicago, Detroit, Dallas, San Francisco and other cities around the country. Here to[o], there has been modest improvement in the employment of performers of color, but there is much still to be done. . . .

Besides the activities described above, SAG has sponsored several national conferences in Hollywood, New York City, Washington, D.C., and Chicago focusing on the issues of employment and imagery for women and ethnic minority performers and performers with disabilities. These national conferences provide the Guild the opportunity to raise the collective consciousness of the motion picture, television and advertising industry about the multicultural and multiracial aspects of the American scene; to underscore the importance of reflecting such diversity in films and commercials and finally, to encourage consumers of films and commercials to get involved in the movement to change existing casting practices which too frequently either exclude or stereotype negatively performers of color.[52]

Since 1993, SAG has sponsored independent research on trends related to race, ethnicity, and gender in American television. In his 1997 report for SAG, George Gerbner concluded:

> Despite slight progress towards more equitable representation, men still outnumber women two to one.

> The representation of African American males (but not females) increased each year until it reached 171 percent of its real-life proportion.

Commercial media shun poor people. Low-income wage earners are virtually invisible.

Asian/Pacific characters are still less than one half of their proportion of the U.S. population.

Latino/Hispanic characters are less than one third of their real proportion of the U.S. population.

Television characters in the nineties are healthier and wealthier than in the eighties.

The characters (especially women) are also younger. The stage is set for more younger women–older men relationships.

There has been a decline in the number of characters with disabilities, and disabled performers still do not play "normal" roles.

Women age faster than men; as they age they become more evil.

Mentally ill characters and "foreigners" fail most often, and commit most crime and violence.[53]

7

Cable Television and America's Diversity

The Era of Choice

America's minorities appear to have been among the beneficiaries of the growth of the cable television industry during the last quarter century. The development of cable has brought increased citizen participation and diversity in broadcasting and has provided Americans with access to many program sources (see chapter 6). Cable programming networks and cable programming companies operated by minorities have contributed to the development of the Era of Choice, as have new technologies, the business practices of mainstream mass media companies (mergers and acquisitions), minority audience demands, the assertiveness of minority entrepreneurs, foreign governments, and federal regulations.

The Cable Industry

The cable broadcasting industry began in 1948 with the experiments of John Walton in Mahanoy City, Pennsylvania, and Ed Parsons in Astoria, Oregon. These pioneers constructed distribution systems by stringing cable from antennae erected on the tops of mountains to homes in the valleys below. Thus they were able to deliver over-the-air commercial network television signals to those homes that were unable to receive them before. The experiments were so successful that they launched the community antenna television (CATV) revolution.[1]

The freeze on the expansion of commercial over-the-air television imposed by the FCC from 1948 to 1952 helped boost demand for cable. By 1958, there were nearly half a million subscribers, about 1 percent of American television households. But the emerging industry was challenged by what Bill Daniels, one of the industry's pioneers, has called a "formidable array of forces," including "the three networks—ABC, NBC, CBS—local stations, local theater owners, movie producers, the FCC, AT&T, most cities, states and counties, the Congress and the power companies."[2]

By 1951, the leaders of the embryonic industry, "a bunch of young crazy guys," were joined by major investors like Irving Kahn, the owner of TelePrompTer. In 1952, in response to its challenges, the industry established the National Community Television Association, which changed its name to the National Cable Television Council and is now the National Cable Television Association (NCTA).

The cable industry grew from 2,490 systems in 1970 to 11,075 in 1992. In 2000, there were 11,800 cable systems in operation in the United States, most offering sixty or more channels. Given the involvement of telecommunications giant AT&T in the cable television industry, 96.7 percent of the United States was theoretically "wired" for cable. Also in 2000, AT&T Broadband and Internet Services was the largest multiple-system operator (MSO), with sixteen million subscribers, and the cable industry's revenue from subscription fees, advertising, and pay cable was more than $48 billion. In 2001, the industry spent over $14 billion to upgrade and expand its infrastructure.[3]

The cable industry has grown from a mere deliverer of video programming to a sophisticated multimedia sector of the American communication environment. At least five thousand of the country's cable systems originate programming from their own studios. Through its infrastructure, the American cable industry has emerged as the "ideal pipeline for delivery of new advanced services, including digital networks, video-on-demand, interactive television, high speed Internet access and telephony," giving the industry a global reach.[4]

Among the expectations associated with the proliferation of cable television in the United States were opportunities for real diversity in programming and, through access practices, the enrichment of the process of making evident "a multitude of tongues," thus giving further substance to the core ideas behind the First Amendment. But until the late eighties, the industry had not fulfilled those expectations. In the earlier days of cable, the heavy hand of federal regulation and narrow corporate perspectives constrained possibilities for diversity. For example, writing in the early nineties, Patricia Aufderhide contended that the cable industry saw itself purely as a technology to support the delivery of commercial network television. Aufderhide identified two other factors that constrained the cable industry's ability to allow access to a multitude of voices. The first was the industry's dependency on advertising: advertisers can and do influence programming practices. The second was the industry's practice of "clipp[ing] the wings of distribution competitors, such as direct broadcast satellites and wireless cable."[5] Those early business practices ensured that cable television was, in fact, a mere distribution arm of commercial network television.

When Waterman and Grant studied the industry's programming practices in the early 1990s, they sought answers to the following questions: "What proportion of cable programs are new and original to cable, and how many are repeated from other media? Of what types (e.g., informational, dramatic) are aftermarket programs and from what sources do they come? How are cable audiences distributed among these programs categories? What is the extent of cable's economic dependence on its role as an aftermarket?" The term *aftermarket* referred to old movies and reruns of programs once aired on the commercial networks. The results of the study showed that aftermarket programming dominated cable menus and, by extension, a higher proportion of cable viewing.[6]

The aftermarket strategy has become an established programming strategy in the industry, feeding specialized channels like American Movie Classics, Turner Classic Movies, Nick at Night, and the History

Channel. Nevertheless, the cable industry had become the "principal engine of change" in American television programming by the nineties. The proliferation of cable channels, developments in distribution technologies, the logic of programming (especially that of niche marketing), and aftermarket opportunities from international sources have helped the development of a number of channels dedicated to minorities in America. In January 2002, it was possible to identify at least fifty-one national cable program networks dedicated to minority (language, religion, race, or ethnicity) communities in the United States. In 1995, there were only nineteen such networks.

As pointed out earlier, the cable industry is technologically sophisticated. Satellites have helped deliver programs to cable headends (distribution nodes) and have helped create competition for the cable industry. One such competitor is the direct broadcast satellite (DBS) sector. DBS was introduced by the United States Satellite Broadcasting Company (USSB) and Direct TV in 1994. In 1999, Direct TV and USSB merged, and the new entity had thirteen million subscribers.

In the nineties, the concept of technological convergence was clearly evident in the cable television industry. The industry utilized all its infrastructure—copper, fiber optics, and satellites—to provide broadband access to the Internet and deliver a raft of other new and advanced services—digital networks, video-on-demand, interactive television, and telephony. The cable industry's technological capacity has strengthened the global reach of American broadcasting and cable television is a significant sector of the industry.

The cable industry has been scrutinized by several entities—including local (municipal) governments, the federal government, industry organizations, and special interest groups—for its performance in the crucial normative areas of access, equality, solidarity, and quality. Municipalities provide operating licenses to cable companies. Typically, cable operators set aside channels on their systems for community and local government use. They are also required to pay a percentage of the subscription revenues they generate to the municipality to pay for running community access television.

Like commercial network television, cable television was also subject to Equal Employment Opportunity regulations. From 1990 to 2001, cable system operators were required to make annual reports to the FCC on their employment practices, especially the processes they had adopted to ensure that minorities are included in recruitment pools. In the cable industry, the quest for racial and ethnic diversity brought many players into contact with each other: for example, the NCTA, the principal trade association; the National Association of Minorities in Communication (NAMIC), an influential special interest group for employees in the industry; and private foundations such as the Walter Katz Foundation and the Emma Bowen Foundation for Minority Interests in the Media.

A 1999 report commissioned by NAMIC concluded that "minorities are severely under represented in the executive suites of the cable industry."[7] As with commercial network television, the researchers concluded that the cable industry mirrored the rest of corporate America in that regard. About 20 percent of NAMIC members surveyed said they perceived discrimination at their companies. A quarter of the African Americans surveyed felt their race or ethnicity had "a negative impact on their opportunities." Asians did not report similar experiences. The report found that African Americans were "more severely under represented in management than Asians" and that minority men fared better than minority women in the cable industry. Further, 20 percent of the respondents perceived discrimination in corporate polices and practices, especially in professional development. They felt they did not have equitable access to "industry conferences, training programs, or . . . social networks and career opportunities" (4). Based on their findings, the researchers recommended that NAMIC's research and policy committee should ensure that the FCC continue to "require the cable industry to maintain and comply with EEO requirements until all disparities are gone." The committee was also encouraged to resist and oppose any "effort to dismantle existing EEO requirements." Specifically, the researchers encouraged the committee to ask the FCC for a clearer definition of *top management* in the cable industry. The working definition included sales as one of the categories. The report considered that to be a deceptive artifact, as most minority "top managers" were in sales and not in finance, legal affairs, or programming.

The report also requested NAMIC to facilitate collaboration among cable companies and industry organizations with the aim of developing programs "focused on moving people of color into the senior-management levels of the cable industry" (5). The study revealed the presence of "diversity fatigue," a condition that supported efforts to discredit and dismantle affirmative action programs in the United States in the last two decades. In April 2001, the cable industry, through the NCTA, established Diversity Partners, which included the Walter Katz Foundation, NAMIC, Women in Cable and Telecommunications, the Cable Television Human Resources Association, and the Emma Bowen Foundation. The partnership had a three-part mission: "To recruit and increase the overall number of diverse employees in the cable industry. To retain and advance diverse employees to the executive ranks in the cable industry. To increase the use of women and minority owned vendors serving the cable industry."[8] The emphasis on human resource development was inevitable. Since the late eighties the cable industry has sought to exploit America's growing minority audiences. (See Cox Cable's premiums for bilingual salespersons, below.)

The cable industry has developed other initiatives to advance the cause of diversity. These include C-Span (the public affairs service of the cable industry) and Cable in the Classroom, highly visible projects organized by the NCTA. The Cable in the Classroom initiative supports multicultural education in American grade (K–12) schools. It is, however, the programming directed to minority communities, the programming produced by minority cable operators, and the products of independent program providers that make the cable industry's contribution to diversity obvious and relevant to this book.

There are two core sectors in the cable industry. One is the infrastructure, the "pipeline" owned by multiple system operators (MSOs). The second includes the content providers. Through the general tendency for vertical integration between the two sectors, large media corporations have been able to dominate the cable television industry in America.

Multiple System Operators and Diversity

Let us focus on AT&T Broadband, AOL Time Warner, and Cox Communications—three corporations that have been among the top five

MSOs for over a decade. In December 2001, they controlled more than 66 percent of all cable households in America.[9] AT&T Broadband and AOL Time Warner were the outcomes of mergers and acquisitions that dominated the broadcasting industry in the nineties. AT&T acquired Tele-Communications, Inc. (TCI), the number one MSO for most of the nineties, and became AT&T Broadband. AOL Time Warner inherited Time Warner Cable, the second-ranked MSO in that period. Cox Communications remained a privately owned company throughout the nineties. AT&T Broadband, AOL, and Cox not only control most of the subscribers in the major national markets but they also control powerful infrastructures, substantial programming sources, crucial elements of the Internet, and they have substantial global visibility. They demonstrate innovative market-based strategies to diversity, such as supplier diversity and community outreach, and in many ways typify the cable industry's responses to the changing composition of racial and ethnic diversity in the United States.

AT&T BROADBAND

In December 2001, the Denver-based AT&T Broadband was the largest cable operator in the United States, with more than fourteen million subscribers. AT&T Broadband, a unit of AT&T, has more than fifty thousand employees and customers in most of America's major media markets. Its operations are concentrated in Chicago, Minneapolis/St. Paul, Dallas, Denver, Salt Lake City, Los Angeles, Sacramento, San Francisco, Spokane, Seattle, and Portland, but it also has a significant presence in the South (Atlanta, Richmond, Miami) and the Northeast (Pittsburgh).

AT&T Broadband is a diversified company, with AT&T Broadband Internet and AT&T Digital Phone in addition to its cable television operations. The company also has partnerships with the Starz Encore Group LLC, a subsidiary of Liberty Media. The Starz! brand includes Black Starz!, a premium service that specializes in black hit movies.

AT&T Broadband has articulated and operationalized its commitment to diversity in several areas: employment, suppliers, business partners, shareholders, and the communities the company operates in.[10]

As at NBC, special emphasis has been placed on supplier diversity, an "imperative" management strategy that allows the company to enhance its service and competitiveness. Specifically, it means that AT&T has been increasing its expenditures with "women and minority-owned businesses." Another element in AT&T Broadband's diversity strategy is community outreach, which includes membership in organizations and sponsoring events that reflect the ethnic makeup of the communities that the company serves. According to the company, "the factors weighed in the decision [to engage in a community activity] include . . . the political/community/customer impact that the [participation] will engender." AT&T Broadband has identified affiliations with Native American, Asian American, women's, African American, Hispanic, and service-disabled veteran associations.[11]

AOL TIME WARNER

AOL Time Warner is the largest media conglomerate in the world. One of its subsidiaries, Time Warner Cable, has more than twelve million cable subscribers and was one of the first digital cable services in the United States. At the end of 2001, over 94 percent of Time Warner Cable's infrastructure was digital. AOL's mission is to "become the world's most respected and valued company by connecting, informing, and entertaining people everywhere in innovative ways that will enrich their lives." Seven core values guide the organization: creativity, customer focus, agility, teamwork, integrity, diversity, and responsibility. For AOL, diversity refers to attracting and developing "the world's best talent [and] seeking to include the broadest range of people and perspectives." The organization has articulated its commitment to "serving the public interest by using our unique talents and resources to enrich people's lives and strengthen communities around the world." The key vehicle in delivering AOL's global commitment to diversity is the AOL Time Warner Foundation, which focuses on empowering citizens and civic participation, engaging communities and the arts, and extending Internet benefits.[12]

AOL Time Warner operates influential cable programming networks such as CNN, HBO, TNT, and TBS Superstation. The organization also manages some of the largest film libraries in the world, which gives the company substantial content leverage. AOL's cable programming networks have substantial capacity and provide access to many independent ethnic program producers.

Cox Cable is one of the businesses of Cox Communications, Inc., a Fortune 500 company majority-owned by Cox Enterprises, Inc. For the past decade, Cox Communications has operated the fifth-largest MSO in the United States. In 1991,Cox Cable, which has a strong presence in the Southwest, had 1,750,000 subscribers. In December 2001, it had nearly seven million subscribers and was recognized as one of the "full-service providers in the field, offering its customers voice, video and data services."[13] The company is also an investor in several programming networks, such as the Discovery Channel.

For the past decade Cox Cable has had an assertive recruitment and development program for people of color:

> We want a work force that represents the people of the communities we serve—a work force that includes employees from all segments of the population. We consider that a sound business policy, a necessity for all our operations—and simply the right thing to do.
>
> Our employees are truly our greatest asset. With their commitment to excellence we will continue to achieve our corporate goals. In return, we strive to provide our people with an environment that encourages them to stay and grow with us.

The active ingredient in that policy was the company's human resources development program, which stated, "Cox Enterprises was committed to providing qualified people of color and women with career opportunities at both entry and management levels." The company has maintained that policy. An employee can be transferred to any one of the core businesses operated by Cox Enterprises—Cox Communications (cable), Cox Newspapers, Inc., Cox Broadcasting, Inc., and Mannheim Auctions.[14]

The company drew upon local, regional, and national organizations in their quest to recruit and retain employees of color. The previously mentioned Walter Katz Foundation has played a major role in this process. In 1991, the Katz Foundation was described as an organization that "identifies and recruits talented minorities for cable television who already have experience working in a variety of other industries, from banking to broadcasting."[15]

In early 1992, accounts from several of the company's field offices showed the initiatives they had taken to address the needs of their changing audiences and the assertive minority recruitment programs that had been instituted. Cox Cable–Omaha had carried out a diversity recruitment initiative in 1990 to "prepare our system for the diversity of the future." Future plans included the "recruiting of the more mature and the disabled worker."[16]

The responses from Cox Cable–Santa Barbara revealed a wide range of programming, personnel, and community outreach initiatives. Among them:

Broadcasting the local ABC evening news with Spanish voice-over at 11:00 p.m. on Telemundo five days a week.

Adopting bilingual pay differential, $0.50/hr. in January 1992, for any staff member who uses Spanish-language skills in their position.

Exploring local production of bilingual/Spanish newscast on the local channel.

Considering to add a third Spanish-language channel in 1993.

Using Spanish radio and newspaper sources to recruit bilingual staff—as well as community organizations.

Participating in the Adopt-a-School partner project. Ninety percent of their schools were predominantly Spanish speaking.

Executive staff actively engaged in local Hispanic organizations. One was a member of the Hispanic Achievement Board.

Sponsoring a $1,000 college scholarship to a local Hispanic communications student.[17]

In the fall of 1991, Cox Cable–Jefferson Parish (Louisiana) organized a job fair that drew more than five hundred people. That event permitted the system to develop an applicant pool that better represented the community's ethnic groups. Besides the development of applicant pools, the system reported that it had recruited bilingual sales representatives from the local school system to serve their ever-increasing Spanish-speaking customer base. The Jefferson Parish branch also reported initiatives focusing on the black audience, including several campaigns with Black Entertainment Television (BET)—among them an essay contest with the school system and the taping of a BET teen show in New Orleans.

In addition to the human resource development initiatives, in 1991 Cox Cable–Jefferson Parish planned to use technological advances to better serve the changing racial and ethnic composition of their marketplace. In his memo of June 14, 1992, to Judy Henke, Fred Bristol indicated that his unit had "ordered equipment that will enable us to cablecast HBO and Cinemax in Spanish on the Secondary Audio Channel."[18] In December 2001, Cox Communications was offering up to eight Spanish-language channels through the Cox TeleLatina package. In addition, through Cox Digital Cable, customers in 2001 were able to use second audio programming (SAP) to receive Spanish audio with certain channels.[19] Consumer relations also received attention at Cox Cable in the early nineties.

A decade ago, Cox Cable–Hampton Roads (Virginia) described its responses to the changing racial and ethnic composition of its marketplace as proactive.[20] Their Foreign Language Ways and Means Coordinating Board included representatives from educational institutions and community organizations such as the Spanish Association. The coordinating board was associated with the development of an extensive foreign-language service offered on Channel 31, the "higher education channel" of the system. The service took three years to develop and offered programming in "Spanish, Russian, French, German, Hebrew, Polish, Japanese and [languages from] smaller countries." In addition, programs were also offered on issues of "social diversity—changing population—urban problems (civil rights and the political process)."

The higher-education focus also included the organization of "four forums a year in association with the School of Education at Norfolk State University, the second largest, predominantly black institution [of higher education] in America." These fora had been in operation since 1987 and focused on educational and social issues. The system also reported its contribution to the promotion of the festivals and pageants of groups such as the Filipino community. Community outreach was provided through Channel 11, the community access channel (see chapter 9). Through this service, the system reported that they had "contributed over five million dollars in community programming during 1991." Many of the programs, by highlighting minority social and political issues and presenting minority role models, aimed at the development of community leadership.

The practices by Cox Cable–San Diego reinforced what was already a corporate pattern:

utilization of Spanish-language advertising on radio and television stations that broadcast in Spanish; also the development of bilingual (English/Spanish) direct mail pieces targeted to the nonsubscribing Hispanic market

addition of four Spanish-language channels to the channel lineup

addition of dedicated telephone numbers to reach bilingual (English/Spanish) agents for customer service or repair service

active recruitment of bilingual (English/Spanish) employees, in particular for customer contact positions

development of bilingual (English/Spanish) communication pieces for customers advising them of any major changes (e.g., pricing or programming issues)

became corporate members of community groups such as the Union of Pan Asian Communities and the San Diego Hispanic Chamber of Commerce; also contributing funds to their programs, including scholarship funds

sponsorship participation of local Hispanic community events, such as the Cinco De Mayo festival

bilingual (English/Spanish) research among nonsubscribing households for attitudes and pricing/packaging/programming decisions

similar efforts within the various Asian communities including the Vietnamese, Filipino, Cambodian, and Chinese communities. In particular, recruitment of bilingual consumer contact employees;

advertising in each language; community event participation and sponsorship; possible addition of more Asian programming to the channel lineup.[21]

Focusing on the future, Cox Cable–San Diego anticipated, "Consideration will be given to the development of a 'Special Markets Manager' position to coordinate company efforts and activities in each of the Asian, Hispanic, and Black communities, or possibly a consultant could be used for this project." In 2001, Cox Communications had reaped benefits from these diversity efforts. Its subscriber base had increased 600 percent, revenues had increased, and the company had consolidated its presence in the South, Southwest, and West and had expanded into New England.

The changing racial and ethnic composition of the United States has influenced the orientation and performance of the cable industry. As the industry has responded to market forces and market logic and has expanded technologically, it has developed strategies to access greater shares of the minority markets. The rapid return on the large investments in the cable industry over the past three decades has been the major motivation, especially among the MSOs. Of equal importance are the programming activities that have responded to America's diversity.

Programming for Minorities on Cable Television

Since the introduction of Univisión, the Spanish-language cable network, the number of cable programming networks that target America's minority communities has increased. In 1961, there was only one such network; in 1991, there were thirteen; in 2001, fifty-one,[22] delivering programming to an impressive array of minority communities (table 7.1).

SPANISH-LANGUAGE CABLE TELEVISION

In 1991, four networks specialized in Spanish programming. In 2001, there were nineteen.[23] Spanish-language cable television in the United

Table 7.1. Minority Communities Served by National and Regional Cable Networks, 2001

Minority Community	Number of Networks
African American	9
Arab American	3
Caribbean	2
Celtic (Irish, Scottish)	1
Chinese	2
Filipino	1
French	2
Greek	1
Iranian/Persian	1
Italian	1
Japanese	3
Jewish	2
Native American	1
Russian	1
Scandinavian	1
South Asian	3
Spanish	19
Women	3
Multicultural	7
Total	63

Figures are for December 2001.
Source: National Cable Television Association, http://www.ncta.com/industry_overview/programList.cfm.

States started in 1961 with Univisión. Galavisión was introduced in 1979, and Telemundo in 1987. The premium network Canal Sur was introduced in 1991. Like Spanish-language radio, Spanish-language television in the United States is also inflected by the internal diversity of Spanish-speaking people here.

Univisión was founded in 1961, when Mexican media giant Spanish International Network (SIN) established affiliate relations with KWEX-TV, Channel 41, in San Antonio. The name Univisión was adopted in 1987. A decade ago, Univisión had a 54 percent share of the

Hispanic households at prime time. (Telemundo, launched in 1987, was reported to have 46 percent during the same period.)[24] Univisión's dominance was evident across all other time periods and was a function of the distribution capacity of the network. In 1991, the Univisión Station Group owned and operated nine full-power and five low-power television (LPTV) stations. In addition, Univisión has seven full-power affiliates and nine low-power affiliates.[25] A third group of affiliates in 1991 was the over five hundred cable systems that carried Univisión programming. The Univisión Television Group operated twelve full-power and seven low-power stations and had 1,354 affiliates and over twenty-nine million subscribers in an area that included the entire United States, Mexico, and Central and South America.

That network of "owned and operated" stations, affiliates, and cable distribution ensured that Univisión served "virtually every major Hispanic market in the country" in the early nineties. But the fact that most of the stations were in the South and the Southwest stimulated discontent among Latino groups. It was felt that Mexican themes and images dominated Univisión's programming. This was not considered acceptable, given the internal diversity of the Spanish-speaking communities in the United States (cf. similar criticism of BET in the late nineties).

Mexican involvement in the network was also legally challenged. U.S. law prohibits foreign nationals from owning more than 25 percent of a broadcasting property in the United States. In February 1988, the network was acquired by Hallmark Cards,[26] another example of what was considered a contradictory trend in Spanish-language broadcasting in America. When Hallmark acquired Univisión from SIN, most major Spanish-language media properties in the United States were owned by non-Latinos. In July 1991, the Tichenor Group, an Anglo corporation, was the most diversified Latino broadcasting group in the United States.

Clearly the creation of Univisión was recognition of the importance of the Hispanic consumer in the American economy. For Hallmark, Univisión was a direct channel to "Spanish gold,"[27] and Hallmark Univisión articulated a "commitment to improve the quality of life and economic well-being of U.S. Hispanics through mass media information, education, and entertainment." Univisión's programming lineup in the early nineties featured a variety of programming genres. The dominant genre was the telenovela (table 7.2).

In 1991, Hispanic audiences between the ages of eighteen and thirty-four identified Univisión programs as their favorites. In May 1991, nine of the ten top-rated shows for Hispanic audiences in America were broadcast by Univisión. Among them: *Sábado gigante* (Big Saturday), *Siempre en domingo* (Always on Sunday), *Cristina*, *Noticiero Univisión* (Univisión news), *De mujeres* (About women), and *En carne propia* (In person). In December 2001, the NCTA described Univisión as the "leading Spanish-language broadcaster in the U.S."

Table 7.2. Programming on Univisión, October 6–November 12, 1991

Program Genre	Hours per Week	% of Schedule
Telenovelas	52.5	31.3
Talk shows	34	20.2
Variety/games	18.5	11.0
News	15	8.9
Public affairs	13	7.7
Sports	7.5	4.5
Cartoons	5	3.0
Movies	4	2.3
Children	3	1.8
Music videos	3	1.8
Cooking	2.5	1.5
Miniseries (drama)	2	1.2
Dance	1.5	0.9
Comedy	1	0.6
Fashion	1	0.6
Talent	1	0.6
Religious	1	0.6
Miscellaneous	2.5	1.5
Total	168	100.0

Source: Memorandum, Carole Baird, Univisión Programming, September 10, 1991.

Its programming continued to be dominated by telenovelas and variety shows.[28] *Sábado gigante* was still in the lineup, and the talk show *Cristina* was just ending its daytime presence. In the nineties, Univisión also developed special programming for children. Other programs on the schedule in 1991 were similar in theme, format, and production values to mainstream American programs. For example, *Fama y fortuna* resembled *Lifestyles of the Rich and Famous,* and *Buscando estrellas con Budweiser* (Looking for stars with Budweiser) was similar to *Star Search.*

In 1989, Univisión introduced *Más* (More), the first magazine to be published by the network. By the early nineties, *Más* had the largest circulation of any Spanish-language magazine in the nation. One key goal was to link the magazine with Univisión's television resources to provide "one-stop shopping" for potential advertisers, marketers, and promoters to the Latino market. The strategy of creating complementary print channels became an industry model and was reproduced by the Black Entertainment Network and other cable networks that targeted America's diversity. Under Hallmark ownership, Univisión's major advertising clients included most of America's largest advertisers: Procter and Gamble, Pepsi-Cola, General Foods, Colgate-Palmolive, McDonald's, Ford, Coors, American Home Products, Scott Paper, Johnson and Johnson, Miller, American Airlines, Coca-Cola, Campbell Soup, Budweiser, and Kraft.

The acceleration in the growth of television advertisements that targeted Spanish-speaking audiences was evident from the fifties. For example, at the Museum of Television and Radio in New York, one can view a 1958 advertisement by Piels Beer that targets the Spanish-speaking audience in the United States. Around the same period, Young and Rubicam developed a campaign for Eastern Airlines based on the heritage that "Old Spain left behind." In 1968, Sears launched a campaign whose central motif was the Spanish matador. By the seventies, television advertisements targeting Spanish-speaking audiences had become less clichéd and more ethnic specific. Consider this description of an advertisement from IBM's 1977 campaign for its System 32 computer. The Rodríguez family were clearly Mexican:

In this commercial for IBM System 32, a young man explains that he came to Southern California in 1967 with his family. His father always wanted to own his own business and decided one day to open a produce company that catered to Spanish-speaking customers. On the first day of business, he sold a grand total of 65 cents worth of onions. But customers kept coming back, and before long, it became difficult to keep track of inventory. Fortunately, the Rodríguez family heard about IBM's System 32, a computerized inventory tracking system custom designed for small businesses. "Now," the young man says, "my father is getting big ideas again." Apparently he wants to open a branch in San Francisco. Slogan: "IBM, helping people find the answers."[29]

Univisión and the other Spanish-language television outlets facilitated this market niching. Other examples of ethnic realism in advertising include the Spanish-language version of the Pepsi's "choice of a new generation" campaign produced by Siboney Advertising. Similar strategies were evident in advertisements for Heinz Baby Food and Sears. We will see this pattern reproduced for other racial and ethnic communities served by American cable television.

Not only has Univisión been a pioneer in ethnic television in the United States, it has also been a leader in the use of emerging communication technologies. In 1976, it was the first commercial broadcaster to distribute programming directly to its affiliates via domestic satellites.[30] In the same year, it was the first commercial network to use ENG cameras and AKAI quarter-inch tape in its news operations.

In the eighties, Univisión's interests appeared to coincide with those of Ronald Reagan's Republican administration. According to Univisión documents, in September 1980, "at the request of the U.S. State Department, SIN [began providing] programming via satellites to Cuban emigres in refugee camps throughout the United States." In March 1986, President Reagan appeared on Univisión's morning program *Temas y debates* to discuss the situation in Nicaragua—before his evening address to the nation on aid to the Contras. This convergence of interests is an example of the reciprocal relations that exist in the industry. Univisión provided the Republican administration with a platform to support its programs, and that could explain why, on

May 10, 1980, the network became the "first U.S. company authorized to receive programming via satellite from a foreign country."

Galavisión was launched in October 1979 as the premium channel of the embryonic Univisión network. The programming then emphasized "recently produced Spanish-language movies along with coverage of select sporting events and special entertainment shows."[31] When Univisión was acquired by Hallmark, Galavisión was not part of the deal. It continued to be operated by SIN, Inc. In 1988, in response to the arrival of the Telemundo service and Hallmark's acquisition of Univisión, a decision was made to "convert Galavisión's cable operations to an advertising-based basic cable service." In 1992, the Galavisión network consisted of three full-power and seven low-power UHF stations.[32] In 1992, the network had affiliate relations with 228 systems. By 2001, the network had 672 cable affiliates and over twenty-two million subscribers.[33]

Galavisión's programming in the early nineties was targeted to "Hispanics of Mexican and Central American origin." That niching reflected an appreciation of the presence of a regional cultural community and the diversity inherent in the Latino market. That programming niche is still present and the network's programming is "tailor-made to appeal to a wide array of Hispanic viewers. Spanish-speaking viewers who have been in the United States for many generations, as well as those who arrived more recently."[34]

In the early nineties, Galavisión broadcast "unfiltered" Mexican television to the United States twenty-four hours a day.[35] The news programming, which totaled about thirteen hours per day, was produced by the Mexico-based system Empresas de Communicaciones Orbital (ECO). In 2001, the network still had solid linkages with ECO, which has been described as the Spanish-language CNN. Its programming, which features movies, telenovelas, sports, comedy, and variety shows, is supplied by Mexico's Televisa and Venezuela's Venevisión—a subsidiary of Televisa—through four satellites. The network reaches the United States, Central and South America, Western Europe, and Northern Africa.

Telemundo Group, Inc., was launched in May 1986 as a result of the acquisition of the debt-ridden "diversified communication businesses of John Blair & Co. by Reliance Capital Group." That acquisition provided the Reliance Capital Group with production and transmitter facilities in Puerto Rico, but it was not the first venture into Spanish-language television by Reliance. In 1985, through its subsidiary Estrella Communications, Reliance Capital Corporation had acquired property in Los Angeles (KBSC). In 1986, Reliance acquired WNJU in New York, a company previously owned by Screen Gems, a subsidiary of Columbia Pictures. Screen Gems also owned WAPA, in Puerto Rico. The later acquisition provided Reliance with access not only to "Columbia's repertoire of films regularly marketed to Latin America, but also to a great variety of Spanish-language programs."[36]

Over the eighties, Reliance Capital, Inc., acquired a number of properties, developed affiliates, and expanded the network. In 1987, it acquired KSTS Channel 48 in the San Francisco area from the National Television Group and, in 1988, KTMD in the Houston/Galveston area. In 1988, it established affiliations with WSNS in Chicago, a station originally affiliated with Univisión. In 1989, Telemundo developed an affiliate relationship with KVDA in San Antonio. In 1990, Telemundo purchased 85 percent of the stock of Nueva Vista, the company that operated KVDA. By 1992, Telemundo owned and operated six full-power and four low-power stations. It also continued to operate WKAQ-TV in San Juan, Puerto Rico, the network's only VHF station. In addition, Telemundo had affiliations with six full-power and sixteen low-power stations plus seven cable carriers that operated in fourteen states and the District of Columbia. In 1992, affiliated stations in Tijuana, Juárez, and Matamoros, Mexico, served the American Hispanic communities in, respectively, San Diego, El Paso, and McAllen/Brownsville.[37] As at Univisión, in 1992, no Hispanic person was a member of the board of directors or worked at the highest echelons of the network.

As at the other Spanish-language networks, the dominant program genre on Telemundo during the nineties was the telenovela, of which thirty-two hours were aired during a typical week. Most of the domestic productions were news, talk, variety, and comedy shows. Telemundo's long-term strategy was to differentiate itself from Univisión and win the viewership of the more acculturated Hispanic.[38]

By 2001, Telemundo reached 89 percent of the Hispanic audience in the United States with a "compelling mix of domestically produced programs . . . and depict[ions of] contemporary U.S. Hispanic lifestyles."[39] The network had eight hundred affiliates and more than twenty-two million subscribers. Its programming was delivered by satellite to audiences in the United States, Canada, Mexico, the Caribbean, Central and South America, and Europe. In 2000, the network launched Telemundo Internacional, a twenty-four-hour service delivering news "from the Hispanic perspective" to audiences throughout the Western Hemisphere. In 2001, Telemundo Internacional had eighty million cable subscribers and 580,000 DBS subscribers.

In 2001, the Telemundo network was owned by Sony Pictures and Liberty Media (which originally had been owned by TCI). When AT&T bought TCI, Liberty Media was not part of the deal. In 2001, Liberty Media held influential shares in cable operations in the United States and around the world. Among its American investments in 2001 were AOL Time Warner, Court TV, Discovery Communications, E! Entertainment Television, Bravo, Fox Family Worldwide, Starz Encore Group, International Channel, and MacNeil/Lehrer Productions. Among its international investments were the New Corporation, Prager SCA (Argentina), the Premium Movie Partnership (Australia), and the UKTV network.

Since the eighties, there have been other players in Spanish-language cable television in the United States. Some have been U.S.-based, and others have been international organizations. Most, like International TeleMúsica, have targeted Spanish-speaking youth and feature, among other things, music videos, entertainment news, and lifestyle programs. That programming service was supported by Radio Programas de México. Spanish-language television, following the lead of MTV's *Second Generation,* also targeted the assimilated, younger, English-speaking Latino community. In 1993, MTV launched MTV Latin America as an advertising-supported network, and by 2001 it had 9.5 million subscribers and was delivering its programming by satellite to audiences in the United States, Mexico, the Caribbean, and Central and South America.

Viva Television was founded by Cuban Mark Careno in June 1992 and had as its target audience Hispanics eighteen to forty-nine. The programming line emphasized "news, public affairs, sports, comedy, children's shows, art films and movies." To become competitive in the Spanish-language market in the United States, HBO also used SAP technology.[40] It had started that practice in 1989, when it introduced the Selecciones en Español service through cable operators in El Paso, Miami, New York, San Antonio, and San Diego. In 1991, 182 cable systems in the U.S. were offering this service. In November 2000, HBO launched HBO Latino. The service now has 5.5 million subscribers in the United States and Puerto Rico. Fox and the Tribune Broadcasting Company are also utilizing the SAP technologies to target Hispanic audiences. In 2001, Fox had two channels dedicated to Spanish-language audiences. So did CNN and Discovery. Liberty Media also had investments in Spanish-language programming. There are eighteen networks serving the Spanish-language community in the United States,[41] thirteen established in the nineties. These networks have a subscriber base of more than fifty-six million viewers in the Americas.

Spanish-language television in the United States is hard-nosed commercial television, controlled by a small group of companies. Spanish-language cable television also has attributes associated with mainstream American television, particularly the tendency to appropriate already successful program genres and formats. *Cristina* (Univisión) and *Cara a cara* (Telemundo) have been described as Spanish-language Oprah Winfrey shows. In the early nineties, Univisión redesigned its news show *Noticiero* to give it a more American look. That decision generated substantial objections from the public and significant organizational turmoil.[42]

There are several explanations for the tendency to reproduce mainstream production values in Spanish-language television in America. One is the acculturation of Spanish-speaking audiences to the production values of American television. Another may be a function of the pre-Americanization process, especially the high consumption of American television programs before immigration to the United States. (The late Sydney Head noted that almost 90 percent of all Latin American broadcasting systems were directly influenced by the American free market broadcasting practices, including production models.)[43] Another explanation could be the dependence that

Spanish-language television in the United States has on products from Mexico, Venezuela, and other parts of Latin America.

Popular Spanish-language television programs not only reproduce U.S. genres and production values, they appear to have reproduced problems associated with racial and ethnic representation: "Latinos span the racial spectrum, with some being blond and blue-eyed and others having African features. A majority of those in the United States are of mixed race, indigenous or African stock. But that reality is not reflected in the offerings on the two networks that dominate Spanish-language television in this country, Univisión and Telemundo." As in real life in Latin America, dark-skinned Latinos are invariably cast as "maids, gardeners, chauffeurs or dabblers in witchcraft." The general counsel of the Puerto Rican Legal Defense and Education Fund concluded, "[The telenovelas] stereotype the hell out of people, . . . you would think they came from Scandinavia or somewhere like that with all the blond, blue-eyed people you see."[44] The practices of exclusion have been challenged by special interest groups such as the National Hispanic Media Coalition and the Screen Actors Guild. In 2000, Brazil's *Xica* featured the first black woman in a leading role of a Latin American telenovela. It is felt that protests from the United States contributed to that change.

BLACK CABLE TELEVISION

The black community in the United States is growing and becoming more internally diverse. Between 1990 and 2000, the population of black America increased by 4.7 million or nearly 16 percent. Migrations from continental Africa, the Caribbean, and Latin America contributed to that diversity. During the same period, the African American population increased by 10 percent, and more than seven hundred thousand Latinos defined themselves as black for the 2000 census.[45] Increased contacts between black Europeans, especially black British television producers, performing artists, and intellectuals, have also added to black diversity in America.

Despite this internal diversity, there is a strong sense of commonality—a transnational ethnicity. In the early nineties, Paul Gilroy, a black British scholar, called for the translation of this "meta-cultural identity" into a major a cultural project for what he called "the black Atlantic world." I have used the term "global Africa" (meaning continental Africa and its diaspora) to refer to this phenomenon of shared identity. The recognition of this shared identity is not new; its roots can be traced to the pan-Africanist ideas and the efforts of Martin Delaney, Marcus Garvey, and W. E. B. DuBois.[46] The mass media has always fostered this idea. The newspapers of Garvey's United Negro Improvement Association and DuBois's NAACP had global circulation and helped to mobilize black awareness and solidarity in the United States, the Caribbean, Central and South America, Europe, and Africa. Toward the turn of the twentieth century, the electronic media, especially black American-based television, began to demonstrate that they had the potential to play a central role in the activation of the "black Atlantic world/global Africa."[47]

Black Entertainment Television, established in 1979 by Robert L. Johnson, is the second cable television network developed in the United States to target a minority community (Univisión being the first). From its first transmission, on January 25, 1980,[48] BET attracted the attention of the broadcasting industry and economic marketplace. For example, in September 1979, Warner Cable, American Telecommunications Corp., and TelePrompTer agreed to carry the network on their systems. In November of that year, TCI became "a minority equity investor." In January 1980, "six companies signed on as BET charter advertisers": Anheuser-Busch, Time, Champale, Pepsi-Cola, Sears, and Kellogg.

BET's program schedule in January 1980 extended from 11 P.M. to 1 A.M. on Friday nights and was delivered to 3.8 million subscribers in 350 markets. By September 1980, BET had grown to "5 million cable households in 499 markets in 47 states, including Alaska and Hawaii." By the end of 1980, programming had been extended to 2 A.M. and included two new half-hour shows, *The Bobby Jones Gospel Show* and *Black Showcase*. By 1991, the BET subscription base reached 30 million in 2,400 markets and was broadcasting twenty-four hours a day. In December 2001, BET had 70.8 million subscribers through 2,622 affiliates and was distributed in the United States, Canada, Europe, Africa, Australia, and the Caribbean.

BET programming has had two tendencies: original productions and aftermarket products. The network's first venture into original programming was "the production of Black Collegiate sports." Since then, it has ventured into other program genres, including news, public affairs, music programs, game shows, and children's programs (table 7.3).

In 1992, just over 60 percent of BET's programs were original productions. Over 45 percent of the original programs were music programs featuring music videos. Key programs in this category included *Video Soul, Video LP, Midnight Love, Video Vibrations, Soft Notes, Sound and Style with Ramsey Lewis,* and *Rap City.* This programming approach was important to black entertainers, especially during the period when black performers were invisible on MTV.[49] It was also a clear demonstration of the parsimony principle at work. The remainder of the original programming (26.5 percent) included programs such as the twice weekly *BET News, BET News Briefs, Personal Diary, For the Record, Our Voices, Live in L.A., Screen Scene,* and *Teen Summit. Teen Summit* was developed during the black youth crisis of the early nineties and has been commended for providing

Table 7.3. Programming on Black Entertainment Television,
April 4–10, 1992

Program Genre	Hours per Week	% of Schedule
*Music	76	45.2
Infomercials	49.5	29.5
*Public affairs/talk	17	10.1
Sitcoms	10	5.9
Soap operas	5	3.0
*Gospel	3.5	2.1
*Sports	2	1.2
*Youth	2	1.2
*News	1.5	0.9
*Children	0.5	0.3
Miscellaneous	1	0.6
Total	168	100.0

*BET original production.
Source: TV Guide, April 4–10, 1992.

positive role models for African American youth and for serving as a forum for issues they value. In December 2001, *Teen Summit* was still on the schedule. In addition, there were thirty-two other original programs on the schedule.

In its early days, especially the mid- to late eighties, BET had to develop innovative strategies to generate income. For example, in 1991, almost 30 percent of BET programs were infomercials. In December 2001, 23 percent of the programming was still infomercials. During 1989, BET was carried on 1,825 of the 7,500 cable systems that were in operation at that time. Further, BET was earning only five cents per subscriber, while other cable networks were earning between fifteen and twenty. Robert Johnson considered that condition to be the result of industry racism. The industry, on the other hand, felt that BET was underresourced and lacked marketing expertise.[50] Johnson would be vindicated (see chapter 3, "urban dictates"). To deal with the cash flow problem, Johnson adopted a number of strategies, including program syndication and the publication of magazines and other businesses that exploited the emerging communication technologies.

The first step in program syndication was the talk show *Live in L.A.,* targeted at those markets that did not carry BET as part of their cable mix. The aim was to permit a local television outlet in a market with African American audiences the opportunity to buy the show and insert it into its general programming. As part of that strategy, BET also produced specials like *Soul by the Sea* and the *Black Agenda 2000* telefora series.

The magazines *Emerge* and *YSB* (*Young Sister/Brother*) were introduced in the early nineties. With those print avenues in place, BET had the infrastructure to offer "one-stop shopping" for advertisers and promoters to a subscriber base of thirty million. *YSB*, the first magazine geared to the African American teenager (ages twelve to eighteen), was promoted as "[a] positive, upbeat, and useful magazine for teens. It provides the latest news on music, sports and fashion, and serves as a guide to personal improvement by building a sense of confidence and self-esteem. More important, *YSB* explores issues of teens in a realistic way." *Emerge* ceased publication in 2000, "a casualty of corporate realignment."[51]

During the same period, BET initiated "Action Pay-Per-View, a national, satellite-delivered, pay-per-view movie channel based in Santa Monica, California; BET International, a provider of BET programming throughout Africa and other foreign markets; Identity Television, a London-based cable service targeting Afro-Caribbean viewers; BET Productions, a subsidiary providing technical and production services to outside companies." In addition, they operated the BET Radio Network and BET Pictures, a joint venture with Blockbuster Entertainment, whose aim was to produce and distribute "black, family-oriented films."[52] In 2001, BET was operating BET.com, which billed itself as the most comprehensive black Internet portal in America.

In 2001, BET's aftermarket use of ex-network programs that featured black talent or the black experience was packaged as Black Star Power. The genesis of this approach can be found in the early nineties. Among the shows that returned to BET are *Frank's Place, Generations, What's Happenin'? Roc, Sanford and Son,* and the British situation comedy *Desmond. Desmond* was originally broadcast on Britain's Channel Four, an important plank in Britain's approach to multicultural television. The sitcom was set in a southeast London barbershop and featured some of Britain's leading black actors and actresses. The cast included actors from Guyana, the Gambia, Jamaica, and Trinidad and native-born black British talent. The interactions among this global African cast were hilarious.

In 1992, *Desmond* had been on BET for more than two seasons and was very popular, especially among West Indian audiences in America. The airing of this show on BET provided visibility for its leading man, Norman Beaton. His popularity resulted in a cameo in an episode of *The Cosby Show* (1991–92 season) in which he and Cosby educated each other about cricket and baseball. The popularity of the *Cosby/Desmond* nexus is another example of cultural similarity and cultural shareability. The relationship also exemplified the recently introduced phrase "black Atlantic world," which is similar to the concept of "cultural areas"— areas of the world that have cultural similarity but are not necessarily bound together as states.[53] This characteristic of contemporary transnational identities makes it possible for different nationalities to consume the cultural products of other nationalities (see chapter 3).

The concept of "cultural areas" is illustrated by the opening sequence of *Desmond,* in which black people are shown coming off a ship. The theme song states, "We come from the sun." This sequence connects the peoples of the most recent wave of black immigration to Britain, which commenced just after World War II and continued unabated until the mid-sixties.[54] The opening sequence also connects the young British blacks with the older generation who still spoke with West Indian accents. This reality also resonates with Caribbean immigrants in the United States and Canada. The show evokes sentiments common to the immigrant peoples of the black Atlantic. They all came from the sun and shared the "same ship."

The editing of the opening sequence of *Desmond* also made the connection with black America clearer. The opening sequence uses a variety of transitional devices, particularly the cutting/scratching style associated with American hip-hop. Further, the action of the sitcom is in a barbershop, a pivotal social institution in black America, indeed global Africa. These visual and audio images provide connection with the African American audience.[55] There was a hope that BET would expand on *Desmond*'s experience and produce other programs that nourish transnational identities. Other than *Caribbean Rhythms,* with Jamaican beauty queen Rachel, there has been few black Caribbean or global African programs on BET since 1991. Music videos of the hip-hop/reggae hybrid are the dominant Caribbean/West Indian presence on BET. Images of continental Africa are rare and have tended to be through news items, especially news of visits by elite Americans to Africa or news of catastrophes. In its coverage and representation of Africa, BET has modeled mainstream American television.

Since 1990, BET has been developing program production partnerships. Besides BET Pictures, ventures have included partnerships with Butch Lewis Productions to produce "special [sports] programs and special pay-per-view events for BET." (Butch Lewis is an influential black boxing promoter.) Another partnership was announced in the early nineties with Tim Reid's production company, United Image Entertainment. (Tim Reid played the lead in the acclaimed *Frank's*

Place.) It does not appear, though, that these production partnerships have been able to sustain BET's programming. However, in BET's diversification strategies, two specialized networks emerged: BET Gospel and BET on Jazz.

BET Gospel was launched in November 1998 and is also a satellite-delivered network. In December 2001, the NCTA said that BET Gospel "showcases the best in gospel talent and programming geared towards uplifting and guiding the spirit in today's world. BET Gospel features notable and legendary gospel artists through music videos, exclusive in-depth interviews and concert performances. BET Gospel also features inspirational speakers and programming." BET on Jazz, launched in January 1996, is a satellite-delivered, advertising-supported network that had 8.4 million subscribers in December 2001. BET on Jazz is distributed in the United States, Africa, and Europe and was America's first television programming service dedicated exclusively to jazz. That genre is explored through "in-studio performances, documentaries, concert coverage and celebrity interviews."[56]

BET has attracted significant audiences. In a 1990 study in Atlanta, Felicia Jones concludes that the "younger and high racially oriented respondents tended to be heavier viewers of and more satisfied with BET programs than black-oriented programming on major network channels." She suggests that the respondents had more confidence in the way black-owned media portrayed black subjects but that "it was premature to generalize these results to the black audience nationwide."[57] By the turn of the century, it was possible to discern a shift in audience reactions to BET. Among the criticisms is that BET's programming, especially the excessive use of "gangsta" and "playa" rap videos, reinforces negative stereotypes of black people in America and provides irresponsible role models for young blacks. It has been argued that the hip-hop reality is not the only black reality in the United States and that the hip-hop images that dominated BET were disrespectful to black women. Since the sale of BET in January 2001 and the increased use of music videos featuring white acts, there have been more assertions that BET had sold out.

BET was sold for $3 billion and became a subsidiary of Viacom International. Viacom's other television properties include the CBS Television Network, CBS Enterprises, MTV Networks, Paramount

Television, Nickelodeon, VH1, the United Paramount Network, the Nashville Network (TNN), Country Music Television (CNT), Showtime Networks, Inc., and Comedy Central.[58] In addition, Viacom owns thirty-four television stations that reach fifteen of the top twenty television markets in the United States. BET is a story of growth and appropriation. With its sale, there was the feeling that there was now no other black television outlet in the United States. This is not an accurate position.

OTHER BLACK CABLE NETWORKS

Since it was introduced in 1980, BET has attracted criticisms for being parochial in its representation of the diversity of the black reality in this country. The creation of the Caribbean Satellite Network in 1992 was undoubtedly a response to this deficiency. Also present in the early nineties were independent black producers such as the Johnson Publishing Company (*The American Black Achievement Awards*) and Percy Sutton's Apollo Productions (*Showtime at the Apollo*).[59] In December 2001, the NCTA identified eleven cable television networks serving blacks, primarily African Americans, in the United States: BET, BET Gospel, BET on Jazz, Black Women's TV, MBC Network, Black Starz!, Hip-Hop Network, NUE TV, Caribbean Visions Television, Sun TV, and VH1 Soul. My fieldwork provided information on cable television programmers that target Caribbean immigrant communities.

Commercial-free Black Starz! has been described as "the first and only movie channel created exclusively to meet the unique entertainment choices of Blacks and others with Black sensibilities." The network's presentations include "hosted movie segments, interviews, movie trivia between films plus original programming."[60] The HipHop-Network, "the official music video film channel," was established in January 1997 as an advertising-supported regional cable network. In December 2001, it was supported by Priority, Def Jam, Universal, and other major record labels. In addition to music, the system offers home shopping.

The Major Broadcasting Cable Network (MBC), an Atlanta-based, satellite-distributed, advertising-supported cable programming network, was launched in November 1998. In November 2001, it had fifteen million subscribers in forty states and twelve hundred markets. The five principals behind the network are Willie Gary, an attorney (chairman and CEO); Cecil G. Fielder, of the New York Yankees; Marlon Jackson, of the Jackson Five (president); Evander Holyfield, former world heavyweight champion (vice chairman); and Alvin James, a twenty-year broadcasting veteran (founder and senior managing partner). The network prided itself as being the only twenty-four-hour, family-oriented cable network in America owned and operated by African Americans. Its wholesome, "uplifting and solution based" programming was geared to African American families and urban communities. Most of the programs were original and most were talk shows. Among them were Willie Gary's *Spiritual Impact* and Cecil Fielder's *Sports Lifestyle,* both of which won awards in 2001 from the Black American Political Action Committee, the NAACP, and the Atlanta Association of Black Journalists.[61]

NUE TV was launched in July 2000 and served the United States and the Caribbean. However, my efforts to contact the system in January 2002 suggested that it had gone out of business. VH1 Soul was launched in August 1998 as a twenty-four-hour digital service, part of the MTV Networks. This "music channel for jammin' classic soul and rhythm & blues" features videos from the greatest names in soul and R&B, including Aretha Franklin; Earth, Wind, and Fire; Stevie Wonder; and the artist formerly known as Prince.[62] Nevertheless, although black television in America is an attractive site for aftermarket products and is attractive to investors from the mainstream media environment—and despite what may appear to be a proliferation of channels targeting the black audience since 1991—the black audience in the United States continues to be underserved.

CARIBBEAN TELEVISION IN AMERICA

The colonial history of the Caribbean brought together many diverse racial, ethnic, and religious groups. Reflecting that diversity are the Caribbean Satellite Network, a now defunct cable television service; Spotlight TV, a service started by and directed to Indo-Caribbean audiences in New York; and Caribscope, a Washington, D.C., cable programming service.

The Caribbean Satellite Network (CSN) was one of the pioneers of Caribbean television in the United States. At the start of transmission in December 1992, CSN described itself as "the heart and soul of the Caribbean" and "TV That Jams." The satellite-distributed network saw its audience as international. The footprint of the satellite used to deliver CSN gave it a potential audience of over six hundred million viewers in over three hundred million homes in all of North and Central America, northern South America, and the Caribbean. The promotional literature also described CSN as "a 24-hour-a-day video party celebrating the music, dance, art, and culture of the Caribbean." The projected programming mix included music videos, interviews, and concerts, emphasizing "Roots Music"—described as "the sound generated by African music [which] has survived, taken root, and flourished in the musics of the Americas, the islands, and around the world. Reggae, Calypso, Ska, Black American blues and Jazz are all descendants from the ritual beat of Africa."[63]

The Caribbean flavor, especially reggae, dominated the music programming. Seventy percent of the lineup was allocated to reggae and "other island" videos, 10 percent to American roots videos, 10 percent to other roots videos, and 10 percent to news capsules. The programming orientation was justified on the grounds that roots music was especially popular within influential sectors of American society. CSN reported that roots music had become popular with major American advertisers such as BIC, Blue Cross/Blue Shield, Budweiser, Chevy, Ford, the Gap, Miller, Safeway, 7Up, and Swatch. The network argued since the target audiences for those products paralleled the target audience for CSN—"teens, college students, and young adults"—there was a good fit. The buying power of teens in the early nineties was projected at $80 billion. The buying power of college and young adults was projected at $30 billion and $700 billion, respectively. Further justification for CSN's roots music orientation was its popularity on campus radio stations. CSN stated that over five hundred college radio stations in America were programming roots music in the early nineties and that "over 940 million Roots Music records" were sold in 1991, representing "12 percent of all record sales." Roots music was also identified as the core of the critically acclaimed 1992 television series *Going to Extremes*. CSN clearly expected to benefit from that popularity. Within three years CSN had failed![64]

Many reasons have been offered for the failure of CSN's pioneering effort, among them the fuzziness of CSN's market and the fickle nature of its product. One Caribbean observer concluded that it was ineffective management that killed CSN but that, despite its failure, the idea behind CSN remained valid.[65] The CSN experience also shows that, even as it was starting up, CSN sought to expand outside the United States and to connect with the Caribbean diaspora. This is currently a tendency of most of the cable programming networks that serve minority audiences in America, such as Spotlight TV, Channel 76, the Indo-Caribbean cable television service in New York.

Spotlight TV is a brokered service delivered by Time Warner Cable to audiences in Brooklyn, Queens, Manhattan, Staten Island, and Jersey City. Spotlight is actually a subbrokered element of a service managed by the Arabic Channel in New York. This means that Spotlight buys time from the operators of the Arabic Channel to air its programs. Spotlight TV's CEO is Mohamed Alim Ali, an Indo-Guyanese Muslim businessman engaged in the distribution of petroleum products in the New York area. He started the television service in 1997 ("Some people invest in stocks, I invested in television") as Spotlight on Guyana, and it emphasized Guyanese news and information. At that time, he was aware that there were other Guyanese engaged in television in New York. These included Herman Singh and Raj Jagopat, who emphasized Asian Indian materials.[66]

The actual motivations for Spotlight TV are associated with the return of the East Indian–dominated People's Progressive Party (PPP) to political power in Guyana in 1992, after twenty-eight years as the opposition party; a visit to the United States by Cheddi Jagan, then president of Guyana; Jagan's death; and Alim Ali's experience with Raj Jagopat, a television presenter in New York. Specifically, it all started in 1996 when Guyana's president, Jagan visited New York en route to the Middle East on an official visit. During that visit to New

York, Jagan met with Alim, the son of Yacob Ali, the former head of the Anjuman (an Islamic collective) in Guyana and a loyal supporter of the East Indian–dominated PPP, led by Dr. Jagan. During that meeting, Jagan indicated that he felt that Guyanese diaspora, especially the New York segment (read: Indo-Guyanese) needed information on what was being done by the PPP since they took over the reins of government.

Alim said that Jagan asked him to use his influence with the Islamic community and the "Arabs [the Arabic Channel] to show what was happening in Guyana." Jagan promised that he would ensure that the producers would be given access to materials produced by media channels operated by the government of Guyana. Those channels included Guyana Television (GTV), Guyana Broadcasting Corporation (the radio service) and the state-owned newspaper the *Guyana Chronicle*. In 2001, Spotlight TV were the distributors of the *Guyana Chronicle* in New York.

Cheddi Jagan died on March 6, 1997, before the launching of the planned television service. His death propelled Alim into action. He had received from Guyana video footage of Jagan's illness; his travel to the United States for treatment on board a U.S. air force plane; his last press conference—in essence he had "breaking" news from Guyana. However, he had no outlet. He contacted Raj Jagopat to air the materials, and she responded in true brokerage form. She charged him eight hundred dollars and also sold commercials to accompany the video footage. That experience showed him the proverbial light that illuminated his venture into television.

Alim's first step was to buy time from the Arabic Channel. He bought eight hours a day (from 6 A.M. to 2 P.M.), seven days a week. He quickly learned that his target audience, Indo-Guyanese aged eighteen to forty-five ("those who were earning and had spending power") worked during the week and were not viewing the programs. In 1998 he began broadcasting only on Saturday and Sunday—eight hours each. In 2001, he still "owned" the Monday-through-Friday slots but was reselling most of that time to Latino programmers. He contended that there were larger stay-at-home groups in the Latino community during the day.

Alim said he quickly realized that television programming required variety. So his intentions were to go bold, beyond the Asian Indian materials carried by Herman and Raj. In 2001, Alim's programming emphasized Caribbean themes, cricket, news and information, cultural materials from the Caribbean, and Islamic programming in English. According to Alim, Spotlight TV acquires most of its programming from Guyana, Trinidad and Tobago, Barbados, England, and Muslim countries. In 2001, tapes from Guyana and Trinidad and Tobago were sent on airlines controlled by the East Indian–dominated governments of those countries, and the owner of Spotlight TV also operated North American Airlines, a service that operated between New York and Guyana. There has been some exchange of programming between Spotlight TV and Channel 9 in Guyana—an outlet aligned with the People's Progressive Party in Guyana, the party founded by Cheddi Jagan. All the major political parties in Guyana appear to have an affiliation with one of the eighteen television stations operating in its capital, Georgetown. These stations share a common characteristic—program piracy. The linkage between Spotlight TV and Channel 9 demonstrates the complex web of relationships that could exist among minority broadcasters in the United States and entities around the world based on race, ethnicity, religion, and other shared attributes.

The Caribbean audience in the tristate area (NY, NJ, CT) was drawn to Spotlight TV because of its programming of cricket matches—no one else was airing this type of program. Then, in late 2001, Fox Sports International began to air cricket matches. Cricket programming is controlled by national cricket boards, and broadcast rights are guarded strenuously. In the English-speaking Caribbean, cricket is a national sport. Indeed, it is essential to the West Indian identity. The West Indies cricket team is probably the only regional institution that transcends race, color, and class. Caribbean governments exert substantial influence on broadcasting. Many broadcasting outlets are still controlled by governments, and the rights to air cricket matches sometimes reside with government-owned stations. These rights are for airing the matches to their citizens. Spotlight TV has benefited from an illegal extension of the term *citizen* to include citizens in diaspora. So the governments of Guyana and Trinidad and Tobago, both controlled by East Indians in 2001, have, on occasion, made cricket programs available to Spotlight TV.

Early-morning Hindu and Islamic devotional programs on Spotlight TV are also popular, particularly among the older audience. These shows feature commercial and social announcements; video clips of scenes and locations from Guyana, Trinidad, and Suriname; and religious music and readings. The form and content of these religious programs are reminiscent of the early-morning programs produced by East Indian independent program producers in those countries. Perhaps this explains the persistence of similar program formats among minority broadcasters in the United States.

Alim reported that he lost about $1.5 million during the two-year period when Spotlight TV broadcast for eight hours per day, seven days per week. Despite these losses, Spotlight remained on the air. It is clear that Spotlight's continued presence is political. The service provides a channel of communication for the Indian-dominated governments of Guyana and Trinidad and Tobago. Indo-Caribbean immigrants in New York own and operate significant real estate, contracting, supermarket businesses, and other enterprises and are important contributors to the coffers of the political parties that control the governments of Guyana and Trinidad and Tobago. Spotlight TV also serves as a communication channel that supports Indo-Caribbean solidarity in New York. The service has been mobilized to back Indo-Caribbean politicians running for office in New York and native-born politicians who appear to support Indo-Caribbean interests.

Like radio, most Caribbean cable television is found in New York City and is developed through the brokerage system. Caribbean cable television programs in New York fall into three categories: the nationality specific, the racially and ethnically specific, and the content specific. Spotlight TV is a hybrid, as it is both nationality and racially specific. Other nationality-specific Caribbean television in New York includes Peter Bouchon's *Caribscope,* which targets Haitians. Music is the dominant genre across all categories of Caribbean television. Shows produced by African Caribbean producers tend to promote reggae, calypso, or soca (*soul* + *calypso*). Programs from Indo-Caribbean producers tend to promote chutney soca and the filmi music of Bollywood. The shows produced by African Caribbean groups have some cross-ethnic appeal.

The fact that most of the Caribbean cable television shows in New York are produced through the brokerage system means that advertising is essential to the life of the programs. Media analyst and editor-in-chief of the *Caribbean Voice* Annan Boodram describes most Caribbean television programs in New York as infomercials, "advertisements interspersed with music." The major advertisers tend to be real estate companies and mortgage bankers. (Boodram believes this is true for all the programs by Indo-Caribbean producers.) Other major advertisers include supermarkets and travel agencies. There are variants to this general pattern. For example, *Caribbean Classroom,* produced by Grenadian John Crow, focuses on the education sector.[67] Another example of what is termed serious Caribbean television is the programming from CaribNation TV in Washington, D.C.

The program *CaribNation,* the "signature broadcast" of Larry Sindass's CaribNation Television, was launched in 1995 and by 2001 aired three times a week on the cable system operated by the University of the District of Columbia. In December 2001, UDC Cable was the only twenty-four-hour, noncommercial adult education service in the nation's capital. The channel was available to over one hundred thousand residents. The magazine format of *CaribNation* included political analysis, news reports, personality profiles, Caribbean arts, and the region's place in the world scene. Important presenters on the show were Guyanese political activists, David Hinds and Paul Tennessee, Darrice Dean of the Voice of America, and John Blake, former host of the radio show *Caribbean Connection* at WHMM, for more than thirty years. *CaribNation* was also syndicated in the United States ("from New York to Florida") and in the Caribbean (Guyana, Jamaica, Saint Kitts–Nevis) and has been described as the *Nightline* of Caribbean television.[68]

Like other Caribbean television shows in the United States, *CaribNation* depended entirely on the Caribbean News Agency (CANA) and the Caribbean Broadcasting Union (CBU) for materials from the region. During the eighties and nineties, most Caribbean television and radio shows provided more news and information about the Caribbean than about Caribbean communities in the United States. This was clearly a function of their news-gathering capabilities. When the Caribbean Media Corporation, the successor agency of the Caribbean News Agency, announced the suspension of its services in early 2002, the following announcement was posted on CaribNation's website: "*News Briefs* is unavailable due to the temporary suspension of services of CANA Radio, CANA Wire and CBU television. The Board says it regrets that the region's only source of indigenous news and programming has had to be suspended, and it looks forward to when it will return to stronger and expanded operations."[69]

In 2001, the NCTA indicated that two other cable networks were targeting Caribbean audiences in the United States—Sun TV and Caribbean Vision Television. Sun TV has been described as an advertising-supported network that provides "quality programming"—news, spots, entertainment, sitcoms, soaps, talk shows, and tourism. The service is delivered by satellite to over seventy thousand subscribers in the United States, the Caribbean, and Central and South America. This network gave the term Caribbean a stronger Spanish-language inflection.

During 2001, AT&T, Comcast, and Cablevision announced that they were planning to launch Caribbean Visions Television during 2002. The service was going to be a "no charge, advertising supported" network. The projected distribution area was to include Georgia, Florida, New York, Washington, D.C., Texas, Chicago, and the U.S. Virgin Islands. The programming plan was to provide "coverage of events taking place in Caribbean communities, in addition to creative and information programs, news, sports, entertainment, travel and other variety programming features."[70]

The importance of Caribbean audiences, especially the growing and economically successful Indo-Caribbean sector, has not been lost on other minority cable television networks in the United States. Two Asian Indian–owned cable networks serving Asian Indians in the New York and New Jersey area—International Television Broadcasting, Inc. (ITV), and TV Asia—took concrete steps to attract this audience.

Annan Boodram felt that ITV had made the most inroads into the Indo-Caribbean community, due to the network's deliberate efforts to feature Indo-Caribbean matters and personalities in its newscasts and regular programming. The network consistently featured interviews with elite Indo-Caribbean personalities such as former prime minister of Trinidad and Tobago Basdeo Panday and the late president of Guyana, Cheddi Jagan. By the end of 2001, New Jersey–based TV Asia had been unable to make similar penetration, even though the Indo-Caribbean population in New Jersey was not as large as that of New York. TV Asia, however, was making efforts to expand into that market by providing some coverage of Indo-Caribbean matters. However, both channels offer Indo-Caribbean audiences a very popular product—current filmi music. Time Warner Cable has also targeted the Indian diaspora in the United States with its ITV, which "serv[es] the needs of viewers from the Indian subcontinent." Launched in April 1986, this regional cable service had more than half a million subscribers in December 2001.[71]

According to Boodram, Caribbean television in New York has shifted from programming for transient people to programming for a rooted people—providing them with essential coping information (not usually available from the mainstream media) and a valuable venue for introducing Caribbean musical talent to the community. He is convinced that most Caribbean television program producers had a tie-in with the Caribbean and filmi music industries and that the programs provide a forum for Caribbean businesses to advertise to the Caribbean market, as it is difficult to access that market through the mainstream media. More significantly, Caribbean television is becoming more informative. Immigration and political developments in the Caribbean are the topics regularly covered by Caribbean television in America.

Asian Cable Television

Just as Asian populations in the United States have experienced dramatic growth in the last quarter century, so has their presence on American cable television. For example, in 1995, six national cable networks delivered programs to Asian communities in America, and, in 2001, at least eight did so. In the early nineties, two tendencies were evident in Asian cable television in the United States—aggressive entrepreneurs and independent programmers using brokered television. Examples of aggressive entrepreneurs included the International Channel and TV Japan. Korean and South Asian television were good examples of brokered television services. These television programs were supplemented by video rental services available at Korean and South Asian grocery stores in those communities. Three tendencies typify Asian cable television in the United States—networks owned by mainstream investors that were developed by aggressive entrepreneurs in the late eighties and early nineties; brokered television provided by independent producers; and the delivery of programming from Asian countries via cable.

THE INTERNATIONAL CHANNEL NETWORKS

The International Channel, the basic cable service of the International Channel Networks (ICN) was launched on July 3, 1990, by John J. Sie, who came from Shanghai to the United States in 1949. From its inception, this advertising-backed network emphasized Asian Pacific languages in its programming. The early lineup included foreign-language news, sports, and comedy. In the early nineties, the network claimed that it allowed "cable operators across the country to penetrate foreign-language speaking communities in their franchise" and thus to provide foreign-language subscribers with "a powerful incentive to maintain their subscriptions." They also contended that "English-speaking subscribers will appreciate the subtitled programming and the opportunity to experience different cultures." In March 2001, ICN launched *Atlas,* an online marketing resource for the network's cable affiliates to help them with marketing to targeted ethnic groups.[72]

In the early nineties, Asian programming on the International Channel was obtained from a variety of sources. Korean programming was acquired from the Korean Broadcasting System. Japanese programming came from Fuji TV. Chinese programming, in both

Mandarin and Cantonese, was acquired from Taiwan, Hong Kong, and the United States. International Channel Networks provides two cable networks—the basic service on the International Channel and a digital premium service. The basic service offered programs in seventeen languages, including Cambodian, Cantonese, Hindi, Hmong, Japanese, Korean, Mandarin, Tagalog, and Vietnamese. This proliferation of languages is, according to the network's management, a reflection of the growing market size and influence of those communities in the United States. The network's twenty-four-hour premium channels include two Chinese channels (CCTV-4, from the People's Republic, and Power TV Zhong Tian, from the Republic of China), the Filipino Channel, TV Asia, TV Japan, Zee TV, a Vietnamese channel (Saigon Broadcasting Network), and a Korean channel (MBC-TV).

The presence of CCTV-4 as a premium service of ICN was the result of collaborations between Encore International—a company developed in 1995 by John Sie—and China Central Television (CCTV). The collaboration required Encore International to supply "daily, prime time programming for CCTV's general entertainment network CCTV-8. In exchange, Chinese programming on CCTV-4 [was] distributed directly in the United States through cable systems and through the International Channel Networks and the C-Span Networks." The programs from CCTV-4 programs are primarily in Mandarin. There are some newscasts in English. Other programs on CCTV-4 include "news and information on China's politics, economy, culture, science, education, and history."[73]

The programming on Power TV Zhong Tian Channel is provided by Taiwan's Power TV and is presented in Mandarin. The channel emphasizes the latest in Chinese entertainment, especially dramas and variety shows. Power TV is reported to be the most popular television service for the Chinese diaspora, with audiences in "Hong Kong, Taiwan, Japan, the Philippines, Singapore, Malaysia, Australia, North America, South America, and a large part of the Asia Pacific region." The programming for The Filipino Channel is provided primarily by two Philippines-based media businesses—ABS-CBN, the dominant broadcaster in the Philippines, and cable operator MSO.

The programming is a mix of news, entertainment, and sports. ABS-CBN is the "first network in Asia to deliver 24-hour programming to the North American Filipino population as well as the Filipino population throughout the Pacific, Europe, and the Middle East."[74]

TV Asia, a New Jersey-based premium network launched in April 1993, has been described as "North America's first coast-to-coast entertainment and information channel for the South Asian community." The network states that it is dedicated to bringing the South Asian American community together by delivering a high-quality channel, both in content and on-screen presentation. According to the NCTA, TV Asia is distributed on three thousand cable systems and has forty-five thousand DBS subscribers. In addition to audiences in the United States (including its courting of the Indo-Caribbean audience in New York), TV Asia reaches Canada, the Caribbean, and South America.[75]

JAPANESE TELEVISION IN AMERICA

TV Japan is a channel of NHK, Japan's influential public television service. TV Japan is the preeminent Japanese-language television service in the United States. The story of its rise to that position provides us with an opportunity to look at the interactions between influential streams in America's diversity—the sojourner (see chapter 2), especially the tourist, and the practices of aggressive international media entrepreneurs.

By the early nineties, the American tourism industry had become aware of the huge economic significance of Japanese tourists and was responding to their needs. American hoteliers were advised not to ignore the growing Japanese market and were offered some strategies for "build[ing] a positive guest experience for Japanese visitors." These strategies included learning to "say essential expressions in Japanese," "understanding and providing the ritual and aesthetics of Japanese cuisine," recognizing that "Japanese travelers want security and comfort," and providing a mechanism for them "to stay in touch with home."[76] TV Japan provided the mechanism for staying in touch.

TV Japan started in April 1991 as an element of the "in-room-entertainment" services provided by some hotels for Japanese tourists. Ninety-three percent of all Japanese tourists to America in the early nineties were staying in hotels an average of nearly eight and a half days. In the late nineties, Japanese businesspersons were also becoming significant consumers of hotel rooms and potential consumers of in-room entertainment and information services. In addition, in the early nineties there were "more than one million Japanese nationals and Japanese Americans living in the United States."[77]

The shareholders of the new cable network included some of the most powerful institutions in Japan: Itochu Group, NHK Group, Media International Corporation, Japan Airlines, ten of Japan's leading banks, major insurance companies, and travel agencies. The only non-Japanese investor is Capital Cities/ABC Video Enterprises. Itochu Group, in 1991 "Japan's leading global enterprise with net sales of $US135 billion," is active in an "extensive range of information, communications, media and entertainment businesses." Among those businesses are Japan's Domestic Carrier; International Common Carrier; a strategic partnership with Time Warner; joint cable programming ventures with ESPN (Japan Sports Channel), and investment in over thirty CATV operators in Japan. In 1991, NHK owned and operated the largest public broadcasting company in Japan, had "extensive holdings" in direct broadcast satellites, and was the only supplier of HDTV technology in Japan. NHK also owned a substantial film library, was a major supplier of information, and had access to global information resources. In July 1990, NHK, Itochu, and several major Japanese banks established Media International Corporation, whose aim is to "co-produce films and television programs on a large, international scale, and the global purchase and sales of TV programs." The fourth major player in the creation of TV Japan was Japan Airlines, one of the largest members of the International Air Transport Association, with passenger and cargo offices in more than eighty cities and more than forty countries around the world. In 1991, JAL owned many affiliates in the travel industry, including Nikko Hotels International, which operated more than thirty resort hotels throughout the world.[78]

Several factors were at play in the development of Japanese television in America: responding to the demands and expectations of the Japanese tourist, the development of strategic alliances and infrastructure, and garnering experiences to become a major participant in the emerging global communication marketplace, especially in television program production and delivery. The development of TV Japan is a good example of *keiretsu,* a "group of commercial investors who have mutually beneficial interests in a venture or project." In 1991, TV Japan described its programming as truly reflecting today's Japan: "It's everything that is happening in Japan, news, drama, variety shows as well as sports, and educational programming. TV Japan's programs are supplied by many of Japan's best known television producers, most predominantly from NHK, Japan's largest broadcasting system."[79]

At the start of its service in the United States, TV Japan offered up to sixteen hours of programming a day. These programs originated in the Tokyo studios of NHK and were distributed by satellite to the Japan Network Group studio in New York. From the start, TV Japan's programming was delivered by DBS and cable technologies throughout the United States to hotels, schools, commercial buildings, industrial locations, and hotels. Over the years, the network has made solid growth. In 1991, TV Japan had three thousand home subscribers. In 1992, the service was available in 57,900 rooms in seventy-two hotels. The goal was to extend the service to "300,000 rooms in eleven cities by the end of 1993." In 2001, TV Japan had forty-three thousand subscribers and twenty-five affiliates.[80]

To establish its niche, TV Japan offered a range of incentives, including providing free of charge the one-meter dishes (manufactured the Itochu Group) required to receive its service. And hoteliers received 5 percent of the hotel rate ($7.95 per day in 1991). TV Japan has an established presence in the United States and has expanded its distribution to include Canada and has a twenty-four-hour premium service. It is one of the flagship premium channels on the International Channel Networks. According to ICN, "TV Japan offers the same programs you can see in Japan today, from some of the most popular current dramas, today's headlines, and sports to children's programs."[81] Also serving the Japanese community in the United

States is the Nippon Golden Network, a pay-per-view cable service based in Hawaii, but it is not offered by ICN.

Another premium Asian programming service delivered by the ICN is Zee TV. Launched in the United States in 1999, this premium channel is the "most popular satellite channel in India." It is watched each day by an average of 180 million viewers across the world and is associated with the launching of the cable and satellite revolution in India. Most of Zee TV's twenty-four-hour programming, in Hindi and other regional languages, comes from India and Pakistan. Its schedule ensures that it can serve "the prime time requirements of both the Eastern and Pacific Time Zones" of the United States. Generally, Zee TV's programming is "aimed at serving the needs of South Asians living abroad" and includes "news, movies, dramas, children's programs and talk shows plus special interactive programs involving social issues."[82]

Ten percent of ICN is owned by John Sie, its chairman and CEO. He identifies as his mentor the late Bill Daniels, one of the fathers of the American cable television industry. From Daniels he claims he acquired the basic value of "giving back to the community." Under Sie's leadership, ICN and Starz Encore have developed a range of programs and community-based activities aimed at supporting the acculturation and assimilation of immigrants to the United States. The initiatives include bringing more ethnic minorities into the cable industry, developing joint-ventures with minority programmers in the United States, developing public service campaigns that promote cultural and religious tolerance, and creating programs that focus on the challenges facing families in multicultural America and that support learning in the classroom and education for citizenship. In addition to programming for Asians in America, ICN also offers programming for Middle Eastern and European communities.[83]

Arab Cable Television

Most Arab Americans were born in the United States. The first wave of Arab immigrants to the United States started to arrive around 1875 and continued until 1920 when immigration was restricted. The second wave started in the 1940s. Most early Arab immigrants came from Syria and Lebanon to escape economic difficulties, but today Arab Americans can also trace their roots to many countries, including Algeria, Egypt, Iraq, Kuwait, Libya, Saudi Arabia, the Sudan, Tunisia, the United Arab Emirates, and Yemen. Although not defined as a minority group by the United States government for purposes of housing and employment, many Arab Americans are "asking for protection from the same issues affecting people in minority groups, such as profiling, stereotyping, and exclusion." Three cable programming networks have dominated Arab television in America—The Arab Channel, ANA Television, and ART.[84]

The Arabic Channel, established in New York in April 1991, has more than a million subscribers. This network broadcasts mainly children's shows, sports, news, and soap operas in Arabic, twenty-four hours a day, seven days a week. It calls itself the "first Arabic television station in the world that is not owned or controlled by a government or group in the Middle East."[85]

ANA Television was also established in 1991, by the Arab Network of America, Inc. The Arab Network was established in September 1989 by Mohammed Basrawi as a reaction to what he considered the inadequate treatment of Arab themes in the U.S. media: "unless there's a calamitous piece of news, or an assassination, there's probably no more than a half-minute of news from the Middle East a week."[86] His first step was the establishment of a radio network that served the major Arab American communities in Detroit, Chicago, San Francisco, and Washington, D.C. That network was the first in the United States to report on Iraq's invasion of Kuwait in 1990 (five hours ahead of CNN), but it closed in 2000.

Since then, television has been the only arm of the ANA. This television network broadcasts in Arabic and English and distributes its programs in the United States, Canada, and Central America. In the United States the service was available in areas with significant Arab American populations—California, Michigan, Illinois, and metropolitan Washington, D.C. In addition to cable delivery, the service was also distributed by satellite to TVRO (television receive only) homes, hotels, colleges, and businesses.[87] Interestingly, this network did not have a website in December 2001. Interviews with the staff suggested that the network was under much pressure as a result of September 11, 2001.

The most recent addition to Arab television in the United States was the international Arab Radio and Television Network. ART was launched in 1993 as a "private network, with administrative headquarters in Jeddah, Saudi Arabia; technical headquarters in Amman, Jordan; and production facilities spanning the entire Middle East." The network's programming was a mix of live and recorded shows. Typically, ART produced over six thousand shows a year, including family dramas, sports, music videos, and documentaries. The network reported that it had access to the "largest Arabic movie library in the Middle East"[88] and that its content was sensitive to the diversity of the Arabic audience worldwide. ART has been available in the United States since 1999 and is distributed to more than twenty U.S. cable systems as a premium channel by International Channel Networks, which also distributes Melli TV, a network launched in 1995 targeting the Iranian community in America.[89]

Ethnic European Cable Television

When Marion Marzolf referred to the persistence of ethnic media in the 1970s, she was commenting on the presence of ethnic European newspapers in the United States (see chapter 3). There has also been significant growth in the electronic media serving European ethnic communities since 1990. In 1995, four networks provided programming for European ethnic communities; in 2001, there were eight—National Jewish Television and Universal Torah Broadcasting, Celtic TV, National Greek Television, RAI International, Russian TV, Scandinavian TV, and TV5-USA.

The National Jewish Television network, established in May 1981, has ten million subscribers. The advertising-supported service, programmed for three hours per week on Sundays, provides America's Jewish community with "relevant, enlightening, interactive family-based programming on the unique Jewish way of life, religion, and people." The dominant genres are documentaries, children's programs, and news magazines. The network is an important link in the broadcasting web that connects Jewish America with Israel and the Jewish Diaspora. Universal Torah Broadcasting was established in December 1998 and now has fifteen million subscribers in North America, Europe, and Israel. Its eight weekly hours of programming could be described as religious and inspirational, with particular emphasis on the Torah and the Bible.

Celtic Vision TV, a basic advertising-supported network based in Boston, was established in March 1995 and has 175,000 subscribers. The twenty-four-hour network offers "exclusive entertainment and current affairs programming from Ireland, Scotland, and the entire Celtic world." A special feature is the evening news from Dublin. Other genres include music, dance, drama, comedy, documentaries, and travel shows. National Greek Television, established in December 1987 is a regional cable network targeting Greek Americans in Brooklyn and Queens. The twenty-four-hour service has half a million total subscribers to its basic and premium services. National Greek Television broadcasts news, sports, talk shows, dramas, comedy series, movies, and documentaries from Greece, as well as locally produced Greek programming.[90]

RAI International is a television service of Italy's national broadcaster, RAI. This twenty-four-hour service is an example of a nation using its broadcasting capacity to maintain contact with its diaspora (see the discussion of Spotlight TV, above). RAI International has been available in the United States since 1999 and is distributed as a premium service of International Channel Networks. Its programming represents the best of the state-owned broadcaster. Particular emphasis is placed on Italian culture, including festivals, concerts, movies, cooking shows, game shows, documentaries, and news.

TV Russia is also offered as a premium channel by ICN and is available in all fifty states. The twenty-four-hour network, launched in 1995, is the only Russian-language network in the United States. The Scandinavian cable programming network ceased operations on May 1, 2001, after about a year of operation. Also distributed by ICN, it was the only twenty-four-hour cable network that featured programs from Denmark, Finland, Iceland, Norway, and Sweden. Its programming was targeted to a projected audience of sixteen million Scandinavian Americans and featured, "daily news, sports, outdoors, reality TV, culture, travel, and general entertainment with English subtitles." The CEO of the Scandinavia Channel said the network folded because it failed to generate capital from potential investors. He added that the marketplace in 2001 had "little tolerance for businesses that were not profitable in a very short time no matter their progress or promise."[91]

TV5-USA, a twenty-four-hour Canadian-based network, targeted French-speaking audiences throughout the world. The network was introduced in January 1998 and features programming from Belgium, Canada (including Quebec), France, French-speaking Africa, and Switzerland: film, dramas, news from five countries, cultural talk shows, kids programs, and documentaries about the art of living. The network subtitles its programming on Saturday nights. In December 2001, the NCTA indicated that the network had 130 million subscribers in 123 countries. It is offered as a basic or a premium service, depending on the market.

SCOLA: Another Network Responding to America's Diversity

Satellite Communications for Learning is a consortium established in August 1987, but its origins can be traced to 1983 and the work of Rev. Lee Lubbers, who was involved in linking the dormitories and classrooms of Creighton University and providing them with "satellite-borne programming." The first priority of the consortium was to "bring [live] news from around the world."[92] In January 1993, the consortium was offering twenty-four hours of news programs from thirty-seven nations daily. SCOLA now has 4.5 million subscribers in the United States, Canada, Mexico, the Caribbean, and Central America and retransmits news programs from forty countries to over eight thousand schools, colleges, and universities across the Americas. It also operates a foreign variety channel and a channel dedicated to

Chinese as well as an audio programming service featuring Radio France International, the World Radio Network, and Vatican Radio.[93]

Since SCOLA, similar cable programming networks have emerged, including the Canadian Broadcasting Corporation's New York–based twenty-four-hour news channel, Newsworld International (NWI). Like SCOLA, NWI presents "unedited newscasts from many nations around the world, available in both English and the originating languages." Other news networks are being planned. For example, Noah's World International plans to focus on Israel, Turkey, and China.[94] Also on the drawing board are Diversity TV, Global Village Network, and the Urban Broadcasting Company. Diversity TV was described as a premium movie network targeting African, Latino, and Asian Americans. Hawaii-based Global Village Network plans to focus on global business and world cultures. The New York–based Urban Broadcasting Company plans to deliver original programming and special musical events from around the world to "multicultural" audiences.

Cable television in America requires sophisticated infrastructures— satellites and reliable landlines. Over the past three decades, a sophisticated and reliable infrastructure with generous capacity has been put in place although its installation was costly. Investors' desire for rapid profit has required agility and the development of strategic partnerships with domestic and international partners. One consequence has been a dramatic concentration of ownership, particularly of infrastructure. AT&T, AOL Time Warner, and Cox Communications alone control 68 percent of the industry systems. An equally small group controls content flow. Liberty Media Corporation, along with its subsidiaries International Channel Networks and Starz Encore, control most cable programming directed to America's minority communities.

The presence of America's minority communities has contributed to the proliferation of cable television networks in America over the past three decades, as has the increasing economic and political importance of these communities. U.S. foreign policy is also responsible for the growth of cable networks, especially those that target America's minorities. The presence of CCTV-4 is directly related to strategies aimed at engaging China and incorporating it into the international trading system and at the same time acquiring access to its substantial media markets.

As a for-profit sector of the American broadcasting industry, the cable industry, like the over-the-air sector, has aimed to contain costs and maximize profits. Cable programmers have demonstrated solid commitment to the parsimony principle. Music videos, talk shows, stand-up comedy, and aftermarket programming dominate cable network programming. The American cable industry is therefore in a position to facilitate intercultural communication. In the last decade, it has appeared that those intercultural interactions that were taking place were among racially and ethnically similar groups (Indo-Caribbeans and South Asians, for instance). However, the conversation among English-, French-, and Spanish-speaking Caribbeans of African ancestry has not really come of age. Intercultural and ethnic dialogue is still relatively rare on American cable.

Despite these limitations, the cable programming that targets America's minority communities has demonstrated positive dimensions. It is contributing to the construction of positive identities and is nourishing self-efficacy. These programs are helping some communities (e.g., South Asians, some Caribbean communities) see their cultural connections beyond the narrow confines of their former homelands. These new transnational identities are helping to bridge cultural areas and may very well be the first steps in discovering the brotherhood of man dreamed by W. E. B. DuBois. That goal is in harmony with the possibilities of the first universal nation.

In 1989, the director of the Friedrich Naumann Foundation in New York observed, "In the United States virtually no television program from the developing countries are broadcast and the few feature films which are shown have a limited audience." That deficiency, she contended, bred insularity and cultural chauvinism and was not in the best interests of a world superpower. Cable television's response to America's increasing diversity is helping to correct that situation and in the process is adding a new dimension to what Hamid Mowlana has called the ethnicization of the media in the industrialized nations of the world.[95]

8

Noncommercial Television and America's Diversity

Public Television

The profit motive alone cannot be counted on to fulfill all the national, cultural, educational, and informational needs that broadcast media could ideally serve. Hence arose the concept of *non-commercial broadcasting*—motivated by public-service goals rather than profit.

—Head and Sterling, *Broadcasting in America*

PUBLIC TELEVISION (PTV) is the clearest manifestation of socially responsible broadcast principles in the United States. It is the only television service in the United States required by law to cater to the nation's minority[1] communities. The origins of noncommercial public television in America are intertwined with the origins of noncommercial radio, especially the struggle during the 1920s to acquire licenses to develop broadcast services that were "devoted explicitly to education." That struggle resulted in the FCC's establishment of "the reserved-channels principle," which allocated a portion of the spectrum to educational radio. When television began to emerge as the dominant mass medium in the late forties, a "new campaign" was launched to extend the reserved-channels principle to the new medium. The FCC extended the principle to television in 1952. Under the FCC's *Sixth Report and Order*, 242 channels of the 2,035 allocated were reserved for educational television (ETV)—80 channels were VHF and 162 were UHF. KUHT in Houston became America's first noncommercial television station in 1953.[2]

From its inception, there have been controversies about the role of educational television, now termed public television. The controversies were engendered in part by the diversity of groups involved in its founding: "The miscellaneous grouping of enthusiasts developed conflicting views about the form educational television should take. One group took the words 'educational television' to mean a broadly inclusive cultural and information service. Another took them to mean a new and improved audiovisual device, primarily important to schools and formal adult education. Some, following the model of commercial broadcasting, favored a strong national network and a concern for audience building. Others, expressly rejecting the commercial model, focused on localism and service for more limited, specialized audiences. Some wanted to stress high culture and intellectual stimulation. Others wanted to emphasize programs of interest to ethnic minorities, children, and the poor."[3] Those strains of thinking are still evident in the discourse about American public television.

The Public Broadcasting Act of 1967 established the structure of what is now termed public broadcasting in America. Under the act, the Corporation for Public Broadcasting (CPB), public broadcasting's central coordinating mechanism, was required to "develop television and radio systems that would reach and serve all Americans with alternative programming, develop connection services that would link the public broadcasting stations nationwide, help support those stations, help ensure production of high quality programs from diverse sources, [and] provide training, instruction, recruitment, research, and development." Public broadcasting has established itself as an important and influential pillar in the American broadcasting environment. National Public Radio (NPR) and the Public Broadcasting Service (PBS) are the primary radio and television arms of this sector. Under the Public Telecommunications Act of 1988, CPB is required to conduct research every three years to assess the needs of America's minority audiences and the plans of public broadcasting entities to meet those needs. The assessments are also expected to explore "the ways radio and television can be used to serve racial, ethnic, and other minority groups," and to offer " projections concerning minority employment by public broadcasting and public telecommunications entities." The Public Telecommunications Act also required CPB to "prepare an annual report on the provision by public broadcasting and public telecommunications entities of service to minority and diverse audiences in regard to programming (including that which is produced by minority producers), training, minority employment, and efforts by the Corporation to increase the number of minority public radio and television stations eligible for financial support from CPB."[4]

At the beginning of the nineties, public television in the United States was a sophisticated, satellite-linked network known as the Public Broadcasting Service (PBS). But despite its legal mandate, PBS has not always been successful in responding to America's diversity. It has thus been subjected to the scrutiny of private media research and watchdog groups. For example, a 1992 report on the biases in PTV documentaries concluded that PBS had failed to be "diverse, objective, or balanced,"[5] that public affairs broadcasting on PTV was dominated by white males, and that racial and ethnic minorities were involved only when the issues under discussion related directly to that racial or ethnic community, reinforcing stereotypes of parochialism. By the end of the century, however, African Americans and Latinos were evident as hosts on PTV public affairs and news programs.

In 1992, the PTV network was made up of 350 stations; in 2001, there were 375. Those stations are owned and managed by four categories of operators: states and municipalities, institutions of higher learning, public school boards, and community foundations. But regardless of ownership, PTV has had to deal with four major influences on the sector's ability to respond to America's diversity: funding, programming, and human resources, and technology.[6]

Funding

Access to adequate funding has been a perennial problem for public television in America. This inadequacy has influenced and continues to influence the way that American PTV is organized and the products it delivers. It was this consistent shortage of funds in the educational broadcasting sector that led to the creation of the Carnegie Commission on Educational Television in 1965, which catalyzed the passage of the Public Broadcasting Act in 1967. The commission emerged out of the First National Conference on Long-Range Financing of Educational Television Stations convened by the National Association of Educational Broadcasters and the U.S. Office of Education in 1964. Fearing federal interference in public broadcasting programming, the commission recommended two strategies to insulate public broadcasting: the collection of a federal excise tax on television sets and a twelve-person supervisory board—"six appointed by the President with the advice and consent of the Senate, the other six chosen by the appointees."[7]

Neither recommendation was accepted. When President Johnson submitted his proposals for a "public television act" to Congress in 1967, he proposed federal financial support, including $9 million in initial funding and promises to return to the issue of funding a year later. The debate in Congress revealed fears that the new public television would reproduce the "liberal bias" associated with the existing national educational television system.[8] The Public Television Act had no provisions for a predictable source of funding for public television. The numerous resulting conflicts were ameliorated in 1989 with the introduction of the Television Program Fund.

In their review of the first twenty-five years of the Corporation for Public Broadcasting, the authors of *Wasteland to Oasis* noted Elizabeth Campbell's observations to illustrate the excitement associated with the introduction of the Television Program Fund: "CPB's Television Program Fund was a terribly, terribly important step forward in bringing good programming to public television. Before it, most stations didn't have the money even to do a pilot, let alone produce programming of national scope. The program fund gave us a great new bank for national programming" (10).

The Television Program Fund was introduced in 1989 to fund independent producers through the Independent Television Service, Inc. (ITVS). In 1990, the fund was expanded to include minority-initiated programming through the Multicultural Programming Fund (10–11). So by the beginning of the nineties, CPB was establishing a network of program-funding mechanisms geared to ensure diversity in public broadcasting. The funding model remained in place throughout the decade. CPB continues to invest in a number of agencies, central among them were five minority programming consortia and the ITVS. The Television Program Fund was only one source in the funding model developed by PTV to ensure it delivered its mission of responding to America's minorities. A decade ago, PTV's several funding sources included "pledgers," public sources (local, state, and federal government, colleges), private sources (memberships, businesses, foundations), and other entrepreneurial activities, such as auctions.[9] The failure of PTV to develop a single dedicated source of adequate income has made it susceptible to threats from the government and criticisms of bias and of pandering to corporate and foundation interests. Underwriting deals with companies such as Archer Daniels Midland were criticized as selling out to corporate interests. It is against this backdrop of funding tensions that we examine PTV's programming responses to America's diversity in the decade 1990–2001.

Programming: A Survey of Genres and Themes

Public television programming in the United States has two strands— the nationally oriented and the locally oriented. A decade ago six categories of programs dominated the national programming: children's programming, public affairs and news, programming for the classroom, cultural documentaries, performing arts, and science and nature (10). By the turn of the century, it was possible to add a seventh category—how-to programs like *This Old House* and *The Frugal Gourmet*. All these categories have delivered programs reflecting America's diversity.

Another PTV strategy to ensure programming that reflects America's diversity is the sharing of programs produced by individual stations within the public television system. An example of that tradition is *Tony Brown's Journal*, an African American public affairs program. One of the first programs to be funded by CPB, it has been shared since it was introduced in 1967 and continues to be distributed by PBS stations across America. Other early examples include *Black Horizons* at WQED, Pittsburgh (since 1970); *Basic Black* at WGBH, Boston (1971); *Detroit Black Journal* at WTVS, Detroit (1973); *Images/Imagenes* at the New Jersey Network (1972); and *Mundo hispano* at WLVT, Bethlehem, Pennsylvania (1976) (2).

CHILDREN'S PROGRAMMING

Public television's children's programming has consistently reflected the racial and ethnic diversity in American society through such popular offerings as *Sesame Street, Degrassi High, Mr. Rogers' Neighborhood, The Electric Company, 3-2-1 Contact, Where in the World Is Carmen Sandiego? Sagwa the Chinese Siamese Cat, Arthur,* and *Clifford the Big Red Dog*. PTV's children's programming has been highly rated by all segments of the national audience, including African American, Hispanic, and Asian American audiences. The conclusion was drawn that America's minority families watch PTV's children's programming together.[10]

In the early nineties, PTV was also producing materials geared for the classroom. In 1991, 65 percent of PTV's air time, when schools were in session, was devoted to classroom materials like *All about You, Newscasts from the Past,* and *The Shakespeare Plays*.[11] More than 24 million students and three-quarters of a million teachers were using those materials. PTV has since developed online services for children through PBS Kids, a program that provides interactive content to supplement many of its popular children's programs.

The term *major-strand programming* is used by PBS to refer to programs (public affairs, drama, documentaries, etc.) that are distributed by PBS nationally, particularly during prime time. Especially in the last decade such programs have clearly been committed to developing America's awareness of its diversity. Much of the national programming has promoted community involvement and has used different languages to bridge cultural differences. Examples of this orientation in the early nineties included *New Immigrants: The Arab-American Experience; Other Voices, Other Songs: The Armenians; Holocaust Survivors Speak; Topaz;* and the award-winning independent productions, *Eyes on the Prize, The Africans, The American Experience, Black Champions, Civilization, Columbus and the Age of Discovery, Heritage: Civilization and the Jews, The Civil War,* and *Color Adjustment.*[12] In 2001, fifty-one programs with minority themes, including shows about America's new immigrants, were broadcast by PBS. Among them:

Turbans, about the struggles of an Asian Indian Sikh family in Oregon.

American Masters—Bob Marley: Rebel Music.

American Experience—Marcus Garvey: Look for Me in the Whirlwind.

Ancestors in America, "the untold history and contemporary legacy of Asian American immigrants to the Americas from the 1700s to the 1990s."

Forgotten Americans, "profiles of the people who live in the Mexico/ U.S. border colonias, most without basics such as water and electricity."

Islam: Empire of Faith.

We Served with Pride: The Chinese American Experiences in WWII.

Wrapped in Pride: The Story of Kente in America, explored "how kente-cloth crossed the Atlantic from Ghana and found its way into everyday American life."[13]

Also in 2001 CPB funded the series *American Family,* about "a Mexican American family in contemporary Los Angeles." It was the "first drama series ever to air on broadcast television featuring a Latino cast," including Sonia Braga, Esai Morales, Edward James Olmos, and Raquel Welch. The series, created and produced by award-winning director Gregory Nava, first aired in January 2002.[14]

BILINGUAL PROGRAMMING AND OTHER COMMUNITY PROGRAMMING APPROACHES

Since 1990, the public television system has adopted three strategies to serve its non-English-speaking audience. The first approach is to provide programs in languages other than English. The second approach is to provide bilingual programs in which people speak more than one language. The final approach is to record the program in English and in another language and thus allow the viewer to select the language through the use of separate audio channels. Among the programs that adopted that strategy was the *MacNeil/Lehrer NewsHour*. Since January 1991, the flagship newscast of American public television was broadcast in English and Spanish. In the early nineties, Miami's WLRN was airing more than five hours of Spanish-language programming a week, and Milwaukee's WMVS broadcast its monthly special on Hispanic issues, *Conciencia,* over two audio channels, one in Spanish and one in English. KUAT, in Tucson, aired *Reflexiones,* "Southern Arizona's longest-running bilingual news magazine," and Louisiana Public Broadcasting produced three programs in French: *Parlez-moi, Images du monde francophone* and *En français.* KYUK, in Bethel, Alaska, broadcast daily news and public service announcements in Yup'ik, a language of the Yukon-Kuskokwim Delta. PTV has also broadcast in other languages in response to emergency situations. For example, Twin Cities Public Television produced and aired a half-hour special in Hmong for the Asian Hmong community during a measles epidemic in St. Paul in the early nineties.[15]

An obviously proactive response to America's diversity has been public television's decision to provide language education services. Through collaborative efforts among state public broadcasting networks, such as the Nebraska Public Television Network and South Carolina ETV and projects such as the Annenberg/CPB Project, public television has offered high school– and college-level courses in Japanese, Russian, French, and Spanish. The Satellite Educational Resources Consortium has played a major role in the distribution of these programs (11).

Broadcasting in different languages has grown, and PTV stations in states with significant minority populations have developed their own foreign-language programming. For example, KENW-TV, in Portales, New Mexico, produced a Latino affairs program in Spanish. In Philadelphia, WYBE-TV aired a "weekly World TV lineup consisting of programs from local and international sources and in native languages," including Ukrainian, Italian, Greek, Hindi, Vietnamese, Korean, and Polish (74). WMVS-TV, in Milwaukee, launched the weekly magazine *¡Adelante!* in 2001, "highlighting the positive aspects of the Latino community" (84).

The use of foreign languages is most evident in the outreach programs organized by American public television. For example, through the Minority Consortia (see below) the Public Television Outreach Alliance, the public television system coordinates much of its outreach programs. Examples of these projects include Project Literacy. Other issues for which community outreach projects have been organized in the last decade, at both the local and national levels, include drug abuse, child care, the unemployed, high school dropouts, troubled youth, the AIDS crisis, the environment, prejudice, and the family.[16] PTV outreach programs also address voter education and consumer education. These outreach programs have become integrated multimedia projects, bringing together the communication resources of communities—print, radio, face-to-face, television, and the Internet. Responding to community needs is central to the idea of the localism that underpins public broadcasting in America. In this process, PTV has pushed the definition of diversity to include persons with sight and hearing impairments.

The Minority Consortia and the Independent Television Service

Five organizations constitute the Minority Consortia: Latino Public Broadcasting, the National Asian American Telecommunications Association, the National Black Programming Consortium, Native American Public Telecommunications, and Pacific Islanders in Communications. These five, along with the Independent Television Service, have played a significant role in ensuring that PTV provides the American public high-quality and culturally diverse programming. Nearly all were established before the passage of the Public Telecommunications Act of 1988.[17] The consortia develop, produce, and distribute programming that appeals to diverse audiences and harnesses the creative talents of minority communities. These organizations also award grants to producers for program production, training, exhibition, and outreach activities.[18]

NATIONAL ASIAN AMERICAN
TELECOMMUNICATIONS ASSOCIATION

San Francisco-based NAATA was founded in 1980—the outcome of the "first national conference of Asian American media makers and activists." Its mission, as stated in 1989, is "to advance the ideal of America as a pluralistic society where diverse cultures and peoples are equally empowered and respected, and to promote better understanding of the Asian Pacific American experience through film, video and radio to the broadest audience" and its specific goals are "to nurture and support Asian Pacific American artists working in film, video and radio; to provide the many Asian Pacific American communities locally and nationally access to works by Asian Pacific media artists; to ensure that works of excellence in film, video and radio by and about Asian Pacific Americans reach broad, mainstream audiences."[19]

At its twentieth anniversary, NAATA stated that it had achieved its founding goals of establishing "a credible organization, securing funding from the Corporation for Public Broadcasting, and [placing] Asian American programming on public television." Its mission has expanded to include the presentation of "stories that convey the richness and diversity of the Asian Pacific American experience to the broadest audience possible . . . [and] to do this by funding, producing, distributing, and exhibiting films, video, and new media." There were also new goals:

to support and encourage Asian Pacific American artists working in film, video, and other electronic media

to provide local and national Asian Pacific American communities opportunities to view works made by Asian Pacific American media artists that illuminate personal and community viewpoints

to use media as an educational tool for learning about the historical and contemporary issues of Asian Pacific American communities

to use artistically excellent works by and about Asian Pacific Americans to reach audiences of all backgrounds, and to introduce diverse Asian Pacific American perspectives into an ongoing dialogue of what it means to be American

to project a global vision that encourages transnational exchange through media—Asian Pacific American media, Asian-themed media products throughout the world, and media from all of the world's cultures[20]

The organization was proud of its productions from its first twenty years. Among the shows that were singled out for special praise were *Who Killed Vincent Chin? Color of Honor, Sa-I-Gu* (April 29), *Days of Waiting,* and *a.k.a. Don Bonus.* NAATA was associated with six programs aired on PBS in 2001. *Hidden Korea* explored South Korea's culture through its unique food and food history, and *Roots in the Sand* focused on the experiences of Punjabi immigrants in the Wild West. *We Served with Pride* addressed "the forgotten and often ignored history of Chinese Americans during World II" through the lives of twenty-eight individuals. *Great Wall across the Yangtze* focused on the conflict-ridden Three Gorges Dam.[21]

Like other sectors of America's broadcasting industry, NAATA has begun to appropriate the Internet, cable, and satellite to deliver Asian American comedies, dramas, children's and public affairs programming twenty-four/seven to an international audience. The organization also has its sights on a bigger challenge, rectifying exclusion in mainstream commercial television: "Asian Americans remain marginal, ephemeral figures on commercial television, the most influential medium in our society. Part of our mission must include working with civil rights and advocacy groups to make Hollywood open up its doors." NAATA sees training and the "nurturing of a new generation of writers, directors, and producers" as a contribution to changing the situation in Hollywood. For the past two decades, it has been organizing film festivals, community screenings, media workshops, and the distribution of works through the broadcast system and to educational markets. It has also emerged as one of the active research-oriented members of the Minority Consortia. NAATA was responsible for the research report that led to the development of the model currently used by CPB to fund the Minority Consortia and the ITVS.[22]

NAATA has operated a media library for over a decade that contains "some of the finest independently-produced Asian American programs." Among the programs offered in the catalogue were the "Classic Series," referring to the early works produced by Visual Communications, "the nation's oldest Asian Pacific media center." The thirty-five titles in the original catalog were divided into five broad categories—history and immigration, history and social science, sociology, classic series, and women's studies. The catalogue service is now called NAATA Distribution and has two hundred titles in thirteen categories.[23] NAATA has maintained an active international program though film and video festivals such as the Asian American International Film Showcase, in which Asian American artists like Loni Ding have participated. Programs produced by NAATA have won several national and international awards.

NATIONAL BLACK PROGRAMMING CONSORTIUM

The National Black Programming Consortium was founded in 1979 to address, among other things, the "paucity and disparity of Black film/video programming, at home and abroad." The NBPC defined its mission as "support[ing] and foster[ing] the development, production and distribution of educationally and culturally specific TV/film by and about Africans/African Americans for promotion and marketing to public television, cable and other telecommunication entities in support of community participation, development and empowerment." From its inception, the NBPC established as its key task the organizing and operation of a "clearinghouse to showcase the best in Black-oriented programming at a national/international level." In the early nineties, the clearinghouse was reported to have over two thousand hours of black productions, making the NBPC "one of the world's largest [black media] centers, archiving and distributing socially significant Black TV/film programs."[24]

The NBPC's annual Prized Pieces awards, established in 1981, have served as the major vehicle for acknowledging and rewarding outstanding black video and film materials. It "has evolved into an international film/video competition/awards festival which continues to attract entries from every facet of the media industry." Its mission has remained consistent: it is "devoted to the production, distribution, promotion, and preservation of diverse films and videos about African Americans and the African diaspora experiences."[25] The NBPC has also funded a number of influential productions, including Julie Dash's *Daughters of the Dust,* which aired on PBS in 1992. NBPC was associated with six programs that were aired on PBS in 2001, including an episode of *The American Experience* titled *Marcus Garvey: Look for Me in the Whirlwind.*

NATIVE AMERICAN PUBLIC TELECOMMUNICATIONS

Native American Public Telecommunications (NAPT) is the successor to the Native American Public Broadcasting Consortium (NAPBC), which was established in 1976 with support from CPB. From its inception, the NAPBC was supported by the Nebraska Educational Television Network, and its declared mission was "to produce and encourage the production and successful use of quality public telecommunications programs by and about Native Americans, for both Native American and general audiences." The consortium operated "the nation's largest [collection of] Native American video programs for public television, instructional and general information use." NAPT now aims to "inform, educate and encourage the awareness of tribal histories, cultures, languages, opportunities and aspirations through the fullest participation of American Indians and Alaska Natives in creating and employing all forms of educational and public telecommunications programs and services, thereby supporting tribal sovereignty." The organization's strategy for accomplishing its mission includes "producing and developing educational telecommunication programs for all media including television and public radio; distributing and encouraging the broadest use of such educational telecommunications programs; providing training opportunities to encourage increasing numbers of American Indians and Alaska Natives to produce quality programs; promoting increased control and use of information technologies by American Indians and Alaska Natives; providing leadership in creating awareness of and developing telecommunications policies favorable to American Indians and Alaska Natives; building partnerships to develop and implement telecommunications projects with tribal nations, Indian organizations, and native communities."[26]

Like the other consortia, NAPT manages a grant program that was established in 1991, when the NAPBC announced it had awarded over three hundred thousand dollars in grants for original Native American projects for public television. The grants were intended to:

identify program priorities and production guidelines in concert with Native American producing communities and public broadcasting for development or completion of programs for national distribution

create visibility, access, and support linkages for Native American producers to national producing and funding resources in public broadcasting and other media

provide direct support to Native American independent and station producers to develop and leverage national program proposals

support emerging Native American producers for the development of national proposals for public television

facilitate and leverage the development of co-productions between Native American producers and public TV, national, and international producers[27]

Programs produced from the grants have been broadcast on PBS as part of its major-strand programming. For example, the influential program *In the White Man's Image* was produced for *The American Experience*. In 2001, four programs on PBS were supported by funding from NAPT: *The Return of the Navajo Boy, Homeland, Lost Bird of Wounded Knee,* and *Lost Kings of the Maya.*

When this Hawaii-based organization became a member of the Minority Consortia in February 1992, its aim was to "assist indigenous Pacific Islander film and video makers to produce programming for national [and international] broadcast." PIC promotes "programming which fosters a deeper understanding of the values inherent in Pacific Island cultures and which enhances public recognition of and appreciation for Pacific Islanders; that is, the descendants of the first peoples of Hawai'i, Guam, the Northern Mariana Islands, American Samoa and other Pacific islands." Like other members of the Minority Consortia, over the past decade PIC has adopted a range of strategies to achieve its mission, including "awarding production grants," "awarding research and development grants," "establishing co-production ventures with national and international entities," "developing and producing program series," "training Pacific Islanders," and "holding public forums."[28]

Among the influential PIC programs aired on PBS have been *The Last Queen of Hawai'i* (for *The American Experience*), which examined the intrigue behind the removal of the Hawaiian royal family. *Holo mai Pele* (Pele travels) featured "chant, dance and mythology of the Hawaiian Fire Goddess Pele and her sister, Hi'aka. [It was] the first *Great Performances/Dance in America* [episode] to feature Pacific performing arts." *Then There Were None* was a personal documentary produced by Hawaiian actress Elizabeth Kapu'uwailani Lindsey. In addition to themes from history, PIC told stories about contemporary life in the Pacific Islands. *Rising Waters: Global Warming and the Fate of the Pacific Islands* was broadcast on PBS on Earth Day 2002. In 2001, PIC awarded, through its media fund, grants for six projects: *Biography Hawai'i,* a series focusing on island life; *Constantly Chamorro,* exploring the forces that influenced life in Guam over the past century; *Hula: The Art of Healing a Community; In the Shadow of Mauna Kea; The Meaning of Food;* and *America Aloha.*[29]

LPB was started in 1974 as the Latino Consortium. According to José Luis Ruiz, the Latino Consortium "was a consortium of ten public television stations, primarily in the Southwest that banded together to share among each other Latino productions for broadcast at the local level. They came together in order to serve an expressed community need for Latino programming, which public broadcasting was not then providing." The new institution became a department of KCET (Channel 28) in Los Angeles. In 1989, however, the consortium became an "autonomous entity" when it was incorporated as the National Latino Communications Center (NLCC) in response to the Public Telecommunications Act of 1988 and demands from Congress and from Hispanics in America.[30]

After the organization became involved in program production in 1974, among the first series produced were *¡Presente!* and *VISTAS*, which both aired on public television. Between 1974 and 1992, the organization produced more than four hundred hours of Latino-themed programs for PBS. Among them were major-strand programs such as *Break of Dawn* for *American Playhouse* and *Los mineros* for *The American Experience.* Luis Valdez's *La pastorela* (The Nativity) and Moctesuma Esparza's *Bowl of Beings* were broadcast in the *Great Performances* series. *Latinos and Politics* was a contribution to PBS's 1992 elections project. Other special programs during the early nineties included specials on AIDS. The NLCC developed several of its programs in the early nineties through coproductions.

The NLCC also supported an influential research agenda in the early nineties. *Multicultural Programming Content in Selected Public Television Series*, conducted by Valdez and Associates, examined the "presence of minorities in [the following] PBS program series: *American Experience, American Masters, American Playhouse, Frontline, Great Performances, Nova, The MacNeil/Lehrer NewsHour,* and *P.O.V.* Chon Noriega conducted the formative research project preparatory to the establishment of national archive of Latino film and video works." In 1992, Jose Luis Ruiz indicated that his organization's plans called for expanding its activities in several areas, including career development assistance to Latino filmmakers; increasing production and programming activity, creating a national Latino film archive, and establishing Latinos in the mainstream of the media landscape.[31]

Latino Public Broadcasting has recently declared that its mission was "to provide a voice to the diverse Latino community throughout the United States. Nurturing and supporting, Latino artists portraying the Latino experience in film, video, radio, and other electronic media, [providing] them with equitable funding and distribution mechanisms to present Latino programs [on] public broadcasting stations in order to educate the global audience to the richness and diversity of Latino cultures." This mission guides LPB's efforts to create a structure that brings together resources from the public broadcasting sector, the community, government, and the private sector with the aim of sharing the diversity of Latino culture with America and the world. Central to this mission is the management of a competitive program managed by a panel of independent professionals to make grants available for most genres of television programs—"dramas, documentaries, comedies, satire, or animation." The key considerations in the awarding of grants are originality, the ability of the project to illuminate the Latino experience in America, ability to engage a national audience, demonstrated experience by the production team, soundness of production and financing plans, and the suitability of the product for PTV. In 2001, two programs supported by LPB were broadcast on PBS—*Forgotten Americans* and *Accordion Dreams.* LPB was also associated with the funding of *American Family; Journeys: Stories of Latino Americans;* and *Visiones: Latino Art and Culture.* In addition, the organization supported the annual conference of the National Association of Latino Independent Producers.[32]

The LPB's leadership reflects the diversity of the Latino population in America. Its chairman, Edward James Olmos, was born and raised in East Los Angeles; the executive director, Marlene L. Dermer, was born in Peru; and the program manager, Luca Bentivoglio, was born in Venezuela. The organization has adopted a multimedia approach to its community outreach efforts. Its website calls itself "a true 'virtual community,' a stopping place for anyone concerned about the representation of Latino culture on television."[33]

In addition to the Minority Consortia, programming that supported PTV's diversity mission was also produced by the Independent Television Service. The creation of the ITVS was the result of "a decade-long struggle by independent media artists and community activists to ensure that diverse voices be championed on public television." From its inception, the organization has been guided by a mission statement with the following elements:

> The mission of the Independent Television service is to bring to public television audiences innovative programming that involves creative risks and addresses the needs of unserved and underserved audiences, particularly minorities and children.
>
> Through the funding of independent producers, the Independent Television Service makes a clear commitment to diverse programming of excellence that is insulated from political pressure and marketplace forces and is available free to public television stations.
>
> Furthermore, the Independent Television Service fosters increased opportunity for cooperation between independent television producers and the public broadcasting system to promote original programming, insure maximum carriage, and develop new audiences through independent production.

The ITVS has reaffirmed its founding mission: "to create and present independently produced programs that engage creative risks, advance issues and represent points of views not usually seen on public or commercial television." The ITVS also has reaffirmed its commitment to programming that addresses "the needs of underserved and underrepresented audiences, and expands civic participation by bringing new voices into public discourse." The ITVS has been an industry leader in giving the voice of gays and lesbians a space on public television. Several works have examined the intersection of race and homosexuality. Marlon Riggs's *Tongues Untied*, a video essay on gay African American life, was aired on PBS in July 1991 as part of the *P.O.V.* documentary series. The show was so controversial that it was condemned by influential senators as a blatant promotion of homosexuality as a lifestyle. Nearly half of PTV stations refused to air the show.[34]

Like the Minority Consortia, the ITVS provides grants to support the program production. In 2001, it distributed $7.7 million. The organization has operated two funding strategies—the "open call" and "focused programming."

> The Open Call invites producers to apply for funding for single programs of any length, subject, or genre, including animation, experimental works, short or feature-length narratives, documentaries, and hybrids that may elude easy categorization.
>
> Focused Programming invites works from producers on common themes, and packages them in series or as special television events. These initiatives are designed to illuminate issues of compelling public interest from different viewpoints in a range of styles and formats, and to establish new program configurations to address national and local issues. Focused Programming will overcome an obstacle often faced by independents—the difficulty of programming single and nonstandard-length works—by combining several short works into a single standard-length program, or by combining several programs into one series.[35]

In 2001, several examples of these programming orientations were broadcast on PBS. *In the Light of Reverence,* which was aired as part of the *P.O.V.* series, profiled "American groups struggling to protect sacred sites." *The Return of Navajo Boy* examined the consequences of a 1950s silent film on a Navajo family. *Five Girls,* also aired on *P.O.V.,* explored the lives of "five diverse teenage girls as they confront the challenges of growing up female in the United States." *Passing Through* and *First Person Plural* followed Korean American orphans who were adopted by an American family. *Homeland* addressed contemporary social problems faced by the Lakotas, a Native American community. In 2001, the ITVS also granted funds for the development of another twenty projects, including *Uncle Sam: Global Pimp,* which examined the "role the United States military plays in fostering and regulating prostitution worldwide."[36]

Beyond contributing to programming diversity, the ITVS has committed itself to ensuring that PTV contributes to a free, open, and informed society. To this end, the ITVS articulated the following statements of principle:

Freedom of expression is a human right.

A free press and public access to information are foundations of democracy.

An open society allows unpopular and minority views to be publicly aired.

A civilized society seeks economic and social justice.

A just society seeks participation from those without power, prominence, or wealth.

A free nation allows all citizens forums in which they can tell their own stories and express their own opinions.[37]

These principles were also embedded in the community outreach programs organized by the ITVS. The ITVS has also developed a global orientation through its engagement with Worldlink TV.

Worldlink TV, launched in December 1999 and distributed in the United States through Direct TV and the Dish Network, offers "globally focused, viewer responsive programming—including current affairs stories, documentaries, narratives and music videos." The motivation for the partnership between the ITVS and Worldlink TV was to position the former in the digital environment and to ensure that American independent producers were actively engaged in an international channel. The venture was also seen as a testing ground for the ITVS, providing it with an opportunity to explore new delivery channels and methods and to ensure that there was a place for diverse and independent voices in the "digital, multi-venue, increasingly monopolized media environment."[38]

The Minority Consortia and the ITVS share several structural strategies in their responses to America's diversity. One strategy is the production and distribution of programs with cross-cultural and intercultural capacity—in other words, programming that can engage most sectors of the national audience. Other structural strategies include a commitment to research, the operation of programming archives, the appropriation of the new communication technologies, and participation in the international arena. Participation in the international arena is an outcome of their recognition of the international connections of the racial and ethnic communities in the United States. Limited access to funding prevents the consortia and the ITVS from doing more programming. These common themes need to be drawn upon in the construction of the next generation of human rights: the right to communicate and the right to be understood.[39]

Human Resources

PTV is also informed by the proposition that the presence of minority professionals in public television will have an influence on program content. Since 1989, the Corporation for Public Broadcasting has been reporting to Congress on the employment of minorities in PTV. In the eighties, both the number and the percentage of minorities employed in public broadcasting increased (see table 8.1).[40]

Table 8.1. Minority Employment in Public Broadcasting, 1981 and 1989

	1981	1989
Total employees	12,342	14,713
Minorities	1,845	2,400
Minorities as percentage	14.9	16.3
Total officials and managers	3,035	3,779
Minorities	218	363
Minorities as percentage	7.2	9.6
Total professionals	4,020	5,288
Minorities	525	790
Minorities as percentage	13.1	14.9

Source: Corporation for Public Broadcasting, *To Know Ourselves: A Report to the 101st Congress* (Washington, D.C.: CPB, 1989), 37.

Since the late eighties, public television has been working with the National Association of Black Journalists and the National Association of Hispanic Journalists to develop materials that encourage young blacks and Hispanics to consider careers in broadcast journalism. That is only one aspect of an active minority recruitment and development program. PTV has also created internships and orientation programs, full-time employment, and graduate education opportunities. Among the initiatives of the early nineties were the Independent Minority Producers Laboratory of WETA in Washington, D.C., South Carolina Minority Internships, and KOCE's outreach project in Los Angeles, KOCE Backstage, which introduced minority communities to the public broadcasting business.

In 1991, the Association of American Public Television Stations reported improvements in the hiring of minority staff: "Public TV also is making progress as an equal opportunity employer, with minority employment rising three times faster than total employment. Of the 11,122 people employed in public TV in 1990, 1,938 are members of minority groups. This amounts to 17.4 percent, up from 16.4 percent in 1989. Further, minority employment among stations' major programming decision makers grew by 16 percent in 1989." A decade later, in its report to the 107th Congress, the Corporation for Public Broadcasting reported a 3.6 percent decline in the number of minorities employed by public television stations from 2000 to 2001 (although the overall percentage of minorities remained constant at 18.4 percent). Thirteen public television stations were reported to have no minorities on their staff. The Corporation for Public Broadcasting defines a station to be minority controlled if at least "50 percent of its full-time employees and 50 percent of its governing board are members of minority racial or ethnic groups." In December 2001, there were six minority-controlled public television stations in America—two controlled by African Americans and one each by Native Americans, Hispanics, Asian-Pacific Islanders; one station was controlled by a multicultural group.[41]

Public television is clearly an important element in American television, and, despite criticism about being elitist and privileging Anglo ethnicity, it has been responding to America's diversity. It has delivered on its mission and in the process has expanded the operational definition of minority to include physical impairment and sexual orientation. Through the development of Closed Captioning and Descriptive Video Services, PTV has made it possible for hearing- and sight-impaired Americans to be included in the national discourse on diversity. Due to a shortage of funding, however, the Minority Consortia and the Independent Television Service can produce only programs that tend to be aired during "heritage months." Such programs thus smack of tokenism. And although the anchors and correspondents on PTV's news and current affairs programming have started to reflect America's diversity, the guests and experts on those shows have remained primarily white.

The public television experience, especially the work of the Minority Consortia and the ITVS, has helped Americans understand the nature of the wider world. The global vistas offered by PTV are extensions of its commitment to community and outreach. PTV continues to be criticized for becoming too bureaucratic and too elitist to be of real value to America. This is a powerful criticism, but it has not been able to undermine the question, If not PBS, then who? Public television in America, with its declared commitment to autonomy for local stations, has nourished the idea that as citizens we should not just watch television, we should make it. That idea finds its most complete flowering in community access television, the focus of the next chapter.

9

Noncommercial Television and America's Diversity

Community Access

Don't Just Watch TV—Make It!
—Deep Dish Network bumper sticker

COMMUNITY (OR PUBLIC) access broadcasting is the third sector of the American broadcasting industry. Philosophically, community access broadcasting in America is guided by the ideals of democratic-participant broadcasting theory (see chapter 4), which holds that in order to advance democracy

Individual citizens and minority groups [must] have rights of access to the media [rights to communicate] and rights to be served according to their own determination of need;

The organization and content of media should not be subject to centralized political or state bureaucratic control;

Media should exist primarily for their audiences and not for media organizations, professionals or the clients of the media;

Groups, organizations and local communities should have their own media;

Small-scale, interactive and participative media forms are better than large-scale, one-way, professionalized media;

Certain social needs relating to mass media are not adequately expressed through individual consumer demands, nor through the state and its major institutions;

Communication is too important to be left to professionals.[1]

The United States has three types of community access cable television—public, educational, and governmental. Public access television is theoretically open to any member of the public, although since 1986 there have been efforts to introduce fees for its use. Citizens have resisted this trend on grounds that it restricts the use of public access channels by all members of the community.[2] Educational access channels tend to be operated by colleges and universities and deliver adult education programs, classroom instruction, and continuing education. Government access channels broadcast programs directly related to municipal governance, like the coverage of council meetings and bulletin boards on local matters and events. In this chapter we will emphasize community expression through the public access channels.

The current system of cable access television in America is the result of recommendations to the FCC from the Sloan Commission on Cable Communication, "community television's counterpart to the Carnegie Commission on public television."[3] The commission's recommendations resulted in the Cable Television Report and Order issued by the FCC in 1972 (39). Under that order all cable systems are required to "reserve three non-commercial 'access' channels: educational, governmental, and public" for their service areas (39). The only restrictions on content are that the programs must not be advertisements and that they satisfy FCC guidelines on obscenity.

Over the past three decades, public access television (PATV) in America has been used as a "direct means of communication among citizens without . . . interference from professional middlemen such as journalists, directors, and producers" (1). This was partly a response to a number of forces, including an increasing dissatisfaction with American commercial and public service television. Commercial broadcasting is perceived by some as having become too capitalistic. Its concentration of ownership, vertical integration, and quest to maximize profits have marginalized substantial sectors of American society. Public broadcasting is perceived in some quarters as having become "too paternalistic, too elitist, too close to the 'establishment' of society, too responsive to political and economic pressures, too monolithic, [and] too professionalized." As a result, PTV has failed to become the "emancipatory" vehicle that would "democratize [the] educational system, provide a showcase for unrecognized talent in the arts, and reaffirm American pluralism" as envisioned by the 1967 Carnegie Commission on Educational Broadcasting (2).

It was not surprising, then, when public access television started to spread in the United States as a result of the FCC's order in 1972, that it was positioned as a "tool of empowerment, for fostering a more responsive government and a more democratic culture" (1). Nevertheless, for many Americans in the early nineties, PATV was loony, fringe, and far-out. Its dominant image in the United States at that time was *Wayne's World,* which began as a *Saturday Night Live* comedy sketch about "two head-banging, heavy metal fans with an amateurish show on public access television" and then a low-budget film that became a box-office smash.[4] But there was another side to public access television in the early nineties: it addressed social, political, and cultural issues. Minorities were producing programs on public access channels that responded to their unmet needs. The cable channel in De-Kalb County, Georgia, for example, has aired an increasing number of locally produced Spanish-language broadcasts in response to its growing Hispanic population.[5] Since then, how has public access television responded to the changing racial and ethnic composition of America?

A Brief History of Public Access Television in the United States

The development of cable access television in the United States is intimately associated with three developments in the late sixties and early seventies. One was a cluster of philosophical ideas, and two were related to communication technologies. One element of the philosophical cluster revolves around the democratic-participant model. Another element was the proposal by Mitchell Stephens and Jerome A. Barron that "access to the press" is a fundamental human right implicit in the First Amendment of the U.S. Constitution.[6] Also at this time, as a result of the civil rights movement, the embryonic cable industry—along with all other American institutions—was scrutinized for racist practices. Ossie Davis, celebrated African American actor and civil rights activist, and Benjamin Hooks, the first black commissioner of the FCC, were engaged in ensuring that African Americans were considered during the development of cable access channels in New York—then the epicenter of the development and diffusion of PATV.

Also of special importance in the development of the philosophical underpinnings of public access television in America was the publication of *Guerrilla Television* by the Raindance Corporation's journal *Radical Software* in 1971. Raindance was a video collective whose origins were associated with the "free speech, civil rights, and antiwar movements of the 1960s. The collective supported the idea of appropriating contemporary communication technologies for roles in creating new and just societies. Michael Shamberg, the author of *Guerrilla Television* pinned his hopes on the portable video camera and recorder unit" (11).

The Portapak, introduced by Sony in 1968, was a major technological influence on PATV. It permitted citizens to experiment with making their own programs and sharing them with their community. Engleman reported that, by 1971, PATV stations in Boston, Philadelphia, Detroit, and San Francisco were providing "any local group the opportunity to air its views free-of-charge" (3). *Catch 44,* a nightly half-hour program on WGBH in Boston, featured various social, political, and cultural groups. In Philadelphia, the program was *Take 12;* in Detroit, *Your Turn;* and in San Francisco, *Open Studio* (3–4). That experiment allowed citizens access to public access television facilities. It was different from what emerged in cable television.

The second technological influence on PATV was the rapid diffusion of cable broadcasting in the seventies (21–22). This expansion demanded substantial investments in infrastructure and, by extension, required a substantial number of consumers in order to ensure rapid return on investments. In its quest to garner franchises to operate, the cable television industry did not resist the FCC's 1972 requirement that all cable systems should set aside channels for community access programming. The 1984 Cable Communications Policy Act reaffirmed that recommendation.

THE ALTERNATE MEDIA CENTER

The Alternate Media Center at New York University played a pivotal role in articulating the place of public access television in the America cable industry. The institute provided vision and organization and supported training for the sector. George Stoney, along with Red Burns, developed the center in 1971 to "inform and educate people who were becoming increasingly confused by the integration of new technologies into their lives; to provide a basis upon which people can control these vital information resources; . . . and to increase communication among diverse groups of people."[7] Stoney had recently returned from Canada, where he had served as guest executive director of the Canadian Film Board's Challenge for Change Project from 1968 to 1970. The project used film and, later, Portapak videotape in Canada's war against poverty in the late sixties. Specifically, Challenge for Change aimed at empowering citizens in the use of mass communication technologies to articulate their problems, mobilize community participation, and negotiate with authority structures. In the process, the Challenge for Change project developed a process model that decentered the director as the auteur and replaced her as a facilitator and social catalyst. The Canadian project had demonstrated that the use of these media could help a community define its problems and initiate steps to resolve them. The project also demonstrated the effectiveness of the strategy in opening dialogue with government institutions.

The Alternate Media Center was the prototype of the media centers that would soon exist across the United States. In its early years, the center became associated with a number of activities, including development of cable television in New York; training a cadre of local, nonprofessional communicators in the use of cable technology; organizing internship programs that led to the creation of media centers across America; and influencing public policy on cable television. Through its engagement with the Sloan Commission, the center influenced the development of the FCC's requirements for public access channels in 1972. Through its direct role in the development of media centers across the United States, the center contributed to the diffusion of community access television across the United States. Finally, it was the Alternate Media Center that facilitated the birth of the National Federation of Local Cable Programmers.

NATIONAL FEDERATION OF LOCAL CABLE PROGRAMMERS/ ALLIANCE FOR COMMUNITY MEDIA

The National Federation of Local Cable Programmers (NFLCP) was established in 1976 as a nonprofit membership organization oriented to promoting the development of local programming on cable television. In 1991 the federation described itself as the only national organization "representing the interests and fulfilling the needs of people interested in community uses of cable television." The organization's goals were to:

encourage the production of community responsive programming

stimulate diverse community use of local cable channels

facilitate the exchange of information among people and organizations concerned with community responsive utilization of cable communications

disseminate innovative programming ideas among cable users

assist in the development of all areas of community programming operations

strengthen the political, regulatory, and industry support for public, education, and government [PEG] access

ensure that public, educational, and governmental access continues as a vital force in local media[8]

In 1976, there were fewer than a hundred community cable programming centers. Since the early nineties, the NFLCP has represented more than a thousand PEG access organizations and community media centers throughout America. In 1995, the federation changed its name to the Alliance for Community Media. The organization manages the Hometown Video Awards, which reward excellence in PATV programming and is considered the premier awards program for this sector of the American broadcasting industry. In 2001, the alliance celebrated its twenty-fifth anniversary and stated that it would "continue to work closely with community groups as well as coalition partners and all levels of government to protect community media centers and work to advance forward-looking policies that will aid the transition to digital communications and other advanced technologies." The latter goal is made easier as the industry can draw upon the experiences of the Deep Dish Network.[9]

THE DEEP DISH NETWORK

In the United States, cable access systems operate at national, regional, and local levels. The Deep Dish Network is a national service. It was established in 1986 by Paper Tiger, a New York City–based television production collective. Deep Dish is described as "the first national satellite network linking community-based producers, programmers, activists and people who support the movement for a progressive television network." In 1991, Deep Dish played a significant role in providing programming to over three hundred cable systems. It had developed the capacity to produce and distribute programs on special themes. To initiate the process for producing special programs, Deep Dish staff would choose a topic, "then send out mailings to cable access channels and independent video producers asking if they can contribute. Those who send in acceptable outlines receive funding (a few hundred dollars) and receive guidance from the Deep Dish staff. Regional coordinators take the finished product and edit the raw footage into a program that is eventually beamed out via satellite. Each program has a budget of about $2,000, half of which goes into production and purchasing satellite time."[10]

Deep Dish programs are shown on more than three hundred cable systems, on select PTV stations, and are received by thousands of satellite-dish viewers across America.[11] The network's orientation is programming that "educates and activates." Deep Dish programs are shown in classrooms and are used by community groups for group screenings and discussion. Deep Dish is committed to "progressive television" and to diversity, and most of the programs assembled by the organization in the early nineties addressed themes and topics not usually addressed by commercial or public television. These included themes and topics related to America's minorities. Between 1986 and 1991, Deep Dish transmitted programming that took a critical look at "AIDS, housing, reproductive rights, the environment, labor, and U.S. military interventions." In 1992, Deep Dish's compelling series *Behind Censorship: The Assault on Civil Liberties* was broadcast in its entirety on PBS stations.[12]

Deep Dish's fall 1992 schedule was dedicated to the examination "of Native American survival in the face of 500 years of colonialism and enslavement." Programs in that lineup included *No hay paz*, produced by Roberto Arevalo and Somerville Community Access TV, which examined the conditions of Salvadoran refugees living in the United States. The two-part series *Native Lands*, produced by Glen Raymond for Indian Visions, examined Indian land issues. Also on that theme was *Una historia* by Luis Valdovino and Don Boord. Other programs subjected the quincentenary of Columbus's encounter with the Americas to critical examination. They focused on "racism and the environment" (*The New Resistance*), "Aztlan/Chicano identity" (*Puro Party*), "Native American Youth" (*Youth Speaks*), "Native American women" (*Women of the First Nations*), and "Gay and Lesbian Native Americans" (*Two Spirits*). The fall schedule also featured programs on the Caribbean, Latin America, new communication technologies, community development, and strategies for social change.[13]

Deep Dish's practice of developing special themed programs continued throughout the nineties. Among the specials was the series *Cable Access: Spigot for Bigots or Channels for Change*, a ten-part series in response to the use of public access channels by white supremacists to promote race hate. During the mid-nineties, public access channels across America had to deal with the problem of free speech and hate speech. Municipalities like Kansas City gave up their cable channels rather than accept programming from the Ku Klux Klan. The airing of the KKK-sponsored program *Race and Reason* created tensions in communities across America and threatened to destroy public access television.[14]

PATV programming in the early nineties revealed many programs for America's racial and ethnic minority communities. In Oak Park, Michigan, local cable producers were creating programs that focused on the ethnic festivals of the large Arabic community in that city. In Long Beach, California, local cable programmers were producing programs for the Cambodian refugee community. Similar services were being provided for Portuguese communities in Rhode Island and Boston. In Miami, Haitians were producing programs. Cajun and Asian Indian programs were being aired in New Orleans. Black, Jewish, and Latino programs were broadcast throughout New York City. In 1991, cable access programming was described as a "vital part of almost 2,000 cable systems."[15]

There are many concerns about PATV, including funding, human resources, and underutilization. Of these, underutilization, especially by nonprofit organizations, attracts most attention. In April 1990, the Benton Foundation published Margie Nicholson's *Cable Access*, whose objective was to "encourage nonprofit organizations to take advantage of the cable access facilities in their community." The handbook provided tips on getting involved in access and offered case studies of effective nonprofit uses of cable access for public education, community organizing, fund-raising, and issues of advocacy.[16] The ideas that informed early public access broadcasting remain alive and relevant as it responds to America's changing racial and ethnic composition.

New York Public Access Television

New York is not only one of the most diverse locations in America but developments in public access television in that city have had influence across America. For example, when Mayor Giuliani considered returning cable access channels to MSO, there were concerns that his action would be replicated across the nation and signal the demise of PATV. Public access broadcasting in New York continues to innovate, having developed Interconnect, "a new cable initiative which allows the simultaneous programming of a show across the public-access stations in every borough."[17]

BROOKLYN CABLE ACCESS TELEVISION

Brooklyn Cable Access Television (BCAT) is available on six channels in Brooklyn.[18] BCAT was established to provide members of the community with the services required to "create, produce, and cablecast video programs—and the opportunity to influence, share, enhance, and preserve the borough's diversity of thought and culture." These services are available to any "individual, organization, corporation, or non-commercial entity."[19]

Over the past decade, BCAT has broadcast both series and non-series programs on government and public affairs, health and sports, education and science, and artistic expression. The programming patterns in winter 2002 are typical and reflect the ethnic composition of Brooklyn.[20] Sundays were dominated by religious programs. Mondays were dominated by programs that focused on health and targeted Caribbean and Latino communities. Public affairs programs and programs for Italian Americans dominated Tuesdays. On Wednesdays, the dominant programs were public affairs and programming for the Jewish community. Municipal programs took priority on Thursdays. The programming on Fridays emphasized Haitian themes and music videos. On Saturdays priority was given to children's programs, Brooklyn themes, and programs for the Latin and Caribbean communities. Programs for other European ethnic communities were also evident. Programs such as *Brooklyn Review,* a biweekly newsmagazine; *Street Games,* a program promoting athletics; and *Health Watch,* addressing current health and medical issues, have attracted critical acclaim.

Brooklyn is the host community for a significant number of immigrants from the Caribbean, and since the early nineties BCAT has provided multilingual Caribbean programming (English, French, Haitian Creole, and Spanish). Local politicians, especially those with Caribbean roots, recognize the influence of public affairs programs, especially the popular talking heads, and readily make themselves accessible. West Indian prime ministers and international politicians have been interviewed on these programs. They recognize the importance of the West Indian diaspora in their nations' politics, and these programs help them connect with the various West Indian diasporas in Brooklyn. European ethnic communities, especially those that are still receiving new immigrants, also use the facilities of BCAT. Like the Caribbean programs, European programs can serve as a vehicle to promote political candidates. And like the Caribbean shows, they serve the other mass communication functions: correlation, orientation, cultural transmission, and entertainment.

In 1991, BCAT launched BCAT Community Calendar, a twenty-four-hour listing of community activities and services, presented on Time Warner Channel 57 and Cablevision Channel 70. BCAT offers training courses in many subjects, including training on field, studio, and editing equipment and the use of studio, editing, and graphics facilities. Since 1998, the center has offered courses in video editing, desktop publishing, and Internet use through its Multimedia Lab.[21]

BRONXNET

Bronxnet, established in the early nineties, is based at Lehman College. Programming is in English and Spanish, since the population of the Bronx is predominantly Hispanic. Many programs on Bronxnet have attracted national attention. For example, in 1996, the network was producing the only regular news show, *BXNY,* on any public access station in the city. The half-hour show aired at 4:30 P.M. and repeated during the evening. Other shows, such as *Bronx Live!* have won CableAce and Hometown Video awards. Also in 1996, the channel launched *Comedy Rhumba,* the only "comedy/variety show catering to English-speaking Latinos." Some segments of the show were shot during stand-up comedy shows at the Gotham Club in Manhattan. The public access program was reported to have increased attendance at the live shows. By December 2001, Bronxnet's programming was extended to twenty-four hours a day and continued to reflect language and thematic diversity. Several of its programs, such as *Bronx Live* and *Perspectives*, were underwritten by Aetna.[22]

Perspectives is "an hour-long interactive call-in television program geared to discussing contemporary topics affecting the African American community on both the national and local levels." The show, developed by Daren Jaime, usually features an expert guest and is taped before a live audience. It is aired twelve times a week in various time slots to allow for different viewing patterns. *Perspectives* is also aired three times a week on New York's Interconnect initiative, can be viewed on the Bronxnet website, and is webcast once a week.[23]

Bronx Live! introduced in September 1995, is a monthly series dedicated to showcasing "the best of Bronx performing artists and arts institutions" and spotlighting the "vibrant multi-ethnic and multi-disciplinary arts community and culture that thrives throughout the borough." *Bronx Live!* has presented artists from around the world, including the Cuban dance band Los Van Van in their first performance in the United States. Other performers have come from Africa, New Guinea, Honduras, and Ireland. In addition to musical performance, *Bronx Live!* also presents world-class cinema and drama. *Bronx Live!* won a Hometown Video Award for the Best Performing Arts Series in 1995 and in 1996 was nominated for a CableAce Award. In 1997, Bronxnet received a CableAce for *Behind the Counter with Mussolini*, presented by the Italian American Playhouse, and an Emmy nomination for *Familias*.[24]

Actualidades y mas, a family-oriented variety show with how-to advice segments, won a Bronx Excellence in Television Access (BETA) award in 1996 for excellence in variety and entertainment. Another how-to show is *PC Survival*, which offers help for beginners and advanced users. The show is produced on location at different appropriate venues and is aired three times a week. Other performance shows include: *I Am Magic*, dedicated to the promotion of the art of magic and featuring magicians from the Bronx and the tristate area; *The Stupid Comedy Show*, "a unique sketch, spoof type comedy show for young adults and older"; *Dancer's Night*, featuring students from the Starlite Dance Studio in the Bronx; and *DBD Presents*, profiling original works in the visual and performing arts. Stacy Ellis, an African American, produced *Blackwash*, which presented positive developments in the Bronx community. According to the producer, "blackwash is one of the few words with the root black that has a positive meaning."[25]

Among the religious programs aired on Bronxnet in the nineties were *Church Alive Broadcast*, presented by the Bronx-based Church Alive Ministries, and *Gospel Today*, a half-hour weekly series that showcased professional gospel singers and promising newcomers in the New York area. The show also featured "interviews, play reviews, on-location reports, and a Church of the Week segment." *Cornucopia Utopia*, described as "télévision vérité," celebrated the culture of "marginalized communities, particularly gay/Lesbian/bisexual/transgenderist persons of color" and was produced by queer leftists of color.[26]

The bilingual *El show de Freddy Lopez* featured freestyle music and was aired six times a week. *First Impressions*, specializing in jazz, Latin poetry, and modeling, was taped in the studio and on location. *Latin Jazz Alive and Kicking*, profiled Latin Jazz artists in venues in the Bronx and Manhattan. That show was aired six times per week. *The Ron Alexander Music Variety Show*, also aired six times a week, profiled up and coming musical talent in all musical genres—"R&B, Jazz, Pop Rock, Gospel, Dance, Hip Hop, etc."

Public affairs shows included the biweekly *Frankie Cruz Show* and *Issues: 10462*, also biweekly, which focused on the Parkchester community. Programs for women included *Homemaking* and *Images, Concepts, and Symbols*, a show produced to "empower women and to focus on their potential strengths and weaknesses." The weekly show also examined topical issues such as child abuse, credit, equal rights, welfare, drugs, and juvenile delinquency.[27] Bronxnet programs also addressed health-related themes. For example, *VA Insights*, produced by the U.S. Department of Veterans Affairs, provided a service for the many veterans in the Bronx community by delivering up-to-date information on the health-related problems faced by a disproportionate number of veterans who reside in the Bronx—Gulf War syndrome, post-traumatic stress disorder, depression, substance abuse, spinal cord injury, and homelessness. The show also provided information on steps being taken by the Department of Veterans Affairs to reduce red tape and provide friendlier service. The show was aired twice weekly. Health-related specials appeared on the series *Dialogo en el Bronx.* The specials, taped before a live audience, had call-in segments. They were funded by the Tony Cox Fund and included participants from the community and from the Centers for Disease Control, the Latino Commission on AIDS, and the Gay Men's Health Crisis. The series was produced and hosted by Glennis Henriques, a middle school teacher. More than half the programs aired on Bronxnet are produced by persons trained by the system.

QUEENS PUBLIC TELEVISION

Queens Public Television (QPTV), a nonprofit corporation, participates in "the training and education of residents of Queens (on a limited basis) in the production, development, and cable casting of programs for, by and about Queens."[28] In 1996, QPTV aired twelve hours of programming a day. In 2000, it produced 1,155 programs at its Jamaica and Flushing facilities. Like the rest of the New York cable access centers, QPTV started to switch to the digital environment in 2000 and launched the QPTV cyber center (QueensNet.org).

QPTV operates a grant program to support community productions. Among those programs, several have addressed themes of diversity. *Musical Bridges* explored relationships between Jewish and Muslim musical traditions from several countries. The program was produced by the Queens Council on the Arts and performed at the Free Synagogue of Flushing. *A Hidden Feud,* an original teleplay produced by Flying Bridge Community Arts, addressed race relations. *Celebrate Jamaica* (the Queens neighborhood), also produced by the Queens Council on the Arts, explored the arts of China in Sun Yat-sen Hall at St. John's University. *Through Immigrant Eyes,* a half-hour documentary produced by the City University of New York, focused on an African immigrant realizing his American dream through participation in the CUNY Language Immersion Program.[29]

CTV, Staten Island's public access television system, started broadcasting in 1988 and now operates four channels. Channel 34 broadcasts eighteen hours a day during the week and twenty-four hours a day on Saturday and Sunday. The second broadcast channel, Channel 35, is on the air about fifty hours a week. The two other channels (channels 56 and 57) serve as twenty-four-hour community bulletin boards. Despite being a predominately white borough, Staten Island does have racial and ethnic diversity, as reflected by several CTV programs.[30] *Black Rodeo* and *Caribbean Festival* have a Black History Month theme and thus smack of tokenism. The jazz show *Just Cooling* features recorded performances by Dexter Gordon, Charles Mingus, and Sarah Vaughan. *Cable to Jewish Life* presents people and issues in Judaism. *African Leadership Council's Vision of Africa* features the views of continental Africans in America. Absent from the schedule are programs for Asians, ethnic Europeans, and Haitians. Spanish-language programming was very limited and unidimensional, not reflecting the internal diversity of Latinos in America. The only Spanish-language program on the channel was the gospel show *Jesucristo, Poder y vida.* However, Channel 34's programming log indicates that it has aired a wider range of ethnic programs in the past. Like most PATV services, the programs mentioned are rebroadcast several times during the month.

MANHATTAN NEIGHBORHOOD NETWORK

Manhattan Neighborhood Network (MNN), established in 1993, is a nonprofit organization responsible for administering all PATV in Manhattan. The organization describes its purpose as ensuring "the ability of Manhattan residents to exercise their First Amendment rights through the medium of cable television and to create opportunities for mutual communication, education, artistic expression and other noncommercial uses of video facilities on an open, uncensored and equitable basis." MNN manages four channels that were originally operated as separate public access channels on the Time Warner and RCN cable systems in Manhattan (an arrangement made in 1993 as part of an effort to reenergize cable access television in the borough). In 1994, Mitchell Mos, director of NYU's Urban Research Center, reflecting on twenty-five years of PATV in New York, described it as an "underachieving medium." He claimed that MNN had not made enough effort to connect the channel with the "organic elements of the community" and that the channel was being used by individuals "fulfilling juvenile fantasies [and] not by community organizations." In response to those criticisms, the network did agree that there was work to be done on increasing the engagement of organizations. Its first priority was training and community outreach.[31]

The programming on MNN has attracted positive attention by the mainstream elite press. For example, the *New York Times* previewed the film *Un viernes social* (A social Friday), about a Latina immigrant who suffers severe beatings from a perpetually drunken husband. The film was shot on location in the apartment of Aida Ayala and produced by the El Barrio Popular Education Project as part of the MNN series *Temas nuestros* (Our ideas).[32] It was clear that despite problems with production values—echoes on the sound track and jerky camera movements—the film was serving a serious social need.

Spanish-language programs such as *Temas nuestros* have proliferated on MNN over the years. The program guide for January 21, 2002, shows the network airing more than forty-eight hours a week of programs for Manhattan's Spanish-speaking residents. Closer examination reveals the internal diversity of the Spanish-speaking community in the broadcasting area. Programs were directed specifically to Mexicans, Cubans, Afro-Cubans, Dominicans, Hondurans, "Central Americans," and Tainos (indigenous Caribbean Americans). There were even programs for Brazilians, as well as for other diverse ethnic groups, such as Hungarians, Israelis, and Chinese. Again, the parsimony principle was evident, as most of the programs were music or talk shows.

In addition to inexpensively produced programming that reflects the internal diversity of minority communities in America, MNN also features some "expensive genres," which have included *Strange Fruit*, a soap opera about drag queens, and *The Next Tomorrow*, a

Caribbean-oriented soap opera. Further, at least 10 percent of the Spanish-language shows have been comedies, providing an opportunity to use more vernacular Spanish, as distinct from the homogenized Spanish that is presented through Spanish-language programming on commercial television.

Boston Public Access Television

SOMERVILLE COMMUNITY ACCESS TELEVISION

Some of the nation's oldest public access centers are to be found in Massachusetts. Community activists in Somerville, adjacent to Boston, were some of the first in the country to organize for public access to the telecommunications infrastructure and develop independent nonprofit management for cable access. These early experiences have led to a high degree of collaboration, responsiveness, and innovation in public access programming in Boston. As a result of negotiations between Warner Cable and a few motivated Somerville residents in 1972, Somerville became one of the first communities in the nation to have public access channels. City Hall ran the government access channel, the public library ran educational access, and Warner managed the public access channel. Warner Cable was licensed for ten years. These first ten years of PATV in Somerville saw both success and failure. "The programs varied: local sports teams watched themselves play on television for the first time, residents could see their aldermen in action, and kids were given a chance to create their own programs. Some shows offended some residents, but many inspired more people to get involved."[33]

In 1982, during the negotiations for the next ten-year license, it was decided to transfer the day-to-day operations of the public access and educational channels to "a new non-profit, community-based organization," Somerville Community Access Television. SCAT began operations in 1983 and "became one of the first non-profit access management organizations in the country."[34] SCAT is still in operation and responding to community challenges in innovative ways. For example,

SCAT recently developed a domestic violence awareness campaign in collaboration with two other community-based organizations.

Forty percent of Boston's non-English-speaking inhabitants live in the Somerville area, and over 60 percent of Somerville's residents do not speak English as their first language. The predominant groups speak Spanish, Portuguese, and Haitian Creole. Domestic violence had been a major social and public health problem in the community. SCAT's response to the problem was the development of a coalition with RESPOND, a local domestic violence organization, to develop a video/television campaign for the Boston area aimed at increasing public awareness. The organizations recognized that local programming increased local awareness. One outcome of the coalition was the production of three short videos for use in community outreach—*Playing for Safety, When Dating Is Dangerous,* and *Immigrants Facing Domestic Violence*—through the participation of the police department, youth groups, immigrant services agencies, and other community organizations. The participants were involved in workshops on domestic violence and video production and presentation. The result was the three videos that have been used in community outreach.[35]

Somerville Community Access Television encourages the free expression of diverse ideas by providing production facilities, technical assistance, and air time. The network also airs programs produced by Boston Neighborhood Network Television for Boston's diverse communities.

BOSTON NEIGHBORHOOD NETWORK TELEVISION

Boston Neighborhood Network Television (BNN-TV) was launched in 1984 with the following mission:

giving a more direct voice to and fostering understanding among various neighborhoods, groups and points of view

expanding the diversity and variety of information on local topics addressing the specific needs of targeted populations increasing the access of residents to educational, cultural, political, health and human service resources of the city

strengthening the ability of all institutions to serve Boston's diverse residents by providing a mechanism though which they can effectively share their resources with the community

providing overall local television programs and opportunities not available on other television venues in Boston[36]

The network broadcasts on two channels (Channels 9 and 23) and presents programs for Boston's multicultural communities, including the many new immigrant and refugee groups: Chinese, Vietnamese, Cambodian, Iranian, Haitian, Russian, and Somali among them. The network also aired programs in Greek, Spanish, Arabic, and in Portuguese for Boston's Cape Verdean community. In addition, there are programs for Boston's Italian and Irish communities.

Among the programs directed to Boston's African American community are the half-hour public affairs program *My Boston* as well as *Thug TV! G.H.E.T.T.O., Strickly Hip-Hop,* and *Nation of Islam.* The hour-long *Asian Spectrum* focused on health care and events in the Asian community. Other programs for Boston's Asian communities were more ethnically specific. For example, *Viet TV* and *Khmer TV* focused on the Vietnamese and Khmer Rouge communities. *The Russian Hour* and *The Blue Globe,* a thirty-minute Russian language magazine show, targeted Boston's Russian community. Available to the Greek community are *Cooking with Georgia, The Greek Program,* and the internationally syndicated *Grecian Melodies. Il mondo in cui viviamo* (The world we live in) and *Ireland on the Move* served the Italian and Irish communities.

The Haitian community could select from *HAT-TV, Presenting Haiti, Festival kreyol* (Creole festival), *Tele kreyol, Christ le seul espoir* (Christ, the only hope) and *La dernière heure* (The final hour). West Indians were served with the program *Caribbean Insight.* BNN-TV offers *Jerusalem On Line,* a half-hour "news and culture program from Jerusalem for the Jewish diaspora and others," as well as *Islamic Perspectives* and *The Arabic Hour. Tu opinión cuenta* (Your opinion counts), *Congregación León de Juda,* and *Consejos de salud* (Health advice) are programs for the Spanish-speaking community. Recent African refugee communities are also targeted. In addition to *Ethiopian Weekly* and *Eritrean Community TV,* the Somalian Development Center presents shows in the Somali language. BNN-TV aired the program *Immigrant Voices* weekly and that program had an immigrant focus.[37]

Among the network's prominent programs is the Monday-through-Friday show *Neighborhood Network News,* produced since 1984 by the Boston Community Access and Programming Foundation "in cooperation with Boston University." The newscast's declared mission is to "concentrate on the news of Boston itself," and its producers claim that, through its coverage of Boston's news and by "serving as a platform for a variety of guests, the show [has become] both a forum and a crossroads for the full range of the city's communities."[38]

BNT-TV has training programs for the new communication technologies, and the BNN Multimedia Center provides training in the new multimedia technologies–website design, digital video production, nonlinear editing, and streaming media. The van operated by the center supports field productions. BNT-TV's declared vision for the future includes stabilizing itself financially, creating long-term organizational viability, and ensuring that BNN continues to "represent the diversity and wealth of experiences among the residents and community institutions of the City of Boston, old and new."[39]

Chicago Public Access Television

CHICAGO ACCESS NETWORK

Chicago Access Network Television (CAN TV), established in 1983, operates five channels, whose programming reflects Chicago's religious, ethnic, and racial diversity. The network reported that, in 1997, 92 percent of Chicago residents believed that CAN TV was valuable to the community. Sixty percent of the programs on CAN TV are locally produced. and many are aimed at Chicago's recent immigrant communities. In 1997, CAN TV introduced *Haiti rencontre* (Haiti encounter), the first Haitian television show in the Midwest. The program presents, in English and Creole, "the people, art and culture of Haiti, with an eye toward debunking some of the myths about the nation." The producer of the show, Jacques Leblanc, considers himself an "ambassador." *Haiti rencontre* has been joined by *Haiti jeunesse* (Haiti youth), and *L'heùre missioniare* (The missionary hour). As for religious diversity, CAN TV also offers *Muhammad and Friends, Taped with Rabbi Doug, El evangelio eterna* (The eternal gospel), and *Conquistando las naciones* (Vanquishing the nations), as well as several programs for Chicago's African American community. Other programs by the African American community have been *The Underground Railroad, African American Contractors' Association,* and *Black Women Lawyers' Association,* the latter aimed at educating the community about the legal process. CAN TV also broadcasts *Latino American Motorcycles,* dedicated to motorcycle touring in Latin America, and *Tropical Riddims and Beats,* showcasing the music of the English-speaking Caribbean community.[40]

Programming for ethnic European communities reminds us of the diversity that was present in Chicago when Robert Park did his groundbreaking work on the intersection of immigration and the press in the early 1920s. *Radio France International,* a two-hour program from France, is broadcast seven days a week, from 7 to 9 A.M. The French news program *La journal* is also aired seven days a week, from 11 to 11:30 P.M., followed by the Italian news show *Notiziario RAI,* produced by Italy's state-owned broadcasting corporation. These broadcasts do more than bring news from France and Italy to audiences in Chicago. They help promote the perspectives of those governments and maintain linkages between the ethnic communities in Chicago and their "old countries" (see chapter 1 on local placement, one of the tactics of public diplomacy). Other European ethnic programs on CAN TV include *Serb View, Irish Journal,* and *Romanian Television. Ashur TV* addressed issues facing Assyrians from northern Iraq.

However, CAN TV's programming does not serve Chicago's internally diverse Asian populations. Chicago has a thriving Chinatown and many Asian Indians. Also absent are programs for the continental African communities, especially the refugee groups, such as the Ethiopians and Eritreans who settled in Chicago in the eighties and nineties. Despite this deficiency, CAN TV provides us with an opportunity to observe the tactics of local placement in public diplomacy and presents public access programming that is intercultural in orientation. Furthermore, CAN TV has received many local and national awards.

An interesting dimension to CAN TV is its intercultural programs—those with themes relevant to more than one community. For example, *African World View: A Different Perspective* "presents current news direct from Africa and the Caribbean, and discusses issues related to the African diaspora that mainstream media often ignores."[41] Clearly, the show intends to support the construction of transnational identities. CAN TV also airs two intercultural immigration-related shows that would have been described by Robert Park as serving an "accelerator role." *CAAELII Immigration* is a call-in program produced by the Coalition of African, Asian, European, and Latino Immigrants of Illinois to support its citizenship program. *Immigration Issues,* produced by Centro sin Fronteras, the Illinois Coalition of Immigrant Refugee Rights, and World Relief, offers "information about the immigration process and advocates for immigrants' rights."[42]

Public Access Television in the Washington, D.C., Area

ARLINGTON COMMUNITY TELEVISION

Arlington Community Television (ACT) is a nonprofit corporation that has provided production facilities, including a mobile production van and training programs, for the residents of Arlington, Virginia. ACT is located at George Mason University's Law School, where it broadcasts telecourses between one and four in the afternoon, Monday through Friday. Over the past three decades, this suburb of Washington has become a very diverse community, and ACT has responded to that diversity. In the early nineties, the system broadcast programs in the Dari language for the more than fifteen thousand Afghanis living in suburban Washington. The shows presented news and information about Afghanistan's civil war, which was twenty years old at that time. The January 2001 schedule featured programming for Spanish-speakers, Ethiopians and other continental Africans, Vietnamese, Chinese, and Muslims. ACT also presents programs for seniors and the disabled. So, like many other public access channels, the ACT program schedule represents a more inclusive definition of diversity.[43]

Like most public access channels, ACT has had its share of controversy. One involved its airing of Jamie Yerkes's award-winning film *Cowboy Jesus* in 1998. *Cowboy Jesus* is on "one level the story of an interracial (black and white) lesbian love affair. It is also an update of the New Testament, set against a modern urban landscape: Jesus comes back as a black lesbian who rides a Harley."[44] ACT has won national recognition for its work since 1990. In 1998, ACT won a national award for overall excellence from the Alliance for Community Media. ACT is also the home of the Rosebud Film and Video Festival, established in 1990, whose goal is to "honor the innovative, experimental, unusual and deeply personal in creative film and video making."[45] A continued survey of public access television in the United States during the last decade will reinforce many of the patterns we have noted so far—a responsiveness to diversity, a propensity toward controversy, a readiness to appropriate the new communication technologies to extend reach and improve citizen access, a readiness to join coalitions to address social challenges, and an increasing tendency to support intercultural communication.

American broadcasting practices have had global influence. The late Sydney Head pointed out that it was America's commercial broadcasting model that influenced the organization and operation of commercial broadcasting in Latin America. Many countries have proceeded with the liberalization of their broadcasting environments, and more and more of them are looking at the practices of American noncommercial broadcasting, including PATV. Has the American experience with public access television had any influence beyond the United States?

American Public Access Television: A Gift to the World?

Britain's Channel 4 started to broadcast American PATV programs in 1993. Packaged together under the title *Manhattan Cable,* they proved to be very popular. According to Tim Lapin, of *The Scotsman,* British audiences watched the show "with an intrigued mixture of voyeurism and cultural condescension." A popular position was that public access–style television would not be popular in the United Kingdom. That turned out to be wrong.[46]

On Saturday, May 6, 1995, Channel 4 started its own version of public access television titled *Takeover TV.* According to Lappin, the eight-week series featured "more than 300 Britons making a complete exhibition of themselves and proving that if the Yanks have a monopoly on kookiness, good old British eccentricity is alive and frolicking." The new program was a collaboration with the American independent producers Fenton Bailey and Randy Barbato, who had produced *Manhattan Cable.* The packaging of American public access television was popular in the United Kingdom because of the mixture of aesthetics and "the regular possibility of profanity, nudity and casually explicit terms."[47]

Efforts to bring American-styled public-access television to Hong Kong were not successful. Many arguments were arrayed against its introduction—first, that there was no precedent for PATV in Asia. Second, that experiences in other countries (clearly referring to the United States) suggested that public access television "can create immense problems, including offences against public morality and taste." Third, that it tends to be difficult to work out who should be allowed to have access and that such a channel would "run out of steam after a few months, ending up being dominated by a handful of interest groups and becoming a drain on public funds." The anti–public access stance was a surprise for many Hong Kong residents, as the decision to introduce cable television was made on the grounds that it would include three public access channels. The reversal by the Hong Kong government was recognized as an accommodation to the politics associated with the reunification of Hong Kong and China.[48]

Other countries have public access television, including the Netherlands and Brazil. An important international forum for public access broadcasters from around the world is the annual conference of the Alliance for Community Media, a venue for the exchange of information on issues facing public access television—among them: programming trends,the First Amendment, court decisions, local government actions, the maneuvering of cable operators, and funding.[49]

Our survey of public access television in the United States suggests that its individualistic, *Wayne's World* image persists, both domestically and internationally. However, that perception is passing as PATV engages in more community-oriented programming. PATV also seems to be responding aggressively to America's diversity. It airs more non-English-language programs than any other sector of the American broadcasting environment.[50]

Further, PATV programming is pushing the boundaries of diversity. It is more inclusive, responding to gender, age, class, disability and sexual orientation. These categories also intersect with race and ethnicity to give new texture and meaning to American's diversity. In the process, public access television is strengthening what is meant by free speech in America and continues to play an ever-increasing role in the American electoral politics at the state and federal levels, as it plays a role in making American municipal government public. An article in the *Christian Science Monitor* in 2002 concluded that PATV was providing "some of the most vibrant coverage of real-life America today" because it has become "more fine tuned to local mores and interests." More and more surveys indicate that audiences are "keeping dates" with their public access channels. The *Monitor's* article mentioned that TV 23 is a regular stop for 80 percent of the residents in Cobb County, Georgia.[51]

By expanding its programming to include genres like documentaries and soap operas, PATV is able to offer a more textured examination of themes relevant to America's diversity. More nationally recognized talent and personalities are being seen on public access, especially in the music and comedy shows. PATV is proving to be an important avenue for making contact with many audience segments. The current reenergizing of PATV is also attributable to access to better equipment. In fact, some public access centers have better equipment that some commercial and noncommercial stations—a far cry from the salvaging that took place to create the first public access center.[52] The new technological capacity of public access television is allowing for improved interactivity.[53]

Potential pitfalls lurking along PATV's path in the twenty-first century are associated with funding, free speech, and the continued expansion of the commercial sector of American broadcasting. Because of the differences in funding approaches, public access television is not under commercial pressure. However, there is increasing dependence on foundation dollars and underwriting. These practices can compromise PATV's programming content and orientation. The emerging practice of introducing user fees, for example, can have a disproportionately negative impact on immigrants, refugees, and people of color. To further mute these groups would undermine American democracy. First Amendment rights will be further challenged as groups that promote hate hijack public access television. Experiences with *Race and Reason,* have shown that some communities even considered shutting down their public access channels as a means of removing racist shows like *Race and Reason* from the air. Public access television will have to find a strategy to respond to that form of terrorism.

In their investments in new technologies and their quest to maximize returns on their investments in the shortest possible time, media monopolies wish to use all available channels to market their new products. The channels allocated for PATV have thus become attractive. It is possible that we will witness the gentrification of public access. As with housing in urban America, the new residents can disregard the old residents or price them out of the market. These potential pitfalls can undermine America's ability to respond to the its own diversity and its ability to be an influential voice in the world.

Responses to Television Programs at the Intersection of Immigration and Diversity

Most of the new immigrants and minorities I interviewed in 1991 on their impressions about broadcasting watched television daily. Most had a favorite commercial television network and favorite shows. It was surprising how popular *The Simpsons* and *South Park* were among the Asian participants. A male Indian respondent suggested that those shows helped new residents acquire American slang and other vernacular skills. Other popular entertainment shows included *Friends, The Late Show,* and C-SPAN's *Books on TV.* News shows produced by the commercial and cable networks were also popular among respondents. These included local shows like *First Watch,* CNN programs like *World Report,* and the nightly newscasts of ABC, CBS, NBC, and Fox. The motivations for watching minority-oriented television programs were similar to those offered for listening to minority oriented radio (see chapter 5). The same Indian interviewee commented, "I love the dances that [are] shown and I can see what's happening at home."[54] Interviewees also indicated a higher level of satisfaction with minority-oriented television programming than with its radio counterpart. Seventy-three percent of the respondents reported some degree of satisfaction with the news and information programming from minority producers.[55] However, nearly half of respondents indicated they were "very dissatisfied" with entertainment programs from minority producers. These descriptive statistics are not offered to prompt generalizations but to give us a flavor of the perceptions associated with the dynamics at the intersection of immigration, diversity, and broadcasting, in New York City, one of the most diverse places in the United States.

During the in-depth interviews, participants were asked the following questions:

What impressions do you think Americans get about your country of origin and its culture from mainstream American television programs?

What impressions do you think Americans get about your country of origin and its culture from television programs produced and presented by people from your home country or the region of the world you are from?

What impressions do you think Americans get about your local community in the United States from television programs produced and presented by people from your home country or the region of the world you are from?

In general interviewees felt that the mainstream media, including television, tend to provide unidimensional, stereotypical treatments of non-American subjects and locales. As with the responses about radio programming, it is evident that the media's treatment is a function of the status the community enjoys in the United States. For example, an Irish female respondent, who had been living in the United States since 1982, remarked that the mainstream media encourage Americans to "imagine that Irish music is only about traditional and folk tunes. They probably think there aren't many contemporary artists or anything interesting going on."[56] A respondent from Israel explained that it is difficult for American media to give an objective perspective on Israel because of the complexity of the ongoing crises in the Middle East. A Chinese respondent commented that "Americans might get the impression that my country of origin is poor." She added that American mainstream media fail to give her nation's culture the same respect they give European nations. She stressed that American "television programs should introduce more Asian actors and actresses" and added, "Producers should be more careful when they arrange exotic scenes. For example, people often combined Japanese and Chinese aesthetics as if Asian countries and their cultures are the same." According to an Iranian respondent, only English people are portrayed as "upright and civil" in the American media. Caribbean participants were concerned that "[t]elevision advertising here [New York] glamorizes Caribbean islands and does not show the day-to-day struggles or triumphs."[57] Guyanese Americans felt that mainstream media coverage of Guyana was inaccurate and not well informed.

IMPRESSIONS OF HOME COUNTRIES FROM
MINORITY-PRODUCED PROGRAMS

Opinions varied. One could detect two tendencies, one positive and the other negative. Like the responses reported in the radio sector,

Irish, Indian, and East Indian Guyanese offered a positive position. According to the Irish respondent, "There is one news program, *Out of Ireland,* that is informative and quite good. If Americans watched, I think they'd get a better understanding of Ireland."[58] The Indian indicated that Indian programming in the United States celebrates India's diversity. The East Indian Guyanese indicated that Americans would get satisfactory impressions of people from his background.

Again, the African Caribbean respondents were dissatisfied with their perceptions of Caribbean-produced media in the United States (New York). According to a Barbadian respondent, "most Americans see the Caribbean as if it were all dread[lock]s and heavy accents." An African Guyanese concluded that Caribbean programming reinforces the perception that Caribbean people are "carefree, rum-drinking people." An East Indian Guyanese offered, "because of the political turmoil in Guyana [it is] being associated with Latin countries that are extremely poor."

IMPRESSIONS OF LOCAL COMMUNITIES FROM
MINORITY-PRODUCED PROGRAMS

According to some of the respondents, minority media practitioners have adopted many of the practices of the mainstream media, especially in the production of news. There is a tendency to go for the sensational. As a result, one Caribbean respondent indicated that American viewers of Caribbean news programming in New York would get the impression that the community was "a dangerous place" with people who were "not serious." The Chinese participant suggested that Americans would "get an impression that Chinatown is a money-making place for gangsters from Taiwan, Hong Kong, and mainland China."

These perceptions will be useful in assessing the performance of the American broadcasting industry and its responses to the nation's diversity.

10

A Map of the Intersection

The intersection of immigration, diversity, and broadcasting in the United States is a very complex environment. In addition to the obvious issues of race and ethnicity, there are issues of politics and governance; economics and trade; culture, gender, values, and morals; peace and war; love and hate. There are several actors engaged in broadcasting at this intersection in the United States—transnational corporations, U.S. governmental agencies, foreign governments, private entrepreneurs (ranging from owners of independent radio and television stations to minority independent producers who use brokerage practices), community activists, and special interest groups. For transnational corporations and the private entrepreneur, America's diversity is an important revenue source that is of increasing significance. For transnational corporations, success with American diversity could signal success in other contexts around the world. For American governmental agencies, this intersection is a site for operationalizing law and demonstrating American political values. For foreign governments, this space provides a site for practicing public diplomacy and a way of maintaining contact with their former nationals now living in the United States.

Racial and ethnic minority producers are motivated to participate in broadcasting for many reasons. An important reason is the opportunity to generate income. However, that is not the only reason. A 1992 survey of independent producers revealed other motivations, including an opportunity to continue a career, responsibility to the community, and an opportunity for personal aggrandizement. Radio Caracol succeeded in Miami because Colombian broadcasters living there were able to continue their careers. Many popular minority broadcasters, like Indo-Guyanese Ishri Singh in New York, bring their homeland popularity with them to the United States.

Community responsibility as a motivation for engaging in minority broadcasting is most evident among broadcasters from minority groups with many refugees. In the 1992 study, this motivation was dominant among Eastern European broadcasters in America. Their programs were developed to support community solidarity and encourage resistance to totalitarian regimes in their home countries. With the fall of the Soviet Union, their roles shifted to support for the development of democratic regimes. Similar patterns are currently evident among the Ethiopian, Eritrean, and Sudanese refugee communities in America. The minority broadcasters who are motivated by community responsibility tend to have some ascribed status within that community, either through family ties, religious office, or former political status. Generally, most of the actors, including the audiences of minority broadcasting in America, appear to subscribe to variations on the libertarian ideological paradigm. In the following sections I shall attempt to answer the three sets of questions I posed in the introduction.

How Has Broadcasting Responded to the Changing Society?

How has broadcasting in the United States, especially between 1991 and 2001, responded to the changing racial and ethnic composition of our society?

What patterns can be drawn from these responses?

What functions have been and are being served?

What stimulates the changing of the roles of broadcasting?

With the end of the Cold War, the United States has emerged as the dominant superpower, a status that has attracted both love and hate. Ideologically, the United States has become more conservative. Hate crimes and other manifestations of intolerance are on the rise. Until recently, the economy enjoyed unprecedented growth. Between 1990 and 2001, the stock market grew dramatically, fueled in part by advances in the new communication technologies. One consequence was the dramatic mergers and acquisitions that changed the way the American broadcasting environment was organized. That, coupled with the nation's power in the world, has given the American broadcasting industry a global influence.

The shift in the racial and ethnic composition of the United States that started with the changes in the nation's immigration laws in 1965 has accelerated. The 2000 census confirmed that communities of color are growing at dramatic rates, which will clearly have architectonic consequences for the United States. One prediction held that, by 2056, people of color would be the numerical majority in the United States. The "browning of America" has stoked the nation's historical ambivalence to immigration. The admissionist and restrictionist voices have been equally strident.

Those were not the only areas of contestation in the domestic reality of the United States in the last decade and a half. Clintonian Democrats and Gingrichian Republicans fought to articulate and establish the nation's political culture, and a phenomenon described as "diversity fatigue" became evident. Policies such as affirmative action were undermined and, in some cases, reversed. As a consequence of this environment, all sectors of the American broadcasting industry responded, each in its own way, to the changing racial and ethnic composition of American society.

THE COMMERCIAL SECTOR

Simply stated, the dominant mainstream commercial sector responded in ways that supported opportunities to increase profitability and developed strategies to quicken the return on its substantial investments in infrastructure. It also responded to legal requirements and moral suasion, particularly to efforts to demonstrate racial, ethnic, and gender inclusion. The pattern of responses by the commercial sector can be described as patriarchal.

THE PUBLIC BROADCASTING SECTOR

The responses of the public broadcasting sector were informed by the nation's legal framework and the assertiveness of community partners. Various telecommunications acts require this sector to respond to the nation's diversity. In these acts, the definition of diversity has been extended to be include physical abilities.

THE COMMUNITY/ALTERNATIVE SECTOR

The community sector's responses were informed by a constellation of factors—legal, technological, and ideological. As cable networks expanded by appropriating the new communication technologies, so did opportunities for alternative broadcasting. Concerns with the concentration of power in the broadcasting industry and the associated muting of the voices of diversity led to demands for a new legal regime. This terrain also encouraged increases in illegal broadcasting—pirate radio, microradio, and expansion in the public access television sector.

In 1989, the director of the Friedrich Naumann Foundation in New York observed, "In the United States virtually no television program from the developing countries are broadcast and the few feature films which are shown have a limited audience."[1] Despite the domination by the mainstream commercial sector—over-the-air and cable—it is possible for Americans to consume broadcast products from around the world. In this context, the United States is sharing a reality with other settler states such as Australia, Canada, and Germany. This reality has been described by Hamid Mowlana as the "ethnicization of the media." Further, there has been a tendency to expand the definition of diversity into new directions. Diversity in the American broadcasting environment appears to have gone beyond race and ethnicity and has incorporated sexual orientation, physical abilities, and religious orientation. In some contexts, these additional categories have been used in an effort to steer away from the still unresolved problems of race and ethnicity. In addition, the notion of diversity has been extended through management practices like supplier diversity and "charter advertising." These approaches to diversity have been undermined by legal reversals in the interpretation of affirmative action and EEO legislation and requirements. In addition to these reversals, structural hindrances, such as a minority dictates, make it clear that racism remains in the operating environment of American broadcasting.

As for the patterns associated with these responses to diversity, clearly the commercial sector responded by seeking to maximize profits. The public sector responded as required by law, and the alternative sector responded in ways that sought to expand public participation. In addition to the classic functions of orientation, surveillance, cultural transmission, and entertainment, American broadcasting has played a number of other roles, including:

a link with sending societies and a vehicle for delivering public diplomatic programming. In this mode, broadcasting at the intersection of immigration and diversity in the United States plays an important role in consolidating and expanding diasporas.

a community resource for resisting racism and exclusion.

a vehicle for protesting and resisting invasions in sending countries.

an educational facilitator, especially in language, health, and civic education.

a facilitator of intercultural discourse through cultural proximity, especially racial and religious proximity, as is evident in the development of the Chinese, Indian, and Islamic diasporas.

Despite evidence of increased intercultural communication, broadcasting at the intersection of immigration and diversity is still predominantly oriented to intracultural discourse. The programming, especially that produced by independent producers, tends to reproduce racial and ethnic schisms evident in sending countries. The functions performed by American broadcasting at the intersection of immigration and diversity are changed by a number of domestic and international factors. At the domestic level they include the assertiveness of the minority community, its economic status, its political salience in the American political environment; the proximity of its values to mainstream American values, and the status its "old country" enjoys in the United States. At the international level, a key factor is the importance of the community in the United States to its sending society (e.g., the recent importance of the East Indian Guyanese to Guyanese politics).

How Do Broadcasting's Responses Measure Up?

Have these responses conformed to society's expectations of the performance of broadcasting in a democratic and multicultural society?

Do these responses advance the nation's founding ambitions of opportunity for all, responsibility for all, and community for all?

To answer these questions we must return to the evaluative concepts associated with normative theory: freedom, equality, diversity, information quality, social order and solidarity, and cultural order (see chapter 4). Although these concepts are interrelated, for this evaluation they will be treated separately.

FREEDOM

It is generally accepted that freedom in the American broadcasting environment has two dimensions. The first dimension can be described as a condition, it refers to the rights of free expression and the free formation of opinion—in other words, access to a wide range of voices. Second, for freedom of expression and free formation of opinion to become operational, citizens must have access to broadcasting channels and audiences must have "opportunities to receive diverse kinds of information."[2] Indicators of a free broadcasting environment include: the legal freedom to transmit or publish, independence from economic and political pressures, opportunities for voices in society to gain access to channels, and assurance that receivers will be able to receive products that are relevant, diverse in perspective, reliable, interesting, original, and satisfying. The industry's response to America's diversity reaffirms a general commitment to freedom. The broadcasting environment provides access through a number of approaches—brokerage in the commercial sector, legal requirements in the public service sector, and public access practices in the community/alternative sector. There is even a window of illegal practice—microradio—that increases access.[3]

There is a general question about the real independence of the American mass media from economic and political pressure. It is generally agreed that there are pressures on broadcasters in every sector of broadcasting in the United States. Large corporate advertisers exert influence on the content and schedules of commercial television. Similarly, public television is influenced by its dependence on funding from corporations and foundations. These pressures are very evident when we look at the practices of independent program producers. Many of these practitioners are influenced by their advertisers. Recall Annan Boodram's description of Caribbean television in New York as "one big infomercial—promoting mortgage bankers and real estate brokers." Many of the programs delivered by independent program producers are de facto local placement vehicles for foreign political parties and foreign governments.

The quality of programs has not been consistent across the American broadcasting industry, from the early days of Polish radio to the persistent equating of cable access television with the aesthetics of *Wayne's World*. Poor quality is generally an indicator of dubious content—not only sound, lighting, and framing but truth, reliability of information, and accuracy. This lack of quality resides primarily in brokerage radio and in the public access arena, where it is accepted as being par for the course. It must be addressed through training so that it does not further undermine the expectations associated with broadcasting freedom in America.

EQUALITY

The idea of equality in broadcasting in the United States also has many dimensions—in politics, business, and citizen access. It is expected that no special favors will be granted to holders of political office and that opposing political views should be given opportunity to be expressed. Those expectations are constrained by environmental factors, especially national security matters. Broadcasting at the intersection of immigration and diversity in the United States offers a special wrinkle. Some minority broadcasters, such as Spotlight TV in New York, are directly related to political parties in foreign countries and do not operate according to the expectations of American broadcasting. Spotlight is not expected to and has not provided access to political operatives from parties or ethnic groups that oppose the PPP and the Indo-Guyanese government. Some would argue that this practice signals the emergence of further constraints to freedom of broadcasting in America.

Equality in broadcasting also dictates that all advertisers should pay the same rates and experience the same conditions. However, under "no buy," "no urban dictates," and "minority discount" practices, minority-owned and minority-operated radio and television stations are not paid the same rates by advertisers, even if such a station is the leader in its market (see chapter 5). The persistence of this practice has attracted the attention of the FCC.[4]

Equality in broadcasting also implies "the absence of discrimination or bias in the amount and kind of access available to senders or receivers, as far as is practicable."[5] The operationalizing of this dimension is a function of channel capacity, the social and economic status of audiences, and their political clout. It is clear that the American broadcasting system has the capacity. However, efforts to introduce user fees for public access television clearly undermine this aspect of broadcasting freedom. Further, poor communities in the United States, including minority groups and white communities like the Appalachian poor, are unable to "pay" for their access. One consequence of this economic inability and the concomitant marginal political status is televisual abuse. On the tabloid shows like *Jerry Springer, The Maury Povitch Show,* and *Judge Joe Brown,* poor whites and urban blacks and Hispanics tend to be portrayed as deviant and aberrant. Because of these practices poor whites, urban blacks, and Latinos are unable to communicate effectively with America. Their muted state serves to reinforce and reinvigorate stereotypes and undermine their participation in the wider American community.

It is clear that freedom and equality inform the state of broadcasting diversity in America. Societies like ours, with declared commitments to libertarianism and participatory democracy, seek to ensure that the structure and the content of their broadcasting systems reflect social, economic, and cultural realities in a proportional way. In addition, broadcasters should ensure that there are "more or less equal chances of access to the voices of the various social and cultural minorities that make up the society." Other factors associated with diversity in broadcasting include the expectation that the media "should serve as a forum for different interests and points of view in a society or community." Finally, the broadcasting industry should offer "relevant choices of content at one point in time and also variety over time of a kind that corresponds to the needs and interests of their audiences."[6]

Given those expectations, we can conclude that efforts are being made to ensure that America's diversity is present in the broadcasting industry's workforce. Starting with the Kerner Commission's report, we note a constant reaffirmation of the importance of hiring minorities in newsrooms, behind and in front of the microphones and camera. Despite efforts by individual corporations and industrywide initiatives, however, the employment of America's minorities in the broadcasting industry still does not approximate their proportions in society. Indeed, evidence suggests a decline in minority employment in American media in general—both print and broadcasting.[7] These realities undermine efforts to build solid and sustainable diversity in America's broadcasting industry.

We can conclude that American broadcasting does make it possible for multiple voices to be heard, but many voices of America's diversity are ghettoized. Our study has shown that the most diversity in American broadcasting is found on the AM radio channels, commercial cable, and public access television. Also, access by America's minorities tends to be paid for primarily through brokerage. In fact, American broadcasting is not doing a good job of supporting intercultural communication. Mainstream broadcasting is homogenized, and minority broadcasting tends to communicate with only its own communities. American broadcasting has yet to initiate and sustain a dialogue that engages all of America's diversity. The development of true diversity in broadcasting is crucial for America. The benefits will include the enriching of American cultural and social life, the limiting of social conflict, and the minimizing of potential misuse of freedom associated with concentrations in the ownership of broadcasting and other media ownership.

INFORMATION QUALITY

The central issue associated with information quality is objectivity. In American society, objectivity is understood to have two basic dimensions—"a particular form of media practice and also a particular attitude to the task of information collection, processing and dissemination."[8] Specifically, broadcasting professionals are expected to adopt positions of detachment, neutrality, and nonpartisanship. And they are expected to strive for accuracy, relevance, and completeness. All the above are predicated on the proposition that the broadcaster does not have ulterior motives. Our exploration of American broadcasting suggests otherwise. The political motivations are clear, as are economic and cultural motivations. To assume that broadcasting in America is neutral is to be naive.

As the quest for impartiality and detachment is honored more in the breach, so is the quest for accuracy, relevance, and completeness. This problem is particularly evident in the news and information programs produced by independent program producers. Their overwhelming presence in minority programming is casting a shadow on the utility of the materials they provide. This reality probably explains the dissatisfaction African Guyanese have with the television programs produced by East Indian Guyanese in New York. It can also explain why Latino broadcasting has been segmenting. It was felt that Cuban Americans were exerting too much influence on Spanish-language broadcasting in America.

This concern may appear to run counter to the ethos of the community/alternative media sector of American broadcasting, as it suggests professionalization. But inaccuracy and lack of completeness is not acceptable from any broadcasting source. Citizens in a democratic society expect "a comprehensive supply of relevant news and background information about events in the society and the world around." More important, broadcasters are expected to strive to provide information that is accurate, honest, "sufficiently complete, true to reality, reliable, and separating fact from opinion" (174). Despite their presence, sensationalism and bias are not acceptable aspects of broadcasting in the United States. Like all normative theory, these considerations about information quality are expectations about what broadcasting ought to be. The practices in all sectors, especially the work of independent producers, leaves much to be desired.

SOCIAL ORDER AND SOLIDARITY

Broadcasting has always been expected to support social integration and promote harmony in American society. For example, the government expects that broadcasters will not transmit materials that will bring injury to citizens and undermine order. The term *order* here refers not only to political and state security but also to cultural (religion, art, mores) and societal structures. Specifically, it is expected that in its quest to promote social order and solidarity, the American broadcasting industry will:

provide channels to support dialogue among all sectors of the society

pay "concerned attention" to socially disadvantaged individuals, groups, and communities

not contribute to "undermining the forces of law and order by encouraging or symbolically rewarding crime or social disorder"

accept that its freedom of action will be limited during times that challenge national security endeavor to observe the publicly acceptable norms on questions of morals, decency, and taste. (177)

Our study shows that in the main all sectors of the broadcasting industry adhere to these propositions. However, there is conflict with free-speech expectations, a conflict that has intensified, especially on some mainstream talk shows and in public access television, which has become the site for many racist and anti-immigrant programs produced by groups such as the Ku Klux Klan. Despite their offensiveness, these programs have been allowed under the First Amendment of the Constitution. Unfortunately some municipalities have considered closing public access channels in order to curb these racist abuses. It is thus fair to conclude that there are elements in American society who will use broadcasting to undermine national solidarity and social order.

CULTURAL ORDER

In broadcasting it is accepted that cultural order includes the twin dimensions of quality of media content and the authenticity of the experiences that are represented. Further, we must also recognize that in plural societies, such as the United States, there are always contestations about whose cultural order to privilege (177). Political power and economic status are important determinants of cultural dominance. This contestation constructs issues of dominant cultures and subordinate cultures. The multicultural discourse that has matured during the last decade has energized this tension. Arthur Schlesinger has argued that multiculturalism will undermine American culture and replace it with a range of transient particularisms.[9]

The dominant cultural values of the United States still have Anglo-Saxon roots. But we must understand that cultures are not static. They are dynamic and are engaged in a dialectical relationship with their environment. New immigrants, most of them pre-Americanized, have selected the United States as their new home because of their acceptance of the nation's commitment to life, liberty, the pursuit of happiness, and the rule of law. The United States, in turn, has always incorporated what the immigrants brought to it. In the last decade, this incorporation has showed signs of accelerating, particularly in the areas of cuisine, furnishings, aesthetics, festivals, music, literature, art, and dance. A quick survey of the new niche cable television channels such as the Food Network, Home and Garden TV, Bravo, and C-SPAN will support this contention. These developments hail a polycultural society.

We can conclude that the United States has responded to the new diversity. We may not be satisfied with the quantity or the consistency of the responses of the American broadcasting industry to the nation's diversity, but efforts are being made to "reflect and express the language and contemporary culture of the nation." Again, despite the nature of the response, the broadcasting industry in the United States is contributing to the preservation of the diverse heritages that make up contemporary American society. We can also agree that the American broadcasting industry is providing a space that supports cultural creativity, originality, and the production of works of high quality.[10] We therefore can give the industry a passing grade for its contribution to cultural solidarity. This solidarity has global dimensions. American broadcasting, especially in its interaction with immigration and diversity has contributed to the creation of larger identities—transnational identities. Further, America enjoys a very ethnicized broadcasting environment.

Can American Broadcasting Improve the World?

Can the responses by the American broadcasting industry contribute to the improvement of race and ethnic relations in other multiracial societies around the world?

The United States is a young, dynamic, unique, and multiracial society. However, we can draw some lessons from the American experience that will be of value globally. The first is that the broadcasting technologies will permit domestic minority communities to make global connections and develop international solidarities. From the American experience it is clear that in developing broadcasting relations in multiracial societies attention must be paid to issues of representation, ownership, employment, education, and training. The American experience has demonstrated the necessity of pushing the definition of diversity to include issues of gender, physical abilities, and sexual orientation.

The American experience has also demonstrated how intractable bias and racism could be in the broadcasting environment, as we have seen with practices such as minority discount and no urban dictates rules. Further, the American experience reveals that groups with entrenched power and privilege will use minorities to front for them to acquire benefits in the broadcast environment aimed at encouraging and facilitating diversity. These realities suggest that a mix of regulation, education, training, and an active citizenry are necessary for effective broadcasting in multiracial societies. The American experience has demonstrated the influential role that industry associations and other professional organizations can play in advancing the development of responsive broadcasting systems. Like the United States, other multiracial societies need to encourage the use of their broadcasting systems to promote intercultural communication. The old paradigm has demonstrated that intracultural communication is necessary. But intercultural communication is needed even more today because existing communication practices seem to be reinforcing old stereotypes and building new ones that consolidate the status quo of racial hierarchies.

Where Are We Headed?

Although the broadcasting industry's response to America's diversity is generally compatible with libertarianism, there is still much work to be done. The proliferation of channels, the growth of new media, and the activism of minority independent producers should not lull us into complacency. There is still significant disparity in access and this does undermine the effectiveness of the American public sphere, "the space between Government and society in which private individuals exercise formal and informal control over the state: formal through the election of governments and informal through the pressure of public opinion."[11]

There are a number of issues on the horizon that will complicate the manner in which American broadcasting will respond to diversity in the twenty-first century. Immigration will continue to be one of those issues. The United States will continue to be one of the most popular destinations for the world's immigrants and this will ensure that race and ethnicity will continue to be crucial issues in America's social, cultural, economic, and political life.

Migration to the United States will be encouraged and supported by many factors, including the policies of nation-states. Some states are "migrant-exporters," promoting the export of their nationals to alleviate domestic unemployment, reduce population pressures, secure access to foreign currencies through remittances, and "gain diplomatic leverage via overseas citizens' political or economic influence in the destination country." This has been a successful strategy and we can expect other countries to join Mexico, the Philippines, India, Pakistan, Bangladesh, the Dominican Republic, Turkey, El Salvador, Guatemala, Jordan, Nicaragua, Vietnam, and Barbados in this practice. We can also anticipate another stream of immigrants from "refugee-producing" states, such as Afghanistan, Rwanda, Zaire, Sudan, Somalia, Guatemala, Bosnia, Kosovo, and Iraq. Those countries, either as a result of deliberate policy, "civil strife, or political collapse," have "disgorged large numbers of their citizens across borders."[12] These flows of migration will bring with them many challenges, including national security and the need for purposive communication.

A number of other factors will cause the United States to promote immigration. These will include the need for skilled workers caused by the expanding economy and by the graying of America. But, the United States will be in competition with other industrial nations for this pool of skilled manpower. We have already witnessed the global acceleration of labor migration among both skilled and unskilled workers. International treaties and conventions surrounding this reality—especially treaties and conventions about seasonal, unskilled workers like farm laborers—require that the information and communication needs of these groups are satisfied by nation-states.[13] American broadcasting will have to add these requirements to the needs that will come with new immigrants in the twenty-first century. Immigration will continue to nourish and expand America's diversity. In addition, increases in interracial and interethnic marriages will begin to add new textures to America's diversity, as indicated by the 2000 census. Mainstream broadcasting, commercial, and public service will have to respond more directly.

We have already noted the emergence of transnational identities and the place of the United States in the consolidation and coordination of multiple diasporas. The broadcasting industry in the United States is important to many diasporas, as seen in our discussions of Polonia, the place of LINKUP radio in the Jamaican diaspora, and the importance of Asian Indian broadcasting in the United States in the construction of global India. These diasporas are already substantial global broadcasting markets and will invite increasing competition from international broadcasters. As evidenced in the American cable sector, international broadcasters have already begun to use race, ethnicity, religion, and gender as segmentation strategies in their search for markets in the United States. America's diversity can give American broadcasters a competitive edge in this new marketplace. To keep this competitive edge, American broadcasters must be better educated and trained—not in the arts of production but in the complexities of the world's cultures. American broadcasters must cast off their ethnocentrism and develop cultural fluency. This approach to the education and training of the next generation of broadcasters is essential not only for domestic and international broadcasting trade but for international relations.

Ongoing concerns about the concentration of ownership of American broadcasting and the global consequences of their homogenized products will make the United States in the upcoming decades an important site of efforts to create a more democratic public sphere. Central to these efforts will be the use of the new technologies to support global solidarities to establish the next generation of human rights, especially the right to communicate and the right to be understood. These rights are essential in the construction of multicultural public spheres. The events of September 11, 2001, made it clear that America's material and political successes have bred envy and hate. Part of the effort to deal with this is to make and keep friends around the world. American broadcasting, the purveyor of American soft power, will have a crucial role to play in this effort. However, for this resource to be effective, it must honestly reflect the diversity that makes America the world's first universal nation and it must be able to communicate with all people and be sensitive to all cultures. This capacity is especially needed if the USA Freedom Corps is to have any success in sharing America's compassion with the rest of the world.[14]

So, what lessons can we distill from the American experience to share with the world? Like the United States, most other nations are addressing the reality of multiculturalism in one way or another. According to Charles Husbands, multiculturalism is more than the recognition of racial and ethnic diversity in a society, it is also about "a political philosophy of how these diverse ethnic identities are supposed to coexist." Vijay Prashad argues that we are living in a polycultural world: "Polyculturalism, unlike multiculturalism, assumes that people live coherent lives that are made up of a host of linkages—the task of the [broadcaster] is not to carve out the linkages but to make sense of how people live culturally dynamic lives." Broadcasting has a responsibility to show us how much of each other we have in each other.[15]

So the American experience at the intersection of immigration, diversity, and broadcasting, especially since 1965, has global value. The American experience has demonstrated the importance of a vibrant public sphere in the nurturing, consolidating, and expanding of multicultural democracies. It has allowed us to distill the following learning points. The creation and nurturing of a vibrant public sphere require, at a minimum, the formulation of policy that

> supports increasing access to the means of broadcasting by all citizens
>
> supports the presence of public service and community local broadcasters in that broadcasting mix

supports the provision of subsidies and grants to minority communities to produce programming

recognizes that there is more to an inclusive broadcasting environment than mere quantitative representation (representation must include presence at the managerial levels of broadcasting and in other "power-brokering" sectors)

supports relevant education and training programs

requires regular performance evaluation

Another lesson we can take away from the American experience is the power of creativity. Our experience has shown that creativity can do unexpected things to support intercultural communication. Given the state of the world's broadcasting infrastructure and the excitement associated with innovations such as LINKUP radio, American broadcasters—commercial, public service, and alternative—in collaboration with their colleagues around the world, may be able to set in motion a new human conversation that will help the world experience the true brotherhood and sisterhood of humankind dreamed of by W. E. B. DuBois a century ago. The twenty-first century must not be marred by the color line.

Notes

Chapter 1

1. The call letters WEVD refer to Eugene V. Debs, a leading American socialist and labor organizer during the 1930s.

2. K. Davis (host), "Yiddish Radio Show 'The Forward Hour' Celebrates Sixty Years," *All Things Considered,* National Public Radio, Washington, D.C., September 27, 1992.

3. Several terms are used to describe the responses of the American broadcasting industry to the changing racial and ethnic composition of the society—multicultural broadcasting, ethnic broadcasting, foreign-language broadcasting, and minority broadcasting. I will use the term *minority broadcasting* extensively.

4. See Dana Calvo, "Bush to Break Language Barrier in Radio Address," *Los Angeles Times,* May 3, 2001. Also available at http://www.ask.com (accessed November 23, 2002).

5. For details on this initiative, visit the Ad Council, http://www.adcouncil. org/crisis/index/html (accessed October 7, 2001).

6. In its report to Congress in 1990, the Corporation for Public Broadcasting reported that the term "multicultural" had become popular and that in many conversations it had replaced ethnic references or even the word "minority" itself. Corporation for Public Broadcasting, *Many Faces, Many Voices: A Report to the 101st Congress* (Washington, D.C.: CPB, July, 1, 1990), 6.

7. W. E. B. DuBois, *The Souls of Black Folk* (New York: Signet Classics, 1969); see the entry "W. E. B. DuBois" in *The Norton Anthology of African American Literature,* ed. Henry L. Gates Jr. and Nellie Y. McKay (New York: Norton, 1997), 607–8.

8. Gates and McKay, "W. E. B. DuBois," 607–8.

9. See U.S. Commission on Civil Rights, *Window Dressing on the Set: Women and Minorities in Television* (Washington, D.C.: U.S. Commission on Civil Rights, 1977), 1.

10. Simon Cottle, introduction to *Ethnic Minorities and the Media,* ed. Simon Cottle (Buckingham, England: Open University Press, 2000), 1.

11. Ben J. Wattenberg, *The First Universal Nation: Leading Indicators and Ideas about the Surge of America in the 1990s* (New York: Free Press, 1990).

12. One respondent, an African Guyanese male, had been in the United States for twenty-nine years. The female respondent from Iran had been here only two years.

Chapter 2

1. U.S. Department of Justice, Immigration and Naturalization Service, *Statistical Yearbook of the Immigration and Naturalization Service* (Washington, D.C.: INS, 1997).

2. Ben Wattenberg, *The First Universal Nation: Leading Indicators and Ideas about the Surge of America in the 1990s* (New York: Free Press, 1990).

3. Philip Martin and Elizabeth Midgley, "Immigration to the United States," *Population Bulletin* 54 (2) (1999): 14.

4. Quoted in Arthur Schlesinger, *The Disuniting of America: Reflections on a Multicultural Society* (New York: Whittle Direct Books, 1991), 1.

5. Robert E. Park, *The Immigrant Press and Its Control* (Westport, Conn.: Greenwood Press, 1970).

6. See Robert W. Gardner and Leon F. Bouvier, "The United States," in *Handbook on International Migration,* ed. W. J. Serow (New York: Greenwood Press, 1990), 341–59. See also R. A. Wells, "Migration and the Image of Nebraska in England," *Nebraska History* 54 (3) (1973): 475–91.

7. NAACP, "The Immigration Bill," Crisis 9 (February 1915): 190; Nicasio Dimas, Donald Chou, and Phyllis K. Fong, *The Tarnished Golden Door: Civil Rights Issues in Immigration,* reprinted in *Race and Ethnic Relations 91/92,* ed. John A. Kromkowski (Guilford, Conn.: Dushkin Publishing Group, 1991), 40–44; for further details on the perception of southern and eastern European immigrants, see Rita J. Simon, *Public Opinion and the Immigrant: Print Media Coverage, 1880–1980* (Lexington, Mass.: Lexington Books, 1985).

8. See John F. Kennedy, *A Nation of Immigrants* (New York: Harper and Row, 1964), 82.

9. See Martin and Midgley, "Immigration," 2.

10. William A. Henry III, "Beyond the Melting Pot," *Time,* April 9, 1990; Latinos: S. Sachs, "What's in a Name: Redefining Minority," *New York Times,* March 11, 2001; Asian Indians: Aziz Haniffa, "Community Records 105.87% Growth in Past Decade," *India Abroad,* May 18, 2001. Also available at http:// www.indiaabroaddaily.com.

11. From Oliver Schmidtke, "Transnational Migration: A Challenge to European Citizenship Regimes," *World Affairs* 164 (1) (September 2001): 3–16.

12. See Gardner and Bouvier, "United States."

13. Ibid., 350.

14. See tables 17, 18, and 19 in INS, *1997 Statistical Yearbook,* 60–66; Donald J. Bogue, *The Population of the United States* (New York: Free Press, 1985), cited in Gardner and Bouvier, "United States," 350. It is obvious that the even distribution of Northwest European migrants is a function of their immigration tradition and the level of assimilation.

15. A. Pohjola, "Social Networks—Help or Hindrance to the Migrant?" *International Migration* 29 (3) (September 1991): 435–41.

16. For details see Gardner and Bouvier, "United States," 354.

17. Martin and Midgley, "Immigration," 20.

18. Martin and Midgley, "Immigration," 6.

19. Martin and Midgley, "Immigration," 20.

20. Simon, *Public Opinion.*

21. Richard Alba, "Immigration and the American Realities of Assimilation and Multiculturalism," *Sociological Forum* 14 (1) (1999): 3–25.

22. Vijay Prashad, *Everybody Was Kung Fu Fighting: Afro-Asian Connections and the Myth of Cultural Purity* (Boston: Beacon Press, 2001), x.

Chapter 3

1. For a detailed discussion of this episode in the history of the foreign-language press in the United States, see chapter 16 of Robert E. Park, *The Immigrant Press and Its Control* (Westport, Conn.: Greenwood Press, 1970). The report of the 66th U.S. Senate titled *Brewing and Liquor Interests and German and Bolshevik Propaganda* details the scope and practices of the manipulation. See ibid., 377. For a report on Hammerling's work on behalf of German propaganda, see ibid., 377–409.

2. Park, *Immigrant Press,* 3, 7.

3. Marion Marzolf, "America's Enduring Ethnic Press," paper presented at the annual meeting of the Association for Education in Journalism, Fort Collins, Colo., August 1973, ERIC EL 083 621.

4. Clemencia Rodríguez, *Fissures in the Mediascape: An International Study of Citizens' Media* (Cresskill, N.J.: Hampton Press, 2001), 133.

5. Internal migration: Nicholas Lemann, *The Promised Land: The Great Black Migration and How It Changed America* (New York: Knopf, 1991); Janette Dates and William Barlow, *Split Image: African Americans in the Mass Media* (Washington, D.C.: Howard University Press, 1991). Dates and Barlow identify and discuss practices that defined the organization and operation of the African American radio.

6. On "new racism," see, among others, Henry Louis Gates Jr., "TV's Black World Turns—But Stays Unreal," *New York Times,* November 12, 1989; Sut Jhally and Justin Lewis, *Enlightened Racism: The Cosby Show, Audiences, and the Myth of the American Dream* (Boulder: Westview, 1992).

7. Dates and Barlow, *Split Image.*

8. Sato Masaharu, "Negro Propaganda Operations: Japan's Shortwave Radio Broadcasts for World War II Black Americans," *Historical Journal of Film, Radio, and Television,* March 1999, http://www.findarticles.com/m3584/1_1/54462177/p1article.jhtml (accessed July 3, 2001).

9. Kenneth Mueller, curator of the ethnic radio collection at the Museum of Television and Radio, New York, stated that before and during World War II, German, Italian, Soviet, and Japanese broadcasters directed programs to the United States. The collection has a program (ref. no.: R76:0143) aired on February 19, 1942, by the Italian Broadcasting Service in which Ezra Pound attacks President Franklin Roosevelt's "abuse of power."

10. Civil Rights Forum on Communication Policy, press release, January 13, 1999, http://www.civilrightsforum.org.

11. For a full discussion of these practices see Kofi Asiedu Ofori, *When Being Number One Is Not Enough* (Washington, D.C.: FCC, 1999). Full text available at www.civilrightsforum.org.

12. Bowker's Database Production Group, *Broadcasting and Cable Yearbook 2000* (New Providence, N.J.: R. R. Bowker, 2000), D-695. For the early development of Polish radio in the United States, see Józef Migala, *Polish Radio Broadcasting in the United States* (Boulder: East European Monographs, 1987).

13. Donald J. Bogue, *The Population of the United States* (New York: Free Press, 1985), cited in Robert W. Gardner and Leon F. Bouvier, "The United States," in *Handbook on International Migration,* ed. W. J. Serow (New York: Greenwood Press, 1990), 350; *What Is Polonia of the Eastern Great Lakes?* http://members.aol.com/pietruska/Pol_Conn_Intro.html.

14. Migala, *Polish Radio,* 121.

15. For the origins and development of polka music in the United States, see ibid., ch. 14.

16. From Donald E. Pienkos, *The Polish National Alliance,* http://www.pna-znp.org/history%20a.htm, select "more detailed version," pp. 1, 2. A fraternal is defined as: "any incorporated society, order or supreme lodge, without capital stock (whose activities) conducted solely for the benefit of its members and their beneficiaries and not for profit (and which is) operated on a lodge system with a ritualistic form of work (and which has) a representative form of government and which makes provision for the payment of benefits."

17. National Fraternal Congress of America, cited in Pienkos, *Polish Na-*

tional Alliance, 1; radio station WPNA 1490 AM, http://www.wpnaradio.com/contact.html.

18. From Halina Paulszek-Gawronski, "Stories about Polish Programs in Chicago," cited in Migala, *Polish Radio,* 124; Polish Radio Syndicate: Migala, *Polish Radio,* 135.

Chapter 4

1. Bowker's Database Production Group, *Broadcasting and Cable Yearbook 2000* (New Providence, N.J.: R. R. Bowker, 2000), xxx; David Croteau and William Hoynes, *Media/Society: Industries, Images, and Audiences* (Thousand Oaks, Calif.: Pine Forge Press, 1997), 4; Nielsen Media Research study, September 1998–June 1999, cited in *Broadcasting and Cable Yearbook 2000,* xxx; *Hispanic,* November 2001, 16.

2. On GDP, trade: William F. Baker and George Dessart, "The Road Ahead," *Television Quarterly* 39 (4) (1998): 2–16; on TV: Bowker's Database Production Group, *Broadcasting and Cable Yearbook 2001* (New Providence, N.J.: R. R. Bowker, 2001), xxx.

3. Bowker's Database Production Group, *Broadcasting and Cable Yearbook 1991* (New Providence, N.J.: R. R. Bowker, 1991), xxx.

4. National Telecommunications and Information Administration, *NTIA TELECOM 2000: Charting the Course for a New Century* (Washington, D.C.: U.S. Department of Commerce, 1988), 539, 540. See also *Broadcasting and Cable Yearbook 2001,* xxx.

5. Baker and Dessart, "Road Ahead," 7.

6. For a recent discussion on this topic, see Clark S. Judge, "Hegemony of the Heart," *Policy Review,* no. 110 (December 2001–January 2002): 3–14.

7. See Sylvia M. Chan-Olmsted, "Mergers, Acquisitions, and Convergence: The Strategic Alliances of Broadcasting, Cable Television, and Telephone Services," *Journal of Media Economics* 11 (3) (1998): 33–46.

8. Bowker's Database Production Group, *Broadcasting and Cable Yearbook 1998* (New Providence, N.J.: R. R. Bowker, 1998), xxxiii.

9. Thomas M. Pasqua Jr., James K. Buckalew, Robert E. Rayfield, and James W. Tankard, *Mass Media in the Information Age* (Englewood Cliffs, N.J.: Prentice Hall, 1990), 1; Paula Bernstein, "PPV Feels Pinch without Punch," *Variety,* April 17, 2000. Also available at http://www.findarticles.com (accessed December 9, 2001).

10. Pasqua et al., *Mass Media,* 1.

11. Wilbur Schramm, *The Story of Human Communication: Cave Painting to Microchip* (New York: Harper and Row, 1988), cited ibid.

12. See Diane Mermigas, "Time Warner Steps into Future," *Electronic Media* 12 (5) (February 1, 1993): 1, 23.

13. For the consequences for civilization of change in communication technologies, see the discussion of the "theory of transitions" in Melvin L. DeFleur and Sandra Ball-Rokeach, *Theories of Mass Communication,* 5th ed. (New York: Longman, 1989), 7–28.

14. Jacques Ellul, *Propaganda: The Formation of Men's Attitudes* (New York: Vintage Books, 1973), 75.

15. Joseph Turow, *Media Systems in Society: Understanding Industries, Strategies, and Power* (New York: Longman, 1992).

16. From Denis McQuail, *Mass Communication Theory: An Introduction,* 3rd ed. (London: Sage, 1994), 65–66.

17. *NTIA TELECOM 2000,* 483; Roper Starch, *America's Watching: Public Attitudes Toward Television* (New York: Roper Starch Worldwide, 1997), 1, 12.

18. Starch, *America's Watching,* 5; George Gerbner, *Casting the American Scene: A Look at the Characters on Prime Time and Daytime Television from 1994–1997,* report to the Screen Actors Guild, 1998. Also available at http://www.media-awareness.ca/eng/issues/minrep/resources/reports/gerbner.htm.

19. Gerbner, *Casting the American Scene,* 2.

20. Tad Friend isolates "ten basic plots" in situation comedies in "Sitcoms, Seriously," *Esquire* 119 (3) (1993): 112–24. Schema and genre theories also explain the formulaic orientation in situation comedies.

21. Jeffrey Escoffier, "The Limits of Multiculturalism," *Socialist Review* 91 (3, 4) (1991): 61–73.

22. Everett Rogers and Thomas Steinfatt, *Intercultural Communication* (Prospect Heights, Ill.: Waveland Press, 1999), 190.

23. McQuail, *Mass Communication Theory,* 3rd ed.; Stanley J. Baran and Dennis K. Davis, *Mass Communication Theory: Foundations, Ferment, and Future* (Belmont, Calif.: Wadsworth Publishing, 1995), 27.

24. For an extended discussion on that metatheoretical formulation statement see Gibson Burrell and Gareth Morgan, *Sociological Paradigms and Organizational Analysis* (Portsmouth, N.H.: Heinemann, 1979), 1–40.

25. Baran and Davis, *Mass Communication Theory,* 27.

26. Shearon A. Lowery and Melvin L. DeFleur, *Milestones in Communication Research,* 2nd ed. (New York: Longman, 1988), 32.

27. Dependency on radio: Paul Lazarsfeld and Frank Stanton, eds., *Radio Research: 1942–1943* (New York: Essential Books, 1944); Baran and Davis, *Mass Communication Theory,* 215.

28. Cited in Denis McQuail, *Mass Communication Theory: An Introduction,* 4th ed. (London: Sage, 2000), 148.

29. For a substantial exploration of this development see Everett Rogers, *A History of Communication Study: A Biographical Approach* (New York: Free Press, 1994). See also Lowery and DeFleur, *Milestones.*

30. Baran and Davis, *Mass Communication Theory*, 15.

31. Ibid., 16, 17.

32. McQuail, *Mass Communication Theory*, 3rd ed., 128.

33. Ibid., 131–32.

34. Tom Graves, "Movies and Home Entertainment," in *Standard & Poor's Industry Surveys*, ed. Eileen M. Bosong-Martines (New York: Standard and Poor's, November 16, 2000), 9; on U.S. TV exports: Tim Walcott, "Euros Warm Up to U.S. Youth Fare," *Variety*, May 22, 2000. Also available at http://www.findarticles. com (accessed December 10, 2001); on cultural identity: Mark P. Orbe and Tina M. Harris, *Interracial Communication: Theory into Practice* (Belmont, Calif.: Wadsworth., 2001), 70; Schmidtke, "Transnational Migration."

35. National Advisory Commission on Civil Disorders, *Report of the National Advisory Commission on Civil Disorders* (New York: New York Times, 1968).

36. Sharon M. Murphy, "From the Kerner Report to the Reagan Era: A Twenty-Year Struggle," in *Readings in Mass Communication,* ed. Michael C. Emery and Ted C. Smythe (Dubuque, Iowa: William C. Brown, 1989), 193–99; for a discussion of the minority ownership initiative, see Howard Kleiman, "Content Diversity and the FCC's Minority and Gender Licensing Policies," *Journal of Broadcasting and Electronic Media* 35 (4) (1991): 411–29.

37. The U.S. Court of Appeals for the District of Columbia Circuit declared the EEO rules unconstitutional and vacated them in MD/DC/DE Broadcasters Association v. Federal Communications Commission, 236 F.3d 13 (2001), also available at http://www.fcc.gov/ogc/documents/opinions/2001/00–1094.txt. On professional training and corporate socializing as influential variables, see Warren Breed, "Social Control in the Newsroom: A Functional Analysis," *Social Forces* 33 (May 1955): 326–35.

Chapter 5

1. In this book the term *community radio* includes pirate radio and microradio.

2. Bowker's Database Production Group, "Radio Formats Defined," *Broadcasting and Cable Yearbook 2000* (New Providence, N.J.: R. R. Bowker, 2000), D-637.

3. Ibid., D-656.

4. See ibid. and Bowker's Database Production Group, *Broadcasting and Cable Yearbook 1993* (New Providence, N.J.: R. R. Bowker, 1993).

5. The complete list: Arabian, Aramaic, Basque, Bohemian, Chinese, Czechoslovakian, Dutch, Filipino, French, German, Gaelic, Greek, Hebrew, Hungarian, Irish, Italian, Jewish, Lebanese, Lithuanian, Norwegian, Polish, Portuguese, Russian, Scottish, Scandinavian, Serbian, Slovenian, Swedish, Swiss, Syrian, Ukrainian, Ute, and Yugoslavian. Broadcasting Publications, *Broadcasting Yearbook 1966* (Washington, D.C.: Broadcasting Publications, 1966), D-30–34.

6. In addition to African Americans, Latinos, and Native Americans: Albanian, Arabian, Armenian, Asian, Assyrian, Basque, British, Calypso, Caribbean, Chinese, Croatian, Czechoslovakian, Dutch, East Indian, Filipino, Finnish, French, German, Greek, Haitian, Hebrew, Hindi, Pakistani, Punjabi, Urdu, Hungarian, Irish, Italian, Japanese, Jewish, Korean, Lithuanian, Norwegian, Polish, Polka, Portuguese, Romanian, Russian, Scandinavian, Serbian, Persian, Swedish, Swiss, Ukrainian, and Yugoslav.

7. Broadcasting Publications, *Broadcasting Yearbook 1976* (Washington, D.C.: Broadcasting Publications, 1976).

8. *Broadcasting and Cable Yearbook 2000.*

9. East Indians started arriving in the Caribbean in 1838 as labor replacements for the soon-to-be emancipated enslaved Africans. For further details on this migration to Guyana, see Dwarka Nath, *A History of Indians in British Guiana* (London: Thomas Nelson and Sons, 1950).

10. Letter in the Guyanese newspaper *Stabroek News,* October 5, 1999. The station owner was Robert Mohammed.

11. Conversation with Halim Majeed, April 4, 2001. See also Brenda Mangru and Madhu Pillai, *Indo-Guyanese: A LOTE-Speaking Community in Richmond Falls, NY,* http://www.nyu.edu/classes/blake.map2001/indo.html (accessed June 10, 2003).

12. National Telecommunications and Information Administration (NTIA), *Minority Commercial Broadcast Ownership in the United States,* http://www.ntia.doc.gov/opadhome/minown98/main.htm.

13. Bowker's Database Production Group, *Broadcasting and Cable Yearbook 2001* (New Providence, N.J.: R. R. Bowker, 2001), D-656–57.

14. Brooklyn has a number of money transfer offices for this purpose in Jamaican, Guyanese, Haitian, Mexican, Puerto Rican, Dominican, Taiwanese, and other ethnic enclaves. These offices, some owned by ethnic businessmen, others by national chains such as Western Union, provide their services in the language of their primary customers. See Manuel Orozco (Inter-American Dialogue), *Remitting Back Home and Supporting the Homeland: The Guyanese Community in the U.S.,* working paper commissioned by the U.S. Agency for International Development (GEO Project), October 25, 2002, 10.

15. For example, Guyanese political parties depend on Guyanese in North America, especially New York, to contribute to their campaign war chests. The leaders of the major political parties are expected to visit these communities as part of their fund-raising activities. The government of Guyana makes materials from its ministry of information available to Guyanese radio and television broadcasters in New York for use in their programs.

16. Annan Boodram, telephone interview by the author, New York, January 11, 2002.

17. For further details see Clear Channel Communications, http://www.clearchannel.com/corporate/index.html (accessed January 15, 2002).

18. Corporation for Public Broadcasting, *Public Broadcasting's Services to Minorities and Diverse Audiences: A Report to the 106th Congress* (Washington, D.C.: CPB, 1996), 3. See Corporation for Public Broadcasting, *Retrospective 1967–1992: Annual Report—Twenty-Five Years from Wasteland to Oasis; A Quarter Century of Sterling Programming* (Washington, D.C.: CPB, 1992), 2.

19. Robert W. McChesney, "The Battle for the U.S. Airwaves, 1928–1935," *Journal of Communication* 40 (Autumn 1990): 29–57.

20. Ibid.; Tona J. Hangen, "Launching the Radio Church, 1921–1940," paper presented at the annual meeting of the Association for Education in Journalism and Mass Communication, New Orleans, August 1999.

21. "Remarks of President Lyndon B. Johnson upon Signing the Public Broadcasting Act of 1967, November 7, 1967," http://www.cpb.org/about/history/johnsonspeech.html.

22. National Public Radio, *Annual Report 1999* (Washington, D.C.: NPR, 2000), 36. Also available at www.npr.org/inside.

23. Corporation for Public Broadcasting, *Public Broadcasting Revenue: Fiscal Year 2000 Final Report,* http://www.stations.cpb.org/system/reports/revenue/, tables 3, 4 (accessed May 5, 2003); NPR, *Annual Report 1999,* 33.

24. Corporation for Public Broadcasting, *Diversity and Public Radio,* http://www.cpb.org/radio/diversity/.

25. G. Chris Taylor, interview by the author, Ohio University, Athens, Ohio, June 1991. Taylor served on the CPB Radio Program Board and worked with public radio in Houston.

26. Robert Farris Thompson, "Afro-Atlantic Music in the Nineties: Making Space for African Futures," in *Afropop Worldwide 1991 Listener's Guide* (New York: World Music Productions, 1991), 2.

27. National Public Radio, "Inside NPR," http://www.npr.org/inside.

28. See Fairness & Accuracy in Reporting, "White Noise: Voices of Color Scarce on Urban Public Radio," *Extra,* http://www.fair.org/extra/0209/white-noise.html (accessed January 24, 2003).

29. Ibid.

30. NPR, *Annual Report 1999*, 3.

31. Von Martin, interview by the author, Havana, August 2001.

32. For further details see Nat Hentoff, "Can WBAI Be Saved? Democracy Now at Pacifica Radio," *Village Voice*, April 17, 2001.

33. The complete mission statement is available at http://www.slip.net/ ~dove/mission.html.

34. For further details see *http://ftp.fcc.gov/Speeches/Kennard/Statements/ stwek847.html* (accessed January 24, 2003).

35. Paul Van Slambrouck, "'Microradio' as Antidote to Mergers: A Push to Reconnect Radio to Local Roots," *Christian Science Monitor*, January 28, 1999. Also available at http://www.csmonitor.com/durable/1999/01/28/p3s1.htm; Nader, press release, October 13, 2000, http://www.slip.net/~dove/nader.html.

36. National Federation of Community Broadcasters (NFCB), http:// www.nfcb.org/.

37. FCC, "Review of the Radio Industry, 2000," http://www.fcc.gov/mmb/ prd/radio.html.

38. Ibid.; Nader press release; Presbyterian Church U.S.A., *Opportunities for Presbyterian Congregations to Invest in Low-Power FM Radio Stations,* http:// www.horeb.pcusa.org/oc/lowpowerfm.htm; Kennard, "The Voice of the People," *Washington Post*, October 23, 2000 (op-ed). Also available at http://www .slip.net/~dove/kennard.html.

39. Admerasia, *Asian Markets,* http://www.admerasia.com/asiantext.html; Sukhjit Purewal, "County Report Cites Immigrants' Problems in Silicon Valley," *India Abroad*, December 18, 2000.

40. See Admerasia, *Asian Markets,* http://www.admerasia.com/asiantext. html.

41. The term "institutional completeness" is associated with comments made by Chris Taylor when she was a student in my class on multicultural broadcasting at Ohio University, 1992.

42. Vibert C. Cambridge, "Immigration, Race, Ethnicity, and Broadcasting in the United States," paper presented at International Conference on Immigration and Communication, Tallinn, Estonia, July 1992.

43. Admerasia, http://www.admerasia.com/southasian.html.

44. *Broadcasting and Cable Yearbook 2001,* D-674–75.

45. http://www.iaol.com/vivdh_bharti.htm (accessed January 22, 2002).

46. http://www.ebcradio.com/ebc1/htmpage and gif/corporateprofile.html.

47. Details in this section were obtained from an telephone interview with Duncan Suh, reporter and public information officer, Radio Korea, Los Angeles, November 10, 1992.

48. Connie Kang, "Airing Differences in Bid for Harmony; Radio: Korean-Language Call-in Show Features Black Guests and Frank Discussions about Cultural Tensions," *Los Angeles Times,* June 22, 1996.

49. Department of Justice, Immigration and Naturalization Service, *Statistical Yearbook of the Immigration and Naturalization Service* (Washington, D.C.: INS, 1997); Brad Edmondson, "Migration: The Newest New Yorkers," *American Demographics* 14 (8) (August 1992): 9, citing details from E. Mann, *The Newest New Yorkers* (New York: Department of City Planning, 1992).

50. Based on responses given during focus group sessions and in-depth interviews with influential community members conducted by the author in 1992.

51. Along with other early pioneers from Jamaica, like Safia Seavright, Ken Williams, Jeff Barnes, John Sandy, Carl Nelson, Gracie Sever, and Amy Sutter.

52. Much of the information in this section is from Annan Boodram and Felicia Persaud, "Caribbean Radio in the Diaspora," *Caribbean Voice* http://www.caribvoice.org/Features/radio.html.

53. For descriptions of the settlement of Indian Guyanese in New York and the consequences of that settlement, see Kim Martineau, "Guyanese Find Opportunity in Schenectady," *Albany Times Union,* July 7, 2002.

54. See, for example, Peter Ruhomon, *Centenary History of the East Indians in British Guiana, 1838–1938* (Georgetown, British Guiana: Daily Chronicle, 1947). Despite efforts to build a unity based on class solidarity, relations between Africans and Indians have always been characterized by suspicion.

55. Félix Gutiérrez, cited in Arminda Trevino, "Spanish-Language Broadcasting in the United States," term paper, Ohio University, July 1999, in possession of the author.

56. In an effort to control costs in a very voracious industry, broadcast practitioners tend to seek low-cost formats. In television the inexpensive programming includes studio-based soap operas, news shows, and situation comedies. Once the set for a program has been created, a major cost has been controlled. For further discussion, see Sydney Head and Christopher Sterling, *Broadcasting in America: A Survey of Electronic Media* (Boston: Houghton Mifflin, 1991).

57. Peter Manuel, "Latin Music in the United States: Salsa and the Mass Media," *Journal of Communication* 41 (1) (1991): 109–10.

58. This section is guided by the work of Colombian mass communication researcher Rafael Obregon, especially "Radio Caracol: Colombian Broadcasting in Miami," report presented to the seminar Multicultural Broadcasting in the United States, School of Telecommunications, Ohio University, fall 1994.

59. For further details see Hertz Herzog, "What Do We Really Know about Daytime Serial Listeners?" in *Radio Research, 1942–1943,* ed. Paul Lazarsfeld and Frank Stanton (New York: Essential Books, 1944), 3–33.

60. Alfred Aversa Jr., "Italian Neo-Ethnicity: The Search for Self Identity," *Journal of Ethnic Studies* 6 (2) (1978): 49–56.

61. Interview instruments completed, respectively, by an Italian male, an East Indian Guyanese male and an African Guyanese female, Manhattan, spring 2001, and by an Indian male student, Brooklyn College, May 5, 2001.

Chapter 6

1. George Lipsitz, "The Meaning of Memory: Family, Class, and Ethnicity in Early Network Television Programs," in *Private Screenings: Television and the Female Consumer,* ed. Lynn Spigel and Denise Mann (Minneapolis: University of Minnesota Press, 1992), 75.

2. Peter Larsen, *Import/Export: International Flow of Television Fiction* (Paris: UNESCO, 1990), 36.

3. Donald L. Shaw, *The Rise and Fall of American Mass Media: The Roles of Technology and Leadership* (Bloomington: School of Journalism, Indiana University, 1991), 10.

4. Roper Starch, *America's Watching: Public Attitudes towards Television 1997* (New York: Roper Starch Worldwide, 1997).

5. Tim Brooks and Earle Marsh, *The Complete Directory to Prime Time Network TV Shows, 1946–Present,* 7th ed. (New York: Ballantine Books, 1997).

6. Lipsitz, "Meaning of Memory," 71.

7. For a good examination of the development of black negative stereotypes during the stage vaudeville era, see Donald Bogle, *Toms, Coons, Mulattoes, Mammies, and Bucks: An Interpretive History of Blacks in American Films* (New York: Frederick Ungar, 1992).

8. For a discussion of the current popularity of *Amos 'n' Andy* videotapes among African Americans, see Henry Louis Gates Jr., "TV's Black World Turns—But Stays Unreal," *New York Times,* November 12, 1989.

9. Brooks and Marsh, *Prime Time,* xv.

10. For further information on enslaved Africans and African Americans during the pioneering era, see Ira Berlin, "The Migration Generation," in *Generations of Captivity: A History of African American Slaves* (Cambridge, Mass.: Belknap Press, 2003), 159–244.

11. Brooks and Marsh, *Prime Time,* xvii.

12. National Advisory Commission on Civil Disorders, *Report of the National Advisory Commission on Civil Disorders* (New York: New York Times,1968), 1.

13. John D. Leckenby and Stuart H. Surlin, "Incidental Social Learning and

Viewer Race: 'All in the Family' and 'Sanford and Son,'" *Journal of Broadcasting* 20 (4) (1976): 481–94.

14. Brooks and Marsh, *Prime Time,* 119.

15. Ibid., 67.

16. For a discussion of "safe" black characters, see Gates, "Black World Turns." Similar ideas have been expressed in Joshua Hammer's examination of blacks in prime-time TV in the 1992–93 season. Hammer, "Must Blacks Be Buffoons?" *Newsweek,* October 26, 1992, 70.

17. Brooks and Marsh, *Prime Time,* xix.

18. Alfred Aversa, "Italian Neo-Ethnicity: The Search for Self-Identity," *Journal of Ethnic Studies* 6 (2): 49–56.

19. Gates, "Black World Turns."

20. Jim McFarlin, "African-Americans Find Their Place on the Air," *Electronic Media,* July 8, 1991, 29, 36. McFarlin adds that "black households view 17 percent more television during prime-time, 65 percent more television at daytime, 90 percent more television weekday late night, 73 percent more television early morning and 32 percent television during early fringe" (36).

21. Ibid., 36.

22. Academic interest in the marriage between education and entertainment appears to have started with Harold Mendelsohn's *Mass Entertainment* (New Haven, Conn: College and University Press, 1966). The federal government has funded projects such as *¿Que Pasa, USA?* a television soap opera whose primary role was the orientation of Cuban émigrés in Miami to American values and civic practices. The practice of using entertainment programming in social and economic development is also being diffused internationally through U.S. based international development agencies. The Johns Hopkins Center for Communication Programs has been extremely visible in developing this methodology as a means to disseminate population control information. Some of their recent efforts have included the production of family planning music video series (*Tatiana and Johnny, Lea Solonga, King Sunny Ade,* etc.), and current ventures into radio and television soap operas. For further details see, for example, Vibert C. Cambridge, "Radio Soap Operas in Global Africa: Origins, Applications, and Implications," in *Staying Tuned: Contemporary Soap Opera Criticism,* ed. Suzanne Frentz (Bowling Green, Ohio: Popular Press, 1991), 110–27; Vibert C. Cambridge, "Radio Soap Operas: The Jamaican Experience, 1958–1989," *Studies in Latin American Popular Culture* 11 (1992): 93–97; M. L. Hazzard and Vibert C. Cambridge, "Socio-drama As an Applied Technique for Development Communication in the Caribbean: Specialized Content and Narrative Structure in the Radio Dramas of Elaine Perkins in Jamaica," in *Caribbean Popular Culture,* ed. J. Lent (Bowling Green, Ohio: Popular Press, 1990), 106–19; Arvind Singhal and

Everett Rogers, *Entertainment-Education: A Communication Strategy for Social Change* (Mahwah, N.J.: Lawrence Erlbaum Associates, Publishers, 1999).

23. From National Association of Television Program Executives, *Minority Programming: A Billion-Dollar Market,* videotape 8, NATPE annual conference, New Orleans, January 16–18, 1991.

24. See Jon Krampner, "Asians Gain in TV: But It Is Still Hard to Reach the Top," *Electronic Media* 8 (July 1991): 29, 34; William Mahoney and Kate Oberlander, "Hispanic Production on the Rise," *Electronic Media* 8 (July 1991): 30, 32; Thomas Tyrer, "Stereotypes Fading from the Small Screen," *Electronic Media* 8 (July 1991): 29, 34; Jackson quoted in NATPE, *Minority Programming;* Sut Jhally and Justin Lewis, *Enlightened Racism: The Cosby Show, Audiences, and the Myth of the American Dream* (Boulder: Westview, 1992).

25. Richard G. Carter, "TV's Black Comfort Zone for Whites," *Television Quarterly* 23 (4) (1988): 29–34, 30.

26. Gates, "Black World Turns" (emphasis in original).

27. Hammer, "Must Blacks Be Buffoons?" 70.

28. Ibid., 71. For a more substantial discussion, see Joshua Hammer and John Schwartz, "Prime-Time Mensch," *Newsweek,* October 12, 1992, 88–89.

29. Jack G. Shaheen, *The TV Arab* (Bowling Green, Ohio: BGSU Popular Press, 1984), 4.

30. Daisy Expósito-Ulla, president and chief creative officer, Bravo Group, to author, July 10, 1991.

31. Based on data collected from a survey of the media educational strategies of Jewish, Arab, African American, and other ethnic organizations.

32. See NAACP, "NAACP Television Report Shows Diversity Remains Unfulfilled Goal," http://www.naacp.org/news/releases/tvdiversity081601.shtml.

33. See the entry "W. E. B. DuBois," in *The Norton Anthology of African American Literature,* ed. Henry Louis Gates Jr. and Nellie Y. McKay (New York: Norton, 1997), 606.

34. For a more complete exploration of media dependency theory, see Melvin DeFleur and Sandra Ball Rokeach, *Theories of Mass Communication,* 5th ed. (New York: Longman, 1989).

35. Michael R. Winston, "Racial Consciousness and the Evolution of Mass Communications in the United States," *Daedalus* 3 (4) (1982): 173.

36. George Comstock, "The Impact of Television on American Institutions," *Journal of Communication* 28 (2) (1978): 12–28.

37. Bowker's Database Production Group, *Broadcasting and Cable Yearbook 2001* (New Providence, N.J.: R. R. Bowker, 2001), xxx.

38. Roberta J. Astroff, "Spanish Gold: Stereotypes, Ideology, and the Construction of a U.S. Latino Market," *Howard Journal of Communications* 1 (4) (1988–89): 155–73.

39. For further discussion on the media and "resource dependency theory," see Joseph Turow, *Media Industries: The Production of News and Entertainment* (New York: Longman Communications Books, 1984).

40. See, for example, the earlier mentioned note on Ad Council's "I Am an American" PSA series and the meetings between the White House and Hollywood. The latter meetings were reported on CNN programs such as *Late Edition* on November 11, 2001.

41. Daisy Expósito-Ulla to author, July 10, 1991.

42. Reports presented at the College of Communication conference on diversity and the media in the United States, 2002.

43. Douglas W. Webbink to author, July 18, 1991.

44. See Pepper and Corazzini, LLP, *EEO Regulations and Employment Practices: A Primer for the Ohio Association of Broadcasters on Current FCC Requirements* (pamphlet) (Washington, D.C.: Pepper and Corazzini, LLP, n.d.), n.p.; Federal Communications Commission, "FCC Proposes New Equal Employment Opportunity (EEO) Rules for Broadcast and Cable," revised FCC press release, December 13, 2001.

45. National Association of Broadcasters, *Broadcast Regulations 89: A Mid-Year Report* (Washington, D.C.: NAB, 1989), 25–26.

46. National Telecommunications and Information Administration, *Minority Telecommunications Development Program* (Washington, D.C.: U.S. Department of Commerce, NTIA, n.d.); Joanna Anderson, interview by the author, December 16, 1992.

47. NTIA, http://www.ntia.doc.gov/opadhome/minown98/tv.htm (accessed December 30, 2001).

48. American Broadcasting Company, *ABC Broadcast Standards and Practices* (New York: ABC, n.d.), 4, 3.

49. Albert R. Kroeger to author, June 14, 1991.

50. Dwight M. Ellis, vice president, human resources development, National Association of Broadcasters, to author, October 23, 1991.

51. National Association of Television Program Executives, *Membership Opportunity: National Association of Television Program Executives* (Santa Monica: NATPE, n.d.), 3.

52. Rodney Mitchell, executive administrator, Affirmative Action, and Elaine Brodey, administrator, Affirmative Action, Screen Actors Guild, to author, December 3, 1991.

53. George Gerbner, *Casting the American Scene: A Look at the Characters on Prime Time and Daytime Television from 1994–1997*, report to the Screen Actors Guild, 1998, 1. Also available at http://www.media-awareness.ca/eng/issues/minrep/resources/reports/gerbner.htm.

Chapter 7

1. Ralph Engleman, *The Origins of Public Access Cable Television, 1966–1972*, Journalism Monographs, no. 123 (October 1990), 21.

2. Daniels quoted ibid., 35.

3. Bowker's Database Production Group, *Broadcasting and Cable Yearbook 2001* (New Providence, N.J.: R. R. Bowker, 2001), D-637; National Cable Television Association (NCTA), http://www/ncta.com/industry_overview?indStat.cfm? indOverviewID=2 (accessed January 2, 2002).

4. *Broadcasting and Cable Yearbook 2001,* xxx.

5. Patricia Aufderhide, "Cable Television and the Public Interest," *Journal of Communication* 42 (1) (1992): 55–56. On the concept of a "multitude of tongues," see Judge Learned Hand's dictum in *U.S. v. Associated Press,* 52 F. Supp. 362, 372 (1943), cited ibid., 54.

6. For further details see David Waterman and August Grant, "Cable Television As an Aftermarket," *Journal of Broadcasting and Electronic Media* 35 (2) (1991): 181.

7. Alisse Waterston, Elvira Gerena, Yihan Xie, and Mariel Gomez, *A Look towards Advancement: Minority Employment in Cable,* report prepared by Surveys Unlimited of Horowitz Associates for the NAMIC Research and Policy Committee, August 1999, 3, 4.

8. Full text available at NCTA, http://www.ncta.com/industry_initiatives/diversity.cfm?indInitID=18 (accessed January 2, 2002).

9. The NCTA reported 72,958,180 basic cable households in December 2001. The top five MSOs were responsible for 48,637,900 subscribers.

10. Full text available at AT&T, "AT&T Supplier Diversity Policy," http://www.attbroadband.com/supplier_diversity/.

11. Full text available at AT&T, "AT&T Supplier Diversity Policy," http://www.attbroadband.com/supplier_diversity/outreach.html.

12. AOL Time Warner, http://www.aoltimewarner.com/about/index.html.

13. Cox Communications, "About Cox: Cox Communications Timeline—2001," http://www.cox.com/Corp/Timeline.asp?LocalSys+LasVegas&dName=LasVegas.

14. James C. Kennedy, quoted in Cox Enterprises, *At Cox, Our Employees Are Our Greatest Asset* (Atlanta: Cox Enterprises, n.d.), 1; Cox Cable Communications, http://www.cox.com/CoxCareer/history.asp?LocalSys=,&dName=.

15. Cox Enterprises, *Our Employees.*

16. Judy A. Henke, vice president, human resources, Cox Cable Communications, to author, June 18, 1992; Henke to Mike Bojanski, personnel manager, Cox Cable–Nebraska, memorandum, June 11, 1992; Bojanski, *The Rules Are Changing: Cox Cable Omaha Preparing for the Diverse Work Force of the Twenty-*

First Century, case study submitted to Cable and Telecommunications Association for Marketing, 1990.

17. Bobbi Didler, director of human resources, Cox Cable–Santa Barbara, to Judy Henke, memorandum, June 18, 1992.

18. All quotations in this section on Cox Cable–Jefferson Parish are from a memo from Fred Bristol to Judy Henke, June 14, 1992.

19. See http://www.cox.com/OKC?DigitalTV/Cox%20Hispanic%20Programming.asp.

20. All quotations in this section on Cox Cable–Hampton Roads are from a memo from Irv Hill to Judy Henke, June 30, 1992.

21. All quotations in this section on Cox Cable–San Diego are from a memo from Brenda Lovitt to Judy Henke, June 17, 1992.

22. National Cable Television Association, Research and Policy Analysis Department, *Cable Television Developments* (Washington, D.C.: NCTA, October 1992). Also available at NCTA, www.ncta.com/industry_overview/programList.cfm.

23. As in chapter 4, I focus on programming for minority communities that have grown in national significance since 1965, concentrating on developments from 1991 to 2001.

24. "SRC May 1991 Network Survey," in Univisión, *Just the Facts* (1991). Unless otherwise specified, all quotations about Univisión in this section are from the *Just the Facts* series and *The Univisión Story* (1991), pamphlets distributed with Univisión's marketing package.

25. The full-powered owned and operated stations were in Miami, Dallas, San Antonio, Albuquerque, Phoenix, Fresno, and San Francisco; the low-powered stations in Hartford, Philadelphia, Austin, Tucson, and Bakersfield. The full-powered affiliates are in Chicago, Houston, Corpus Christi, El Paso/Juárez, Reno, Sacramento and Salinas; the low-power affiliates are in Washington, D.C., Tampa, St. Louis, Lubbock, Denver, Las Vegas, and Palm Desert, San Diego, Santa Maria, and San Luis Obispo, California.

26. For details on that process see Federico Subervi Vélez, "Mass Communication and Hispanics," in *Handbook of Hispanic Cultures in the United States, Sociology,* ed. F. Padilla (Houston: Arte Público Press, 1994), 304–57.

27. See Astroff, "Spanish Gold."

28. NCTA, http://www.ncta.com/industry/_overvieew/programList.cfm?network (accessed January 6, 2002).

29. Description of an advertisement produced by Conahay and Lyon and available at the Museum of Television and Radio, New York; accessed by author, May 2001.

30. PBS was the first American broadcaster to use satellites to distribute television programs.

31. Subervi Vélez, "Mass Communication."

32. The full-power stations were KTFH 49, Houston; KWHY 22, Los Angeles; and KSTV 57, Santa Barbara. The low-power stations were K22BH 22, Corpus Christi; K17BY, San Antonio; K43CW, Tucson; K67FE, Phoenix; K06MB, Palm Springs; K58DJ, Bakersfield; and K22DD, San Jose.

33. National Cable Television Association (NCTA), http://www.ncta.com/industry_overview/programList.cfm?network (accessed January 7, 2002).

34. Subervi Vélez, "Mass Communication"; "Galavisión—A Look of Its Own," Galavisión pamphlet, n.d. [1996].

35. Subervi Vélez, "Mass Communication."

36. Ibid.

37. Ibid. This is also reminiscent of the "border blasters"—commercial radio stations in the radio era established on the Mexican side of the border so as to be free of FCC regulations. See Gene Fowler and Bill Crawford, *Border Radio: Quacks, Yodelers, Pitchmen, Psychics, and Other Amazing Broadcasters of the America Airwaves*, rev. ed. (Austin: University of Texas, 2002).

38. Subervi Vélez, "Mass Communication."

39. NCTA, http://www.ncta.com/industry_overview/programList.cfm?network _id+98&detail+1 (accessed January 4, 2002).

40. Subervi Vélez, "Mass Communication," 50.

41. Canal Sur, MGM Networks Latin America, Canales ñ, MTV Latin America, Discovery en Español, Puma TV, Fox Sports Latin America, Fox Sports World Español, Telemundo, Galavisión, Telemundo Internacional, GEMS Television, Univisión, HBO Latino, Video Rola, HTV, Weather Channel Latin America.

42. Subervi Vélez, "Mass Communication."

43. Sydney W. Head, *World Broadcasting Systems: A Comparative Analysis* (Belmont, Calif.: Wadsworth Publishing, 1985), 25–26.

44. Michael A. Fletcher, "The Blond, Blue-Eyed Face of Spanish TV," *Washington Post,* August 3, 2000.

45. John R. Logan and Glenn Deane, "Black Diversity in Metropolitan America: A Report Based on Data from the 1990 and 2000 Census of Population Supplementary Survey," www.mumford1.dyndns.org/cen2000/Black-White/BlackDiversityReport/black_diversity01.htm; Mireya Navarro, "For New York's Black Latinos, a Growing Racial Awareness," *New York Times,* April 28, 2003.

46. Paul Gilroy, "Cultural Studies and Ethnic Absolutism," in *Cultural Studies,* ed. Lawrence Grossberg, Cary Nelson, and Paula Treichler (New York: Praeger, 1992), 191; Vibert C. Cambridge, "Radio Soap Operas in Global Africa: Origins, Applications, and Implications," in *Staying Tuned: Contemporary Soap*

Opera Criticism, ed. Suzanne Frentz (Bowling Green, Ohio: BGSU Popular Press, 1991), 110–27.

47. Hong Kong's regional program production centers have demonstrated since the early eighties that it could play a significant role in nurturing and promoting global China identity and ambition. See Robert L. Bishop, "Regional Media Export Centers: The Case of Hong Kong," *Gazette* 35 (1) (1985): 61–70.

48. BET, "Black Entertainment Television Highlights," pamphlet (BET, 1991), n.p.

49. The first black entertainer to be featured on MTV was Michael Jackson, in the *Thriller* video.

50. Darnell M. Hunt, "Black Entertainment Television," http://www .mbcnet.org/ETV/B/htmlB/blackenterta/blackenterta.htm (accessed January 9, 2002).

51. BET promotional literature, n.d.; Judy Dothard Simmons, "The Rise and Fall of *Emerge* Magazine," http://www.africana.com/DailyArticles/index_20000614 .htm (accessed January 26, 2002).

52. Hunt, "Black Entertainment Television," 2.

53. Michael Vlahos, "Culture and Foreign Policy," *Foreign Affairs* 82 (Spring 1991): 59–78.

54. For a good exploration of West Indian migration to the United Kingdom since World War II, see Mike Phillips and Trevor Phillips, *Windrush: The Irresistible Rise of Multi-Racial Britain* (London: HarperCollins, 1999).

55. In the movies *Coming to America* and *Barbershop,* the barbershop is a pivotal connection point. For African Americans the barbershop is as important an interpersonal channel as the church.

56. NCTA, http://www.ncta.com/industry_overview/programList.cfm?network.

57. Felicia G. Jones, "The Black Audience and the BET Channel," *Journal of Broadcasting and Electronic Media* 34 (4) (1990): 477, 484.

58. Full text available on-line at Viacom, http://www.viacom.com (accessed January 9, 2002).

59. For details on Johnson Publishing Company television, see "JPC-TV," *Ebony* 48 (1) (1992): 76–82; for details on Apollo Productions, see A. Victoria Hunter, "Percy Sutton/Inner City Broadcasting—A Family Affair," *Class,* February 1990, 33–37.

60. Hunter, "Percy Sutton."

61. Ibid.; telephone conversation with Jamie Carlington, publicist, MBC, Atlanta, January 11, 2002.

62. National Cable and Telecommunications Association, http://www.ncta .com/ industry_overview?programList.cfm?network.

63. Caribbean Satellite Network, "CSN 36 MHZ C-Band Satellite Video Signal: Coverage Map" and "Roots Music Is the World's Music"; "CSN: The Heart and Soul of the Caribbean" [1992]; "Roots Music: The Sound That Started It All" [1992]; all publicity leaflets.

64. Caribbean Satellite Network, "CSN Programming" [1992]; "CSN Reaches a Receptive Market" [1992]; "The Music of the 90's" [1992]; all publicity leaflets.

65. Conversation with Lester Spaulding, Grenada, June 2001.

66. Mohamed Alim Ali, interview by the author, New York, April 11, 2001.

67. Annan Boodram, interview by the author, New York, January 11, 2002.

68. University of the District of Columbia, Cable TV 19, http://www.udc.edu/cabletv19/caribtv.htm (accessed January 12, 2002).

69. CaribNation TV, http://www.caribnationtv.com/programfacts.html (accessed January 12, 2002).

70. NCTA, http://www.ncta.com/industry_overview/programList.cfm?network (accessed January 4, 2002).

71. Boodram interview; NCTA, http://www.ncta.com/industry_overview/programList.cfm?network_id=126&detail=1 (accessed January 4, 2002).

72. International Channel promotional materials, n.d.; International Channel, "International Channel Networks Launches Atlas: An Online Multicultural Marketing Tool for Affiliates," March 26, 2001, http://www.internationalchannel.com, press release page (accessed January 12, 2002).

73. John J. Sie, "Entertainment and Media in China" (speech, Asia Society's Eleventh Annual Corporate Conference, Los Angeles, May 24, 2000), n.p., reported in "Starz Encore's John J. Sie: China Cable TV Can Lead the World with Passage of PNTR and WTO Membership," PR Newswire, May 25, 2000; also available at http://www.findarticles.com/cf_0/m4PRN2000_May_25?62439684/print.jhtml (accessed January 12, 2002); "Premium Networks Overview," http://www.internationalchannel.com.

74. "Premium Networks Overview."

75. Communications Department, National Cable and Telecommunications Association, Cable Television Developments 2001 25 (1) (2001): 132.

76. From Ronald F. Chichy, "Iras-shai-mase (Welcome)," Hotels, June 1992, 40.

77. David Biagini, "Spotlight on In-Room Entertainment," Hotel and Resort Industry (January 1992): 42–50; TV Japan, "TV Japan Research: Reasons for Travel and Types of Accommodations," leaflet based on data from Travel and Tourism Administration, U.S. Department of Commerce; TV Japan, "TV Japan: The Big Picture: An Overview," leaflet in TV Japan's marketing package [1992].

78. TV Japan, "Japan Network Group, Inc.: Corporate Profile," leaflet. The shareholders of TV Japan are listed as: ITOCHU Group, NHK Group, Japan

Airlines, Dai-Ichi Kangyo Bank, Fuji Bank, Sakura Bank, Sanwa Bank, Industrial Bank of Japan, Bank of Tokyo, Long-Term Credit Bank of Japan, Mitsubishi Bank, KDD, Yasuda Fire and Marine Insurance, Maruben Corp., JHC Co., OCS America, Asahi Mutual Life Insurance, Tokyo Dome, Seiyu, Japan Travel Bureau, TP Oceania, Dai-Chi Mutual Life Insurance, Capital Cities/ABC Video Enterprises, Tokyo TV Broadcasting, and Asahi Homecast.

79. Tom Kerver, "Japan's Newest Import," *Cablevision*, November 4, 1991, 44–45; TV Japan, "Big Picture."

80. TV Japan, "TV Japan: From Japan to the United States Instantly" [1991]; TV Japan, "TV Japan: Homes, Hotels, Schools and Businesses via Direct Broadcast Satellite and Cable Television Systems" [1992].

81. International Channel, "Premium Programs Overview," http://www.internationalchannel.com.

82. Ibid.

83. "Denver Business Journal Names Starz Encore Group Chairman John J. Sie 'Business Leader of the Year,'" *PR Newswire*, August 28, 2001; International Channel Networks, "International Channel Networks Produces Public Service Announcement Urging Cultural and Religious Tolerance in the United States," corporate press release, September 24, 2001, http://www.internationalchannels.com, "press releases" (accessed January 12, 2002).

84. "One Hundred Questions and Answers about Arab Americans," *Detroit Free Press*, http://www.freep.com/jobspage/arabd2.html (accessed December 25, 2001); http://www.freep.com/jobspage/arabs/arab4.html (accessed December 25, 2001).

85. EthnicNet.com, http://www.ethnicnet.com/arabic/aboutus.html (accessed January 4, 2002).

86. In Laurie McGinley, "All-Arabic Broadcaster Makes Waves with a Big Scoop," *Wall Street Journal*, December 6, 1990.

87. NCTA, http://www.ncta.com/industry_overview/programList.cfm?network (accessed January 4, 2002).

88. Arab Radio and Television Network (ART), http://www.art-tv.net/corporate.asp (accessed January 13, 2002).

89. NCTA, http://www.ncta.com/industry_overview/programList.cfm? network (accessed January 4, 2002).

90. Ibid.

91. Ibid.; Scandinavian TV, "Scandinavia Channel Shuts Down Operations," http://www.scanchan.com (accessed January 13, 2002).

92. From Julie Anderson, "Educational Superstation Grows: Creighton Getting Larger Satellite Dish," *Omaha World Herald*, June 13, 1988.

93. NCTA, http://www.ncta.com/industry_overview/programList.cfm?network.

94. Ibid.

95. Manina Lassen-Grzech, foreword to *Third World Television Access to U.S. Media: Distributing Television Programs from Developing Countries in U.S. Television, New Electronic, and Nontheatrical Markets,* by Claus Mueller (New York: Friedrich Naumann Foundation, 1989), ix; on Mowlana's concept, see Hamid Mowlana, "Globalization of Mass Media: Opportunities and Challenges for the South," *Cooperation South,* no. 2 (1998): 22–39.

Chapter 8

1. As stated in chapter 5, under the Telecommunications Act of 1988 the term minority refers to "racial and ethnic minorities, including African Americans, Asian Americans, Hispanics, Native Americans and Pacific Islanders; recent immigrants; persons who do not speak English as their native language; and adults who lack basic reading skills." Corporation for Public Broadcasting, *Public Broadcasting and the Needs of Minority and Diverse Audiences and Public Broadcasting's Services to Minority and Other Groups: A Report to the 107th Congress and the American People Pursuant to Pub. L. 100–626* (Washington, D.C.: CPB, 2001), 5. Also available at http://stations.cpb.org/system/reports/minority. Practice has shown that PTV also includes persons with physical disabilities in the definition of *minority* and *diversity.*

2. John Witherspoon et al., *A History of Public Broadcasting* (Washington, D.C.: Current, 2000), 12; Bowker's Database Production Group, *Broadcasting and Cable Yearbook 2001* (New Providence, N.J.: R. R. Bowker, 2001).

3. Sydney Head and Christopher Sterling, *Broadcasting in America: A Survey of Electronic Media* (Boston: Houghton Mifflin, 1991).

4. For further details, see Corporation for Public Broadcasting, *Retrospective, 1967–1992: Annual Report—Twenty-Five Years from Wasteland to Oasis; A Quarter Century of Sterling Programming* (Washington, D.C.: CPB, 1992), 5; Corporation for Public Broadcasting, *To Know Ourselves: A Report to the 101st Congress on Public Broadcasting and the Needs of Minorities and Other Groups Pursuant to PL 100–626* (Washington, D.C.: CPB, 1989), 4.

5. S. Robert Lichter, Daniel Amundson, and Linda Lichter, *Balance and Diversity in PBS Documentaries* (Washington, D.C.: Center for Media and Public Affairs, 1992).

6. *Broadcasting and Cable Yearbook 2001,* xxx.

7. Witherspoon et al., *History of Public Broadcasting,* 14, 17.

8. For details on this liberal bias proposition, see Lichter, Amundson, and Lichter, *Balance and Diversity.*

9. Pledgers donated 21.1 percent of the $1.53 billion CPB generated in 1991. Auctions generated 1.6 percent. In 1992, CPB reported that 50 percent of its income came from private sources. In 1997, 45 percent of the system's revenue of $2 billion came from public sources—local governments (3 percent), public colleges (9 percent), state governments (16 percent), and federal government (17 percent). Fifty-five percent came from private sources—memberships (24 percent), businesses (14 percent), other entrepreneurial activities such as auctions (11 percent), and foundations (6 percent). In 2000, the system's gross revenues were $2.2 billion and just over 15 percent came from the federal government. See Corporation for Public Broadcasting, *Public Broadcasting Revenue Fiscal Year 2000,* http://www.cpb.org.

10. See Corporation for Public Broadcasting, *A Year of Achievement: Public Broadcasting's Services to Minorities and Other Groups; A Report to the 102nd Congress and the American People* (Washington, D.C.: CPB, 1992), 47–48. For more information on Asian American PTV viewing, see Corporation for Public Broacasting, *Making a Difference: A Report to the 102nd Congress, 1st Session on Public Broadcasting's Services to Minorities and Other Groups* (Washington, D.C.: CPB, 1991), 19–20.

11. For details, see CPB, *Wasteland to Oasis,* 16.

12. For a more extensive illustration of that tendency, see ibid., 4.

13. Corporation for Public Broadcasting, *Public Broadcasting and the Needs of Minority and Diverse Audiences: A Report to 107th Congress* (Washington, D.C.: CPB, 2001), 112–16.

14. Ibid., 8; Corporation for Public Broadcasting, http://www.pbs.org/americanfamily/series.html.

15. CPB, *Minority and Diverse Audiences,* 11.

16. For details see CPB, *Wasteland to Oasis,* 25–26.

17. The Latin consortium was established in 1974, the Native American consortium in 1976, and the National Asian American consortium in 1980. The National Black Programming Consortium, created in 1979, joined the Minority Consortia in 1990.

18. National Minority Consortia, http://www.cpb.org/tv/diversity/partners/mconsortia/ (accessed January 30, 2002).

19. National Asian American Telecommunications Association (NAATA), http://www.naatanet.org (accessed January 30, 2002); *NAATA Media Grants* (San Francisco: NAATA, [1991]), 4.

20. NAATA, "NAATA at Twenty," www.naatanet.org (accessed January 30, 2002).

21. Ibid.; CPB, *Minority and Diverse Audiences,* 112–16.

22. This report is NAATA, *Final Report and Recommendations of the Task*

Force on National Minority Programming, available at http://www.naatanet.org. All other quotes in the paragraph are from NAATA, "Background," http://www.naatanet.org (accessed January 30, 2002).

23. NAATA, *CrossCurrent Media: Asian American Audiovisual Catalog* (San Francisco: NAATA, 1990), 1. The NAATA distribution categories are: aging, activism, culture clash, family, history, human rights, identity, Japanese American internment, lesbian/gay/bisexuals, multiracial and ethnic heritage, new immigrants and refugees, racism, personal stories, and youth. Complete details available at http://www.naatanet.org/shopnaata.

24. National Black Programming Consortium (NBPC), "Conceptualization to Realization," http://www.nbpc.tv (accessed January 30, 2002); *NBPC History*, pamphlet from a set of promotional materials produced by the National Black Programming Consortium (Columbus, Ohio: NPBC, n.d.), n.p.; NBPC, *Vision Statement*, pamphlet (n.p.: NBPC, [1991]), n.p.

25. NBPC, *Vision Statement;* "Conceptualization to Realization."

26. From Native American Public Broadcasting Consortium (NAPBC), *NAPBC Overview* (Lincoln, Nebr.: NAPBC, n.d.); Native American Public Telecommunications (NAPT), "Mission Statement," http://www.nativetelecom.org/mission.html (accessed January 30, 2002).

27. NAPBC, *Native American Program Grants* (Lincoln, Nebr.: NAPBC, n.d.), 1.

28. Lurline McGregor to author, undated (before March 18, 1992, the date of other correspondence); Pacific Islanders in Communications (PIC), *Corporation for Public Broadcasting Supports Pacific Islander Media Consortium,* press release; PIC, "What Is Pacific Islanders in Communications (PIC)?" http://www.piccom.org/ (accessed January 30, 2002).

29. PIC, "Executive Productions" and "2001 Media Fund Awardees," http://www.piccom.org/ (accessed January 30, 2002).

30. José Luis Ruiz, executive director, National Latino Communications Center, to Gina Jalon, March 5, 1992.

31. Ibid.

32. Latino Public Broadcasting (LPB), http://www.lpbp.org/page/about/latin (accessed January 30, 2002).

33. Ibid.

34. International Television Service (ITVS), "Everything You Always Wanted to Know about ITVS," http://www.itvs.org/aboutFAQ.html (accessed January 30, 2002); "ITVS Mission Statement," in ITVS, *A New Vision of Television As Varied As the American People,* (n.p.: ITVS, n.d.; Witherspoon et al., *History of Public Broadcasting,* 105–6.

35. ITVS, "Everything You Always Wanted."

36. CPB, *Minority and Diverse Audiences,* 112, 114; International Television Service, "Recently Funded," http://www.itvs.org/producers/recentlyfunded.html (accessed January 30, 2002).

37. ITVS, "About Us," http://www.itvs.org/producers/recentlyfunded.html (accessed January 30, 2002).

38. From "ITVS and WORLDLINK TV," http://www.itvs.org/producers/recentlyfunded.html (accessed January 30, 2002).

39. The idea of the next generation of human rights is associated with the concepts of public sphere and with the work of Hans Einzenberger, Jurgen Habermas, and Charles Husbands in *Ethnic Minorities and the Media,* ed. Simon Cottle (Buckingham, England: Open University Press, 2000).

40. Ibid., 38.

41. Ibid., 2; CPB, *Minority and Diverse Audiences,* 107, 109.

Chapter 9

1. From Denis McQuail, *Mass Communication Theory: An Introduction,* 2nd ed. (London: Sage, 1987), 123.

2. For reports on this trend across the United States, see Miguel Bustillo, "Channeling Creativity: Public Access TV Deal is Putting Amateur Auteurs in the Spotlight for Next to Nothing," *Los Angeles Times,* September 15, 1996; Bob Pool, "Pulling the Plug on Public Access TV?" *Los Angeles Times,* March 25, 1999; Caitlin Liu, Seema Mehta, and Neda Raouf, "Public Access, Spotty Success," *Los Angeles Times,* July 16, 1999; Leslie Williams, "Fees Raised for Use of Public Access TV," *New Orleans Times-Picayune,* August 10, 2001.

3. Ralph Engleman, *The Origins of Public Access Cable Television, 1966–1972,* Journalism Monographs, no. 123 (October 1990): 37.

4. From Simon Rose, "Oldest Head-Banger in Town: The Huge Success of Heavy Metal Comedy *Wayne's World* Has Made Penelope Spheeris a Hot Property," *London Daily Telegraph,* May 20, 1992.

5. From Keith J. McGrew, "Public-Access TV Diverse," *Atlanta Journal and Constitution,* March 6, 1992.

6. Engleman, *Origins of Public Access,* 1, 2.

7. Alternative Media Center, *AMC: The Alternative Media Center, Tisch School of Art* (New York: New York University, n.d.), 2, cited in Engleman, *Origins of Public Access,* 18.

8. National Federation of Local Cable Programmers, *National Federation of Local Cable Programmers,* brochure, n.p., n.d.

9. Ibid.; see also National Federation of Local Cable Programmers/Alliances

for Community Media, "The Alliance for Community Media," http://www.alliancecm.org/about/acm.htm (accessed February 2, 2002).

10. Dwight Oestricher, "Activism on the Airwaves," *City Limits,* January 1992 (photocopy provided by Deep Dish Network); *Deep Dish TV: 1992 Fall Schedule.*

11. From Deep Dish Network, "History," http://www.igc.org/deepdish/history/index.html (accessed January 14, 2002).

12. Ioannis Mookas, operations manager, Deep Dish TV Network, to author, January 1, 1993.

13. Ibid.

14. Deep Dish TV Network, "Catalog," http://www.igc.org/deepdish/aboutus/cat/cat05.html (accessed January 14, 2002). See, for example, Bob Black, "Here's Looking at You," *Chicago Sun-Times,* April 25, 1997; Wayne Washington, "Cable TV Panel Considers Steps to Counter Extremism," *St. Petersburg Times,* May 10, 1997; "Eliminate Public Access," *Tampa Tribune,* September 10, 1998; Jo Thomas, "A City Takes a Stand against Hate," *New York Times,* September 21, 1999.

15. Douglas Davis, "Public Access TV Is Heard in the Land," *New York Times,* June 11, 1989.

16. Margie Nicholson, *Cable Access: A Community Communications Resource for Nonprofits* (Washington, D.C.: Benton Foundation, April 1990).

17. Bronxnet, "Perspectives," http://www.bronxnet.com/bronxnetw/pages/perspectives.html (accessed February 6, 2002).

18. Channels 34, 35, 56, 57, 67, and 80 of the Time Warner system and Channels 67–70 of the Cablevision system.

19. Brooklyn Cable Access Television (BCAT), "About BCAT/Brooklyn Community Access Television," http://www.brooklynx.org/bcat/aboutbcat.asp (accessed February 2, 2002).

20. Based on data at BCAT, http://www.brooklynx.org/bcat/pguide/whatson.asp (accessed February 2, 2002).

21. Ibid.

22. Tom Robbins, "$50 Million and Nobody's Watching the Weird, the Wacky, the Off-the-Wall, All on the Cable System You are Paying For," *New York Daily News,* December 8, 1996; Robert Domínguez, "TV's 'Rhumba' in the Bronx," *New York Daily News,* January 31, 1997; Bronxnet, "Program Profiles," http://www.bronxnet.com/bronxnetw/pages/publicaccess.html (accessed February 6, 2002).

24. Bronxnet, "Bronx Life," http://www.bronxnet.com/bronxnetw/pages/bronxlive.html (accessed February 6, 2002).

25. Ibid.

26. Ibid.; Bronxnet, "Program Profiles."

27. Bronxnet, "Program Profiles."

28. Queens Public Television (QPTV), "A Memorandum from the Programming Department," http://www.qptv.org/memo.htm (accessed February 7, 2002).

29. QPTV, "QPTV Grant-Aid Programs," http://www.qptv.org/grantaid. htm (accessed February 7, 2002).

30. SICTV, "Staten Island Community Television Schedule," http://www. sictv.org/2.3.02.35.html (accessed February 7, 2002).

31. Manhattan Neighborhood Network, http://www.mnntv.com (accessed February 2, 2002); Alex Witched, "Vox Pop Video: A Public Access TV Guide," *New York Times,* October 30, 1994.

32. Constance L. Hays, "New York Stories: The View from Behind the Camera," *New York Times,* October 30, 1994.

33. Somerville Community Access Television (SCAT), "Mission," http://www.access-scat.org (accessed February 2, 2002).

34. Ibid.

35. SCAT, "Media Action Project for the Prevention and Education of Domestic Violence," http://www.access-scat.org/mapped/mapped.htm (accessed February 2, 2002).

36. Boston Neighborhood Network Television (BNNTV), "Mission," http://www.bnntv.org/pages/mission.html (accessed February 2, 2002).

37. Jewish diaspora: "Channel 23 Highlights," http://www.bnntv.org/pages/channel23.html (accessed February 2, 2002); Ethiopians and Eritreans: "Channel 9 Highlights," http://www.bnntv.org/pages/channel9.html (accessed February 2, 2002).

38. "Neighborhood Network News," http://www.bnntv.org/pages/nnnews. hrml (accessed February 2, 2002).

39. BNNTV, "Vision," http://www.bnntv.org/pages/mission.html (accessed February 2, 2002).

40. Kevin M. Williams, "Here's Looking at You: Access Channels Offer TV by, for the People," *Chicago Sun-Times,* April 25, 1997; Chicago Access Network (CAN TV), "Who We Are," http://www.cantv.org/profile.htm (accessed February 3, 2002); "CAN TV Program Descriptions," http://www.cantv.org/descrip .htm (accessed February 10, 2002).

41. CAN TV, "CAN TV Program Descriptions."

42. Ibid.

43. Sylvia Moreno, "Students in the Studio: Access Channel Produces Shows, Experience," *Washington Post,* July 23, 1997; Arlington Community Television (ACT), "January 2002 Programming Schedule," http://www.channel33. org/programming/programming.htm (accessed February 3, 2002).

44. Sylvia Moreno, "Public Airwaves, Private Opinions: Film on Arlington Cable Channel Assailed," *Washington Post,* November 15, 1998.

45. ACT, http://www.channe133.org/rosebud/rosebud.htm (accessed February 3, 2002).

46. Gillina Harris, "Access TV Is about to Hit Britain in a Big Way," *Scotsman,* November 7, 1994; Tom Lappin, "Risqué Business," *Scotsman,* May 4, 1995.

47. Lappin, "Risqué Business."

48. The Political Staff, "Public-Access TV Rejected," *South China Morning Post,* May 7, 1995.

49. Jackie Loohauis, "Anything Goes: Public-Access TV Voices for All: Five Hundred Gather to Examine Role, from Wise to Wacky," *Milwaukee Journal Sentinel,* July 12, 1997.

50. Colin Somerville, "MCWAYNE'S WORLD?" *Scotland on Sunday,* April 11, 1999; community-oriented programming: Caitlin Liu, Seema Mehta and Neda Raouf, "Public Access Spotty Success," *Los Angeles Times,* July 16, 2002.

51. Patrik Jonsson, "Public-Access TV Gains Cachet and New Viewers," *Christian Science Monitor,* January 2, 2002.

52. An excellent visual record of this era is the video *Everybody's Channel.*

53. Jonsson, "Public-Access TV Gains Cachet."

54. Based on comments by an Indian respondent to a survey conducted in New York during Spring 2001.

55. "Satisfied": 45 percent; "acceptable": 18 percent; "very satisfied": 9 percent.

56. Questionnaire, New York, spring 2001.

57. Questionnaire completed by a Barbadian male, New York, spring 2001.

58. Questionnaire, Brooklyn College, spring 2001.

Chapter 10

1. Manina Lassen-Grzech, foreword to *Third World Television Access to U.S. Media: Distributing Television Programs from Developing Countries in U.S. Television, New Electronic, and Nontheatrical Markets,* by Claus Mueller (New York: Friedrich Naumann Foundation, 1989), ix.

2. From Denis McQuail, *Mass Communication Theory: An Introduction,* 4th ed. (London: Sage, 2000), 166.

3. Based on materials ibid., 166–67.

4. Kofi Asiedu Ofori, *When Being Number One Is Not Enough* (Washington, D.C.: FCC, 1999).

5. McQuail, *Mass Communication Theory,* 4th ed., 169.

6. Ibid., 171.

7. See, for example, American Society of Newspaper Editors (ASNE), "2001 ASNE Census Finds Newsrooms Less Diverse: Increased Hiring of Minorities Blunted by Departure Rate," http://www.asne.org/kiosk/diversity/2001survey/ 2001CensusReport.htm (accessed June 11, 2003).

8. McQuail, *Mass Communication Theory,* 4th ed., 172.

9. Arthur Schlesinger, *The Disuniting of America: Reflections on a Multicultural Society* (New York: Larger Agenda Series, Whittle Direct Books, 1991).

10. McQuail, *Mass Communication Theory,* 4th ed., 178.

11. James Curran, "Rethinking the Media as Public Sphere," in *Communication and Citizenship: Journalism and the Public Sphere in the New Media Age,* ed. Peter Dahlgren and Colin Sparks (London: Routledge, 1991), 2, cited in Charles Husbands, "Media and the Public Sphere in Multi-Ethnic Societies," in *Ethnic Minorities and the Media,* ed. Simon Cottle (Buckingham, England: Open University Press, 2000), 201.

12. Michael S. Teitelbaum, "The Role of the State in International Migration," *Brown Journal of World Affairs* 8 (2) (2002): 157–58.

13. For details see Taisto Hujanen, ed., *Information, Communication and the Human Rights of Migrants,* report of the Final Conference of the Joint Study on the Role of Information in the Realization of the Human Rights of Migrant Workers, Lausanne, Switzerland, October 23–27, 1988.

14. On multicultural public spheres: Husbands, "Media and the Public Sphere," 207. The creation of the USA Freedom Corps was announced by President George W. Bush, during his state of the union speech on January 29, 2002. Further details on the organization are available at http://www.usafreedomcorps .gov/.

15. Husbands, "Media and the Public Sphere," 200; Vijay Prashad, *Everybody Was Kung Fu Fighting: Afro-Asian Connections and the Myth of Cultural Purity* (Boston: Beacon Press, 2001).

Selected Bibliography

Alternative Media Center. *AMC: The Alternative Media Center, Tisch School of Art.* New York: New York University, n.d.

American Broadcasting Company. *ABC Broadcast Standards and Practices.* New York: ABC, 1996.

Astroff, R. "Spanish Gold: Stereotypes, Ideology, and the Construction of a U.S. Latino Market." *Howard Journal of Communications* 1 (4) (1989): 155–73.

Aufderhide, P. "Cable Television and the Public Interest." *Journal of Communication* 42 (1): 52–65.

Aversa, A. "Italian Neo-Ethnicity: The Search for Self Identity." *Journal of Ethnic Studies* (Western Washington U.) 6 (2) (1979): 49–56.

Biagini, D. "Spotlight on In-Room Entertainment." *Hotel and Resort Industry,* January 1992, 42–50.

Baker, W., and G. Dessart. "The Road Ahead." *Television Quarterly* 39 (4) (1998): 2–16.

Baran, S., and D. Davis. *Mass Communication Theory: Foundations, Ferment, and Future.* Belmont, Calif.: Wadsworth, 1995.

Berlin, I. *Generations of Captivity: A History of African American Slaves.* Cambridge, Mass.: Belknap Press, 2003.

Bishop, R. "Regional Media Export Centers: The Case of Hong Kong." *Gazette* 35 (1) (1985): 61–70.

Bogle, D. *Toms, Coons, Mulattoes, Mammies, and Bucks: An Interpretive History of Blacks in American Films.* New York: Frederick Ungar, 1992.

Bowker's Database Production Group. *Broadcasting and Cable Yearbook 1991.* Washington, D.C.: R. R. Bowker, 1991.

———. *Broadcasting and Cable Yearbook 1998.* Washington, D.C.: R. R. Bowker, 1998.

———. *Broadcasting and Cable Yearbook 2000.* Washington, D.C.: R. R. Bowker, 2000.

———. *Broadcasting and Cable Yearbook 2001.* Washington, D.C.: R. R. Bowker, 2001.

Breed, W. "Social Control in the Newsroom: A Functional Analysis." *Social Forces* 33 (May 1955): 326–35.

Broadcasting Publications. *Broadcasting Yearbook 1966*. Washington, D.C.: Broadcasting Publications, 1966.

———. *Broadcasting Yearbook 1976*. Washington, D.C.: Broadcasting Publications, 1976.

Brooks, T., and E. Marsh. *The Complete Directory to Prime Time Network TV Shows, 1946–Present*. 7th ed. New York: Ballantine Books, 1997.

Burrell, G., and G. Morgan. *Sociological Paradigms and Organisational Analysis*. Portsmouth, N.H.: Heinemann, 1979.

Cambridge, V. "Immigration, Race, Ethnicity, and Broadcasting in the United States." Paper presented at International Conference on Immigration and Communication, Tallin, Estonia, July 1992.

———. "Mass Media Entertainment and Human Resources Development: Radio Serials in Jamaica from 1962." Ph.D. diss., Ohio University, 1989.

———. "Radio Soap Operas in Global Africa: Origins, Applications, and Implications." In *Staying Tuned: Contemporary Soap Opera Criticism*, ed. S. Frentz, 110–27. Bowling Green, Ohio: BGSU Popular Press, 1991.

———. Radio Soap Operas: The Jamaican Experience, 1958–1989. *Studies in Latin American Popular Culture* 11 (1992): 93–97.

Carter, R. "TV's Black Comfort Zone for Whites." *Television Quarterly* 23 (4) (1988): 29–34.

Chan-Olmsted, S. "Mergers, Acquisitions, and Convergence: The Strategic Alliances of Broadcasting, Cable Television, and Television Services." *Journal of Media Economics* 11 (3) (1998): 33–46.

Chichy, R. "Iras-shai-mase (Welcome)." *Hotels*, June 1992, 40.

Comstock, G. "The Impact of Television on American Institutions." *Journal of Communication* 28 (2) (1978): 12–28.

Corporation for Public Broadcasting. *Building on a Common Core*. Washington, D.C.: CPB, 1992.

———. *Many Faces, Many Voices: A Report to the 101st Congress*. Washington, D.C.: CPB, 1990.

———. *Public Broadcasting and the Needs of Minority and Diverse Audiences and Public Broadcasting's Services to Minority and Other Groups: A Report to the 107th Congress and the American People Pursuant to Pub. L. 100–626*. Washington, D.C.: CPB, 2001.

———. *Public Broadcasting Revenue: Fiscal Year 2000 Final Report*. Washington, D.C.: CPB, 2002.

———. *Public Broadcasting's Services to Minorities and Diverse Audiences: A Report to the 106th Congress*. Washington, D.C.: CPB, 2000.

———. *Retrospective, 1967–1992: Twenty-Five Years from Wasteland to Oasis; A Quarter Century of Sterling Programming*. Washington, D.C.: CPB, 1992.

————. *To Know Ourselves: A Report to the 101st Congress.* Washington, D.C.: CPB, 1989.

Cottle, S., ed. *Ethnic Minorities and the Media.* Buckingham, England: Open University Press, 2000.

Croteau, D., and W. Hoynes. *Media/Society: Industries, Images, and Audiences.* Thousand Oaks, Calif.: Pine Forge Press, 1997.

Curran, J. "Rethinking the Media as Public Sphere." In *Communication and Citizenship: Journalism and the Public Sphere in the New Media Age,* ed. P. Dahlgren and C. Sparks, 27–57. London: Routledge, 1991.

Dates, J., and W. Barlow, eds. *Split Image: African Americans in the Mass Media.* Washington, D.C.: Howard University Press, 1991.

DeFleur, M., and S. Ball-Rokeach. *Theories of Mass Communication.* 5th ed. New York: Longman, 1989.

DuBois, W. E. B. *The Souls of Black Folk.* New York: Signet Classics, 1969.

Edmondson, B. "Migration: The Newest New Yorkers." *American Demographics* 14 (8) (1992): 8.

Ellul, J. *Propaganda: The Formation of Men's Attitudes.* New York: Vintage Books, 1973.

Emery, M. C., and T. C. Smythe. *Readings in Mass Communication.* Dubuque, Iowa: W. C. Brown, 1989.

Engleman, R. *The Origins of Public Access Cable Television, 1966–1972.* Journalism Monographs (Columbia, S.C.), no. 123 (1990).

Escoffier, J. "The Limits to Multiculturalism." *Socialist Review* 21 (3, 4) (1990): 61–73.

Featherstone, M., ed. *Global Culture: Nationalism, Globalization, and Modernity.* Newbury Park, Calif.: Sage, 1990.

Federal Communications Commission. *Review of Radio Industry, 2000.* Washington, D.C.: FCC, 2001.

Fowler, G., and B. Crawford. *Border Radio: Quacks, Yodelers, Pitchmen, Psychics, and Other Amazing Broadcasters of the American Airwaves.* Austin: University of Texas Press, 2002.

Friend, T. "Sitcoms, Seriously." *Esquire* 119 (3) (1993): 112–24.

Gardner, Robert W., and Leon F. Bouvier. "The United States." In *Handbook on International Migration,* ed. W. J. Serow, 71–107. New York: Greenwood Press, 1990.

Gates, H. L., Jr., and N. McKay. "W. E. B. DuBois." In *The Norton Anthology of African American Literature,* ed. Henry Louis Gates, Jr., and Nellie McKay, 606–8. New York: Norton, 1997.

Gilroy, P. "Cultural Studies and Ethnic Absolutism." In *Cultural Studies,* ed. Lawrence Grossberg, Cary Nelson, and Paula Treichler. New York: Praeger, 1992.

Graves, T. "Movies and Home Entertainment." In *Standard and Poor's Industry Surveys,* Eileen M. Bosong-Martines. New York: Standard and Poor's, 2000.

Hammer, J. "Must Blacks Be Buffoons?" *Newsweek,* October 26, 1992, 70.

Hammer, J., and J. Schwartz. "Prime-Time Mensch," *Newsweek,* October 12, 1992, 88–89.

Hangen, T. "Launching the Radio Church, 1921–1940." Paper presented at annual meeting of the Association for Education in Journalism and Mass Communication, New Orleans, August 1999.

Hazzard, M. L., and V. C. Cambridge. Socio-Drama as an Applied Technique for Development Communication in the Caribbean: Specialized Content and Narrative Structure in the Radio Dramas of Elaine Perkins in Jamaica. In *Caribbean Popular Culture,* ed. J. Lent, 106–19. Bowling Green, Ohio: BGSU Popular Press, 1990.

Head, S. *World Broadcasting Systems: A Comparative Analysis.* Belmont, Calif.: Wadsworth Publishing, 1985.

Head, S., and C. Sterling. *Broadcasting in America: A Survey of Electronic Media.* Boston: Houghton Mifflin, 1991.

Herzog, H. "What Do We Really Know about Daytime Serial Listeners?" In *Radio Research 1942–1943,* ed. P. Lazarsfeld and F. Stanton, 3–33. New York: Essential Books, 1944.

Hujanen, T., ed. *Information, Communication and the Human Rights of Migrants.* Report of the Final Conference of the Joint Study on the Role of Information in the Realization of Human Rights of Migrant Workers. Lausanne, Switzerland, 1988.

Hunter, A. "Percy Sutton/Inner City Broadcasting: A Family Affair." *Class,* February 1990, 33–37.

Jhally, S., and J. Lewis. *Enlightened Racism: The Cosby Show, Audiences, and the Myth of the American Dream.* Boulder: Westview, 1992.

Johnson Publishing Company. "JPC-TV." *Ebony* 48 (1) (1992): 76–82.

Jones, F. "The Black Audience and the BET Channel." *Journal of Broadcasting and Electronic Media* 34 (4) (1990): 477–86.

Judge, C. "Hegemony of the Heart." *Policy Review,* no. 110 (December 2001–January 2002): 3–14.

Kennedy, J. *A Nation of Immigrants.* New York: Harper and Row, 1964.

Kleiman, H. "Content Diversity and the FCC's Minority and Gender Licensing Policies." *Journal of Broadcasting and Electronic Media* 35 (4) (1991): 411–29.

Krampner, J. "Asians Gain in TV: But It Is Still Hard to Reach the Top." *Electronic Media* 8 (July 1991): 29, 34.

Kromkowski, J. A., ed. *Race and Ethnic Relations, 91/92.* Guilford, Conn.: Dushkin Publishing Group, 1991.

Lappin, T. "Risqué Business." *Scotsman,* May 4, 1995, 16.

Larsen, P. *Import/Export: International Flow of Television Fiction.* Paris: UNESCO, 1990.

Lassen-Grzech, M. Foreword to *Third World Television Access to U.S. Media: Distributing Television Programs from Developing Countries in U.S. Television, New Electronic, and Non-Theatrical Markets,* by C. Mueller. New York: Friedrich Neumann Foundation, 1989.

Lazarsfeld, P., and F. Stanton, eds. *Radio Research, 1942–1943.* New York: Essential Books, 1944.

Leckenby, J., and S. Surlin. "Incidental Social Learning and Viewer Race: *All in the Family* and *Sanford and Son.*" *Journal of Broadcasting* 20 (4) (1976): 481–94.

Lichter, S., D. Amundson, and L. Lichter. *Balance and Diversity in PBS Documentaries.* Washington, D.C.: Center for Media and Public Affairs, 1992.

Lipsitz, G. "The Meaning of Memory: Family, Class, and Ethnicity in Early Network Television Programs." In *Private Screenings: Television and the Female Consumer,* ed. Lynn Spigel and Denise Mann. Minneapolis: University of Minnesota Press, 1992.

Lowery, S., and M. DeFleur. *Milestones in Communication Research.* 2nd ed. New York: Longman, 1988.

Mahoney, W., and K. Oberlander. "Hispanic Production on the Rise." *Electronic Media* 8 (July 1991): 30, 32.

Mann, E. *The Newest New Yorkers: A Statistical Portrait.* New York: Department of City Planning, 1992.

Manuel, P. "Latin Music in the United States." *Journal of Communication* 41 (1) (1991): 104–16.

Martin, P., and E. Midgley. "Immigration to the United States." *Population Bulletin* 54 (2) (1999): 3–44.

———. "Immigration to the United States: Journey to an Uncertain Destination." *Population Bulletin* 49 (2) (1994): 1–40.

Marzolf, M. "America's Enduring Ethnic Press." Paper presented at annual meeting of the Association for Education in Journalism, Fort Collins, Colo., August 1973.

McChesney, R. "The Battle for U.S. Airwaves, 1928–1935." *Journal of Communication* 40 (Autumn 1990): 29–57.

McFarlin, J. "African Americans Find Their Place on the Air." *Electronic Media* 8 (July 1991): 29–36.

McQuail, D. *Mass Communication Theory: An Introduction.* 2nd ed. London: Sage, 1987.

———. *Mass Communication Theory: An Introduction.* 3rd ed. London: Sage, 1994.

————. *Mass Communication Theory: An Introduction.* 4th ed. London: Sage, 2000.

Mendelsohn, H. *Mass Entertainment.* New Haven, Conn: College and University Press, 1966.

Mermigas, D. "Time Warner Steps into Future." *Electronic Media,* February 1, 1993, 1, 23.

Migala, J. *Polish Radio Broadcasting in the United States.* Boulder: East European Monographs, 1987.

Mowlana, H. "Globalization of Mass Media: Opportunities and Challenges for the South." *Cooperation South,* no. 2 (1998): 22–39.

Mueller, C. *Third World Television Access to U.S. Media: Distributing Television Programs from Developing Countries in U.S. Television, New Electronic, and Non-Theatrical Markets.* New York: Friedrich Neumann Foundation, 1989.

Murphy, S. "From the Kerner Report to the Reagan Years: Twenty Years of Struggle." In *Readings in Mass Communication,* ed. M. C. Emery and T. C. Smythe, 193–99. Dubuque, Iowa: William C. Brown, 1989.

National Advisory Commission on Civil Disorders. *Report of the National Advisory Commission on Civil Disorders.* New York: New York Times, 1968.

————. *Native American Program Grants.* Lincoln, Nebr.: NAPBC, n.d.

National Asian American Telecommunications Association. *CrossCurrent Media: Asian American Audiovisual Catalog.* San Francisco: NAATA, 1990.

————. *NAATA Media Grants.* San Francisco: NAATA, [1991].

National Association of Broadcasters. *Broadcast Regulations '89: A Mid-Year Report.* Washington, D.C.: NAB, 1989.

National Association of Television Program Executives. *Membership Opportunity: National Association of Television Program Executives.* Santa Monica: NATPE, n.d.

————. *Minority Programming: A Billion-Dollar Market.* Videotape 8, NATPE annual conference, New Orleans, January 16–18, 1991.

National Telecommunications and Information Administration. *Minority Telecommunications Development Program.* Washington, D.C.: NTIA, n.d.

————. *NTIA Telecom 2000: Charting the Course for a New Century.* Washington, D.C.: U.S. Department of Commerce, 1988.

Native American Public Broadcasting Consortium. *NAPBC Overview.* Lincoln, Nebr.: NAPBC, n.d.

Nicholson, M. *Cable Access: A Community Communications Resource for Nonprofits.* Washington, D.C.: Benton Foundation, 1990.

Obregon, R. "Radio Caracol: Colombian Broadcasting in Miami." Paper presented at seminar on Multicultural Broadcasting in the United States, School of Telecommunications, Ohio University, Athens, 1994.

Oestricher, D. "Activism on the Airwaves." *City Limits*, January 1992. Photocopy provided by Deep Dish Network.

Ofori, Kofi Asiedu. *When Being Number One Is Not Enough*. Washington, D.C.: FCC, 1999.

Orbe, M., and T. Harris. *Interracial Communication: Theory into Practice*. Belmont, Calif.: Wadsworth, 2001.

Orozco, M. *Remitting Back Home and Supporting the Homeland: The Guyanese Community in the U.S.* Working paper commissioned by U.S. Agency for International Development (GEO Project), 2002.

Park, R. *The Immigrant Press and Its Control*. Westport, Conn.: Greenwood Press, 1970.

Pasqua, T., Jr., J. Buckalew, R. Rayfield, and J. Tankard, eds. *Mass Media in the Information Age*. Englewood Cliffs, N.J.: Prentice-Hall, 1990.

Pepper and Corazzini, LLC. *EEO Regulations and Employment Practices: A Primer for the Ohio Association of Broadcasters on Current FCC Requirements*. Washington, D.C.: Pepper and Corazzini, n.d.

Phillips, M., and T. Phillips. *Windrush: The Irresistible Rise of Multi-Racial Britain*. London: HarperCollins, 1999.

Pohjola, A. "Social Networks: Help or Hindrance to the Migrant." *International Migration* 29 (3) (1991): 435–41.

Prashad, V. *Everybody Was Kung Fu Fighting: Afro-Asian Connections and the Myth of Cultural Purity*. Boston: Beacon Press, 2001.

Rodriguez, C. *Fissures in the Mediascape: An International Study of Citizens' Media*. Cresskill, N.J.: Hampton Press, 2001.

Rogers, E. *A History of Communication Study: A Biographical Approach*. New York: Free Press, 1994.

Rogers, E., and R. Steinfatt. *Intercultural Communication*. Prospect Heights, Ill.: Waveland Press, 1999.

Roper Starch. *America's Watching: Public Attitudes toward Television*. New York: Roper Starch Worldwide, 1997.

Ruhomon, P. *Centenary History of the East Indians in British Guiana, 1838–1938*. Georgetown, British Guiana: Daily Chronicle, 1947.

Schlesinger, A. *The Disuniting of America: Reflections on a Multicultural Society*. New York: Whittle Direct Books, 1991.

Schmidtke, O. "Transnational Migration: A Challenge to European Citizen Regimes." *World Affairs* 164 (1) (2001): 3–16.

Schramm, W. *The Story of Human Communication: Cave Painting to Microchip*. New York: Harper Row, 1988.

Serow, W. J., ed. *Handbook on International Migration*. New York: Greenwood Press, 1990.

Shaheen, J. *The TV Arab*. Bowling Green, Ohio: BGSU Popular Press, 1984.

Shaw, D. *The Rise and Fall of American Mass Media: The Roles of Technology and Leadership*. Bloomington: School of Journalism, Indiana University, 1991.

Simon, R. *Public Opinion and The Immigrant: Print Media Coverage, 1880–1980*. Lexington, Mass.: Lexington Books, 1985.

Singhal, A., and E. Rogers. (1999). *Entertainment-Education: A Communication Strategy for Social Change*. Mahwah, N.J.: Lawrence Erlbaum Associates, Publishers.

Subervi Vélez, F. "Mass Communication and Hispanics." In *Handbook of Hispanic Cultures in the United States, Sociology*, ed. F. Padilla, 304–57. Houston: Arte Público Press, 1994.

Teitelbaum, M. "The Role of the State in International Migration." *Brown Journal of World Affairs* 8 (2) (2002): 157–58.

Thompson, R. "Afro-Atlantic Music in the Nineties: Making Space for African Futures." In *Afropop Worldwide: 1991 Listener's Guide*. Brooklyn: World Music Productions, 1991.

Trevino, A. "Spanish Language in the United States." Paper TCOM 367, School of Telecommunications, Ohio University, 1999.

Turow, J. *Media Industries: The Production of News and Entertainment*. New York: Longman Communication Books, 1984.

———. *Media Systems in Society: Understanding Industries, Strategies, and Power*. New York: Longman, 1992.

United States. Department of Justice. Immigration and Naturalization Service. *Statistical Yearbook of the Immigration and Naturalization Service*. Washington, D.C.: INS, 1997.

United States Commission on Civil Rights. *Window Dressing on the Set: Women and Minorities in Television*. Washington, D.C.: United States Commission on Civil Rights, 1977.

Vlahos, M. "Culture and Foreign Policy." *Foreign Affairs* 82 (Spring 1991): 59–78.

Waterman, D., and A. Grant. "Cable Television as an Aftermarket." *Journal of Broadcasting and Electronic Media* 35 (2) (1991): 179–88.

Waterston, A., E. Gerena, Yihan Xie, and M. Gomez. *A Look Towards Advancement: Minority Employment in Cable*. Report prepared for the National Association for Minorities in Cable (NAMIC), Research and Policy Committee, August 1999.

Wells, R. "Migration and the Image of Nebraska in England." *Nebraska History* 54 (3) (1973): 475–91.

Winston, M. "Racial Consciousness and the Evolution of Mass Communication in the United States." *Daedalus* 3 (4) (1982).

Witherspoon, J., R. Kovitz, R. Avery, A. Stavitsky, S. Behrens, J. Yore, and R. Barbieri. *A History of Public Broadcasting*. Washington, D. C.: Current, 2000.

World Music Productions. *Afropop Worldwide: 1991 Listener's Guide*. Brooklyn: World Music Productions, 1991.

Index

ABC, 146, 179, 237, 272n48, 278n78
accelerator and brake, 29
Ad Council, 3, 258, 272
advertising
  advertisers, 91, 94, 153–54, 160, 168,
    171
  ethnic realism in, 154
  Siboney Advertising, 154
  Young and Rubicam, 119, 153
African Americans, 5, 9, 14, 15, 124, 166,
    167, 270n10, 277n55, 280n1
  employment in media, 141
  radio and, 31-37
  stereotyping of, 115, 116, 134
  television, presence on, 51, 112, 114,
    115
  viewing habits of, 42, 124
  See also blacks
Africans, 9, 12, 68, 74, 89, 108, 115, 194,
    199
  slavery and, 9, 89, 108, 265, 270n10
  See also African Americans; blacks
Afro-Brazilians, 115
Afro-Caribbeans, 99, 115, 163, 164, 172,
    239
Afro-Cubans, 226
Afropop Worldwide, 73, 74, 267n26
aftermarket, 108, 139, 140, 161, 163, 167,
    187
Ali, Mohamed Alim, 169–72
Ali, Yacob, 170
Alliance for Community Media, 216,
    217, 233, 234, 283n9
All India Radio, 83
All in the Family, 107, 111, 112, 270n13
All Things Considered, 78, 259n2
Alternative Media Center, 283n7

American Association of Foreign Lan-
    guage Newspapers, 27
American Family, 194, 204
American Indian Radio on Satellite
    (AIROS), 73
Americanization, 29
  pre-Americanization, 6, 45, 108, 158
Amos 'n' Andy, 33, 60, 105, 106, 107, 117,
    270n8
Angel, 105
Anglophone Caribbeans, 99
Annakie, David "DJ Squeeze," 89
AOL Time Warner, 142, 143, 144–45, 157,
    186, 274n12
apartheid, 4, 14
Arab Anti-Defamation League, 120
Arab cable television, 181
  ANA Television, 182
  The Arabic Channel, 169, 170, 182
  ART, 182, 183
Armed Forces Radio Service (AFRS),
    35
Armed Forces Radio and Television
    Services (AFRTS), 71, 75, 84
Asian American Journalists Associa-
    tion, 74
Asian Americans, 15, 69, 71, 79, 129, 131,
    186, 198, 279
Asian cable television, 175–76
  ABS-CBN, 177
  CCTV-4, 177, 184
  The Filipino Channel, 177
  Fuji TV, 176
  The International Channel, 176, 177,
    180
  Korean Broadcasting System, 176
  MBC-TV, 177

McQuail, Denis, 60, 264n16, 18, 265n32, 283n1, 286nn2, 5, 287n8
Mega-Media Twelve, 44, 45
mergers and acquisitions, 44, 45, 137, 143, 242. *See also* Mega-Media Twelve
Mexican War 1848, 10
Mexico and Mexicans, 10, 16, 18, 23, 151, 155, 185, 194, 226, 254
Miami, 2, 22, 91, 100, 130, 131, 143, 158, 195, 241
microradio, 76, 77, 78, 243, 246, 265n1, 268n35
Migala, Joseph, 262n14, 263n18
Minneapolis, 22, 143
Minority Consortia, 196, 199, 202, 205, 206, 207, 210, 281n18
minority discounts, 36
minority equity investor, 160
Minority Programming Consortia, 192
minority role models, 148
Missing Persons Program, 32
model immigrants, 84, 119
Mohammed, Robert, 88, 265
Motion Pictures Research Council, 55
Mowlana, Hamid, 187, 243, 280n95
Mr. Rogers' Neighborhood, 193
MTV, 117, 157, 161, 165, 167, 277n49
multiculturalism, 18, 251, 256, 261n21, 264n21
Multiple System Operators (MSOs), 142, 142–214
Murdoch, Rupert, 45
Murphy, Sharon, 63, 265n36
Museum of Television and Radio, New York, 8, 153, 262n9, 275n29
music
    balada romántica/canción romántica, 91
    bhajan, 82
    black music, 33, 35
    calypso, 66, 168, 173, 265
    chutney, 68, 173
    cumbia, 91
    filmi, 68, 70, 82, 173, 175, folk, 77, 238
    geet, 96
    gospel, 35, 36, 40, 160, 161, 165, 166, 223, 225, 231

    Gujarati, 80, 82
    hip hop, 36, 164, 165, 166, 223, 229
    jazz
    Latin hip hop, 91
    musica norteña, 91
    oldies, 68, 84
    polka, 38, 39, 40, 65, 95, 261, 265
    Punjabi, 82
    race music, 32, 70
    ranchera, 91
    reggae, 67, 70, 72, 86, 89, 164, 168, 173
    roots music, 168, 169, 278n63
    salsa, 91, 268
    South Indian, 70, 82
    urban pop, 86
    world music, 72, 73, 74

Nader, Ralph, 77, 268n38
National Advisory Commission on Civil Disorder (Kerner Commission), 5, 14, 58, 63, 111, 126, 248, 265n35, 270n12
National Asian American Telecommunications Association, 197, 281n19
National Association of Broadcasters (NAB), 41, 64, 78, 120, 126, 128, 132–33, 273n50
National Association for the Advancement of Colored People (NAACP), 12, 33, 51, 119, 120, 125, 160, 167, 260n7, 272n32
    Television and Film Diversity Initiative, 51, 120
National Association of Black Journalists, 74, 209
National Association of Educational Broadcasters (NAEB), 71, 191
National Association of Hispanic Journalists, 74, 209
National Association of Minorities in Communication (NAMIC), 141, 142, 274n7, 295
National Black Programming Consortium, 197, 199–200, 281n17, 282n24
National Cable Television Association, 138, 141, 142, 150, 165, 174, 178, 185, 275n22, 276n33